GENERATION INNOVATE

UNLEASHING THE CREATIVE REVOLUTION OF MILLENNIALS AND GEN-Z

DAVID S. MORGAN

DEDICATION

To Andrew,

Designer, maker, entrepreneur, son,

And a wonderful human being.

You embody the spirit of innovation.

CONTENTS

PART III: INNOVATING IN THE MODERN ERA

PREFACE

THE DAWN OF GENERATION INNOVATE

We stand at the threshold of a new era of creativity and innovation, one shaped by the dynamic forces of Millennials and Gen-Z. These generations, which I collectively call "Generation Innovate," are not just adapting to change—they're driving it, rewriting the rules of creativity, entrepreneurship, and problem-solving in ways that will define our future.

Over the past decade, I've had the privilege of witnessing firsthand the incredible energy, talent, and determination of these young innovators. As an advisor, mentor, judge, and Board Member for programs like Accelerate at Wentworth Innovation + Entrepreneurship Center, Harvard Innovation Labs, Design Museum Everywhere, MassChallenge, and Boston Architectural College (BAC), I've been continually inspired by the audacious vision and relentless drive of Generation Innovate.

These young leaders are not just developing breakthrough technologies or launching disruptive startups. They're reimagining entire industries, tackling global challenges with unprecedented creativity, and forging a new creator economy that blends purpose with profit. Their approach to innovation is holistic, empathetic, and deeply rooted in a desire to make a meaningful difference in the world.

What sets Generation Innovate apart is not just their technological fluency, but their unique mindset. They've grown up in a world of constant change, global connectivity, and information abundance. As a result, they bring to the table a remarkable adaptability, a collaborative spirit, and a comfort with complexity that is transforming how we approach innovation.

This book is a celebration of their innovative spirit and a roadmap for harnessing their potential. We'll explore how Generation Innovate is leveraging digital platforms, embracing cross-disciplinary thinking, and championing sustainable and inclusive approaches to problem-solving. We'll delve into the emerging Creator Economy, where passion meets profession, and examine how professional (Pro-C) creativity is reshaping our understanding of professional innovation.

At the heart of this book is the Complex Adaptive Systems (CAS) Model of Innovation—a new framework that captures the dynamic, interconnected nature of creativity and innovation in the digital age. This model, inspired by the approaches of Generation Innovate and my own experience developing new products, innovating processes, and leading for-profit and nonprofit organizations offers a fresh perspective on how ideas emerge, evolve, and transform into world-changing innovations.

To be sure, Generation Innovate faces significant challenges. From navigating economic uncertainty to grappling with the pressures of a hyperconnected world, these young innovators are charting their course through uncharted waters. We'll examine these challenges honestly, exploring how they're fueling resilience and driving new approaches to work, life, and innovation.

As we embark on this exploration of Generation Innovate, prepare to have your assumptions challenged and your perspective on innovation transformed. Whether you're a member of this generation looking to maximize your innovative potential, or a leader seeking to harness the creativity of young talent, this book offers insights and strategies for thriving in the new landscape of innovation.

The future of creativity and innovation is being written now, by the bold, purpose-driven members of Generation Innovate. It's time to understand, celebrate, and join their revolution. Welcome to the age of Generation Innovate!

— David S. Morgan

INTRODUCTION
THE CREATIVE REVOLUTION OF GENERATION INNOVATE

Picture this: A 22-year-old college dropout turns her passion for makeup into a multimillion-dollar cosmetics brand using just a smartphone and social media. A teenager's dance videos on TikTok skyrocket him to stardom, landing major brand deals and a budding music career. A young entrepreneur develops an AI-powered app, revolutionizing fashion by making personalized style accessible to millions.

Welcome to the age of **Generation Innovate**, where Millennials and Gen-Z are rewriting the rules of creativity and entrepreneurship. These aren't isolated stories—they are snapshots of a profound shift in how we work, innovate, and solve problems. These generations are driving a creative revolution fueled by technology, collaboration, and empathy.

By 2025, Millennials will make up 75% of the global workforce, with Gen-Z right behind them. Together, they are shaping the future with an approach that goes beyond tech-savviness; it's their **mindset**, rooted in digital fluency, empathy, and creativity, that is setting them apart.

This book is your guide to understanding how **Generation Innovate** is transforming industries, creating new economic paradigms, and shaping the future of work. At its core, we explore how they leverage **empathy**, **flow**, **creativity**, and **social networks**—all integral parts of the **Complex Adaptive Systems (CAS) Model of Innovation**—to lead breakthrough innovations in today's fast-evolving world.

The Empathy-Driven Revolution

Empathy isn't just a soft skill for Generation Innovate—it's the foundation of how they approach everything from product design to team collaboration. Understanding user needs, feelings, and pain points enables them to create solutions that resonate on a deeper level. This book will explore how empathy fuels creativity, enhances problem-solving, and drives successful innovation.

The Power of Flow and Creativity

Flow states—those moments of deep, focused immersion in work—are critical to unlocking creativity. **Generation Innovate** has mastered the art of finding flow in digital environments, combining intense focus with creativity to generate high-impact innovations. We'll delve into how flow, creativity, and innovation are intertwined, and how you can cultivate these states to achieve professional success.

Social Networks as Innovation Catalysts

Social networks—both digital and human—are the connective tissue of innovation for Generation Innovate. These networks don't just help uncover novel ideas by exposing innovators to diverse perspectives, trends, and cutting-edge solutions; they also accelerate implementation. By facilitating rapid feedback loops, resource-sharing, and collaboration, social networks allow innovators to scale their ideas quickly, turning concepts into tangible outcomes faster than ever before. In today's fast-paced world, leveraging social networks is key to both finding creativity and bringing innovation to life.

The Complex Adaptive Systems (CAS) Model of Innovation

At the heart of this book is the **Complex Adaptive Systems (CAS) Model of Innovation**, a framework that captures the dynamic, interconnected nature of creativity and innovation in today's world. The CAS Model shows how empathy, flow, creativity, and social networks work together in an adaptive, evolving system, allowing innovation to thrive in complex environments.

This model helps us understand that innovation is not a linear process—it is shaped by constant interactions, feedback loops, and collaborations. Whether you're leading a team, launching a startup, or navigating your career, understanding the CAS Model will help you foster a mindset that embraces the fluidity and complexity of modern innovation.

What You Will Gain

This book offers practical strategies to:

- **Leverage empathy** to connect with users, customers, and teams for deeper insights and innovation.

- **Harness flow and creativity** to generate breakthrough ideas and solutions.
- **Build and utilize social networks** to collaborate effectively and scale innovations.
- **Apply the CAS Model** to navigate complexity and adaptability in your creative and professional pursuits.
- **Balance innovation with well-being**, ensuring sustainable, long-term success in a rapidly changing world.

Pro-C Creativity and Professional Innovation

A key theme of this book is **Pro-C creativity**, which refers to the type of creativity used by professionals to innovate at high levels. Generation Innovate doesn't just create for the sake of creativity—they create to **solve problems, lead industries, and redefine markets**. Their ability to harness Pro-C creativity has made them leaders in the Creator Economy, turning passions into professions and building sustainable careers.

The Future of Work and Innovation

The innovations of Millennials and Gen-Z are driving the future of work, business, and even education. They are blending **empathy, creativity, technology, and collaboration** to challenge traditional business models and develop new ways of thinking about work. This book will explore how these approaches are reshaping industries, from media to tech, and how you can apply them to your own career and organization.

A New Type of Leader

The leaders of **Generation Innovate** are defined by their ability to **empathize, collaborate, and adapt**. Their innovation is not just about creating new products—it's about creating more inclusive, adaptive, and innovative systems that work in real-time with the complexities of the modern world. As we explore their methods, you'll learn how to lead with these same principles, fostering creativity, collaboration, and innovation in your own work and teams.

Ready to Innovate?

The creative revolution is here, and **Generation Innovate** is leading the charge with a blend of empathy, creativity, and collaboration that's never been seen before. By understanding the **Complex Adaptive Systems Model** and leveraging the tools of this generation, you can position yourself at the forefront of this new wave of innovation.

So, are you ready to explore the future of creativity and innovation? Let's dive into the world of **Generation Innovate** and discover how Millennials and Gen-Z are shaping the future.

PART I

THE GENERATIONAL SHIFT

CHAPTER 1

UNDERSTANDING THE GENERATIONAL SHIFT

In our rapidly evolving world, a new force is reshaping the landscape of creativity and innovation. This force is Generation Innovate - the Millennials and Gen Z who are not just entering the workforce, but actively transforming it. This chapter delves into the unique characteristics of these generations, exploring how their experiences have shaped their approach to work, life, and innovation.

We'll examine how Generation Innovate differs from previous generations, not just in their behaviors and values, but in the very wiring of their brains. From their digital fluency to their desire for purpose-driven work, we'll uncover the neurological underpinnings of their innovative potential. Furthermore, we'll explore the profound impact of digital technology on these generations, seeing how growing up in a hyper-connected world has not only influenced their skills and preferences but has literally rewired their neural pathways.

By understanding the generational shift embodied by Millennials and Gen Z, we lay the foundation for harnessing their immense creative and innovative potential. This chapter sets the stage for a deeper exploration of how Generation Innovate is reshaping the future of work, creativity, and problem-solving in ways that previous generations could scarcely imagine.

1.1: CHARACTERISTICS OF MILLENNIALS AND GEN Z

Picture this: in today's workplace, the intern is showing the CEO the ropes of a new social media platform, while the youngest team members are often the ones driving innovation. Welcome to the world of Generation Innovate, where the lines between teaching and learning have blurred, and fresh perspectives lead the way.

But who exactly are these generations, and what makes them so different from those who came before? More importantly, how have their experiences shaped their brains, influencing their approach to creativity and innovation? Let's dive in and explore.

Millennials, born roughly between 1981 and 1996, were the first generation to come of age in the new millennium. They're often called digital pioneers – old enough to remember a time before smartphones and social media, but young enough to have adapted to the digital world with ease. This adaptation isn't just behavioral; it's neurological. Studies have shown that internet use can alter brain structure and function, particularly in areas associated with attention, memory, and social cognition (Small et al., 2020). It's as if their brains have been rewired for the digital age.

Gen Z, born from about 1997 to 2012, are the true digital natives. They've never known a world without Wi-Fi, smartphones, or social media. For them, the digital and physical worlds are seamlessly integrated. This integration is reflected in their neural pathways. Research using fMRI scans has found that digital natives show different patterns of brain activation when performing online tasks compared to digital immigrants, suggesting more efficient information processing (Small et al., 2020). It's like their brains have been optimized for the digital world from the start.

But it's not just their relationship with technology that sets these generations apart. They bring a unique set of values and expectations to the table, shaped by their experiences and reflected in their cognitive processes.

So what's driving this shift? It's not just about job titles or paychecks anymore – Millennials and Gen Z want their work to matter. They crave purpose and meaning, and they aren't afraid to demand it. A study by Deloitte (2023) found that 86% of Millennials and Gen Z believe the success of a business should be measured by more than just its financial performance. They want to work for companies that are making a positive impact on society.

This desire for purpose isn't just about feeling good – it's a fundamental driver of their career choices and work engagement. Neuroscientific research by Immordino-Yang and Damasio (2007) emphasizes the importance of integrating emotional and social experiences with cognitive processes for effective learning and problem-solving. For Generation Innovate, this integration not only drives their pursuit of meaningful work but also enhances their ability to innovate in ways that are emotionally and socially resonant.

They're also incredibly adaptable. Having come of age during times of economic uncertainty (the Great Recession for Millennials, the COVID-19 pandemic for Gen Z), they've learned to be flexible and resilient. A report by McKinsey (2022) found that 65% of Gen Z see continuous adaptation as essential for success in the workplace. They're not just rolling with the punches – they're expecting them and preparing accordingly.

This adaptability is mirrored in their brains' neuroplasticity – the ability to form and reorganize synaptic connections, especially in response to learning or experience. While neuroplasticity decreases with age, research suggests that engaging in novel experiences and continuous learning can help maintain brain flexibility well into adulthood (Voss et al., 2013). Generation Innovate's tendency to seek out new experiences and skills may be actively supporting their cognitive adaptability. They're not just learning new skills – they're keeping their brains young and flexible in the process.

This adaptability manifests in their approach to learning and skill development. They're lifelong learners, constantly upskilling and reskilling to stay relevant in a rapidly changing job market. According to LinkedIn's 2023 Workplace Learning Report, 86% of Millennials and Gen Z would stay at a company longer if it invested in their career development. They're not just employees – they're students of their craft, always looking to grow and improve.

From a neuroscience perspective, this continuous learning approach is optimal for brain health and cognitive function. Learning new skills creates new neural pathways and can even lead to the growth of new neurons in certain brain areas, a process known as neurogenesis (Shors, 2014). Every time they learn something new, they're literally growing their brains.

Another key characteristic is their entrepreneurial spirit. The 2023 Amway Global Entrepreneurship Report found that 84% of Millennials and Gen Z have a positive attitude towards entrepreneurship, compared to 74% of Gen X and 58% of Baby Boomers. They're not just dreaming about starting their own businesses – they're doing it. The rise of the gig economy and the creator economy are testament to this entrepreneurial drive.

Take Maya, a 27-year-old product manager who negotiated her role to be fully remote so she could travel the world while working. Her story is far from unique – 75% of Millennials and Gen Z would leave their job if they weren't allowed to work remotely, according to Deloitte (2023). This entrepreneurial mindset may be linked to differences in risk perception and decision-making. Studies have shown that the adolescent and young adult brain is more sensitive to reward and less sensitive to risk, which can drive innovative and entrepreneurial behavior (Steinberg, 2008). While this can sometimes lead to impulsivity, it can also foster the kind of bold thinking needed for innovation. They're not just risk-takers – they're opportunity-seekers.

But it's not all rosy. These generations also face unique challenges. They're entering the workforce with unprecedented levels of student debt. According to the Federal Reserve (2023), Millennials hold an average of $38,877 in student loan debt, while Gen Z (those who have attended college) hold an average of $20,900. This financial burden has significant implications for their career choices and life decisions.

Chronic stress, such as that caused by financial pressure, can have profound effects on the brain. It can lead to changes in the structure and function of the amygdala, hippocampus, and prefrontal cortex – areas involved in emotion regulation, memory, and decision-making (McEwen, 2012). Understanding these neurological impacts is crucial for developing strategies to support Generation Innovate's mental health and cognitive function. They're not just dealing with debt – they're navigating its neurological impacts as well.

Moreover, they're navigating a job market that's increasingly volatile and uncertain. The concept of a 'job for life' is alien to most Millennials and Gen Z. Instead, they're building portfolio careers, often juggling multiple gigs or side hustles. A survey by Upwork (2023) found that 50% of Gen Z workers have engaged in freelance work, compared to 44% of Millennials and 30% of Gen X. They're not just employees – they're career entrepreneurs, constantly adapting to market demands.

This constant switching between tasks and roles may be enhancing their cognitive flexibility – the mental ability to switch between thinking about two different concepts, and to think about multiple concepts simultaneously. Cognitive flexibility is associated with creativity and problem-solving abilities (Ionescu, 2012), potentially contributing to Generation Innovate's aptitude for innovation. Their varied work experiences aren't just building their resumes – they're building more flexible, creative brains.

Mental health is another crucial issue for these generations. They're more likely to report feelings of anxiety and depression than previous generations. A study by the American Psychological Association (2023) found that Gen Z adults were the most likely of all generations to report poor mental health. This openness about mental health issues is reshaping workplace cultures and pushing for more supportive, empathetic work environments. They're not just acknowledging mental health – they're demanding that it be taken seriously in the workplace.

Interestingly, this increased awareness and openness about mental health may be linked to enhanced emotional intelligence. Emotional intelligence involves brain areas such as the amygdala and prefrontal cortex, which are involved in recognizing and regulating emotions (Goleman & Boyatzis, 2017). Generation Innovate's focus on mental health may be cultivating stronger neural networks in these areas, potentially enhancing their ability to understand and manage emotions – a crucial skill for innovation and leadership. They're not just talking about feelings – they're developing brains that are better equipped to handle the emotional complexities of the modern workplace.

As we move forward in this book, we'll explore how these characteristics – their digital fluency, their desire for purpose, their adaptability, their entrepreneurial spirit, and their focus on mental health – are shaping a new paradigm of creativity and innovation. We'll see how they're not just participating in the workforce, but actively reshaping it to align with their values and expectations, all while their brains adapt and evolve in response to these unique experiences and challenges.

The story of Generation Innovate is still being written, both in the world around us and in the intricate neural networks of their brains. They face significant challenges, but they also have unprecedented opportunities to create, innovate, and make a positive impact on the world. Understanding their characteristics, and the neuroscience behind them, is the first step in harnessing their creative potential – and perhaps in unlocking our own.

As we dive deeper into the world of Generation Innovate, remember this: we're not just observing a generational shift. We're witnessing the emergence of a new kind of thinker, a new kind of creator, shaped by unique experiences and equipped with brains that have evolved to thrive in a digital, fast-paced world. The future of innovation isn't just about new technologies or business models – it's about the remarkable, adaptable, purpose-driven brains of Generation Innovate.

1.2 DIFFERENCES FROM PREVIOUS GENERATIONS

When we talk about Generation Innovate, it's not just about their unique characteristics – it's about how those characteristics differ from previous generations. To truly understand the seismic shift happening in our workplaces and society, we need to look at how Millennials and Gen Z compare to their predecessors. And here's the kicker: these differences aren't just cultural or behavioral – they're wired into their brains.

Let's start with the Baby Boomers, born between 1946 and 1964. This generation grew up in a time of economic prosperity and social change. They're often characterized by their strong work ethic, competitive nature, and goal-oriented approach to their careers. Boomers tend to value face-to-face communication and hierarchical structures in the workplace (Twenge et al., 2010). Their brains developed in a world of relative stability and linear career paths.

Now, contrast this with our Millennials and Gen Z. These younger generations are more likely to prefer digital communication, even for important conversations. A study by Slack (2023) found that 76% of Millennials and Gen Z prefer to use instant messaging for work communications, compared to just 44% of Baby Boomers. This isn't just a preference – it's a fundamental shift in how business gets done, and it's reflected in their neural pathways.

Research by Small et al. (2020) has shown that the brains of digital natives (like Gen Z) and digital adapters (like Millennials) show different activation patterns when processing digital information compared to digital immigrants (like many Boomers). It's as if their brains have been optimized for the digital age, with more efficient neural pathways for processing digital information.

But the differences go deeper than just communication styles. While Baby Boomers often viewed their careers as linear progressions within a single company or industry, Generation Innovate sees their careers as a series of experiences and skills to be accumulated. They're job hoppers, but not without purpose. This shift towards continuous learning and adaptability is further supported by Immordino-Yang's (2018) findings, which suggest that social and emotional contexts significantly influence cognitive processes, particularly in dynamic and complex environments. For Millennials and Gen Z, the blending of their personal values with their professional lives enhances their cognitive flexibility, making them more adept at navigating the uncertainties of modern career paths.

According to the Bureau of Labor Statistics (2023), the average tenure of workers aged 25 to 34 (which includes younger Millennials and older Gen Z) is just 2.8 years. Compare this to workers aged 55 to

64 (mostly Boomers), who have an average tenure of 9.9 years. This isn't because Generation Innovate is flighty or uncommitted – it's because they're constantly seeking growth, learning, and new challenges.

This constant change and learning is actually beneficial for their brains. Novel experiences and learning new skills promote neuroplasticity – the brain's ability to form new neural connections and adapt to new situations (Voss et al., 2013). In essence, Generation Innovate's job-hopping tendencies may be keeping their brains young and adaptable.

Now, let's look at Generation X, born between 1965 and 1980. Often called the "forgotten generation," Gen X grew up as latchkey kids during a time of rising divorce rates and economic uncertainty. They're known for their independence, skepticism, and desire for work-life balance (Twenge, 2017).

Gen X brought its own revolution to the workplace, pushing for more flexible work arrangements and challenging the rigid hierarchies preferred by Boomers. But Generation Innovate has taken this a step further. They don't just want flexibility – they demand it. A study by Deloitte (2023) found that 75% of Millennials and Gen Z would consider leaving their job if they weren't allowed to work remotely at least some of the time.

This desire for flexibility isn't just about convenience – it's about how their brains function best. Research has shown that autonomy and control over one's work environment can lead to increased motivation and productivity by activating the brain's reward centers (Leotti et al., 2010). When Generation Innovate pushes for flexibility, they're not being entitled – they're creating conditions that allow their brains to function at their best.

But here's where it gets really interesting. While Gen X sought work-life balance, often seeing work and life as separate spheres to be juggled, Generation Innovate is more likely to seek work-life integration. They don't want to balance work and life – they want work to be a meaningful part of their life.

This ties back to what researchers Edward Deci and Richard Ryan call intrinsic motivation – the drive to do something because it's inherently interesting or enjoyable (Deci & Ryan, 2000). Generation Innovate isn't just working for a paycheck – they're working for meaning, for impact, for the opportunity to grow and create. And this sense of purpose activates the brain's reward centers in a way that external rewards like money often can't match (Ulrich et al., 2014).

Another crucial difference lies in attitudes towards authority and hierarchy. Baby Boomers and even Gen X were more likely to respect authority based on position or seniority. Generation Innovate, however, respects expertise and authenticity over titles or years of service.

A study by Gallup (2023) found that 87% of Millennials and Gen Z say that professional development and career growth opportunities are very important to them in a job. They're not content to wait their turn for promotions or opportunities – they want to be constantly learning and growing, regardless of their position in the organizational hierarchy.

This constant quest for growth and learning isn't just about career advancement – it's about how their brains are wired. The brain thrives on novelty and challenge. Learning new skills and tackling new problems triggers the release of dopamine, a neurotransmitter associated with pleasure and reward (Gruber et al., 2014). In a very real sense, Generation Innovate is addicted to learning and growth.

This shift is having profound implications for leadership styles and organizational structures. We're seeing a move away from top-down, command-and-control leadership towards more collaborative, coach-like approaches. Companies that can't adapt to this new reality are finding it increasingly difficult to attract and retain top talent from Generation Innovate.

Now, let's talk about attitudes towards entrepreneurship and risk-taking. While entrepreneurship has always been part of the American dream, Generation Innovate has taken it to new heights. The Global Entrepreneurship Monitor (2023) found that 51% of entrepreneurs in the U.S. are now Millennials or Gen Z, despite making up only about 38% of the adult population.

This entrepreneurial spirit isn't just about starting businesses – it's about a mindset of innovation and problem-solving that Generation Innovate brings to everything they do. They're more likely to challenge the status quo, to ask "why not?" instead of "why?", and to see opportunities where others see obstacles.

This entrepreneurial mindset may be linked to differences in how their brains process risk and reward. Research has shown that the adolescent and young adult brain is more sensitive to reward and less sensitive to risk, which can drive innovative and entrepreneurial behavior (Steinberg, 2008). While this can sometimes lead to impulsivity, it can also foster the kind of bold thinking needed for innovation.

Let's not forget about technology. While Gen X was the first generation to grow up with personal computers, and many Boomers adapted admirably to the digital revolution, for Generation Innovate, technology is as natural as breathing. They don't just use technology – they live and breathe it.

A report by Pew Research (2023) found that 95% of teens now have access to a smartphone, and 45% say they are online "almost constantly." This deep integration of technology into their lives has profound implications for how they work, create, and innovate. It's not just about being tech-savvy – it's about having brains that have developed in symbiosis with digital technology.

Neuroscientific research has shown that extensive internet use can alter brain structure and function, particularly in areas related to attention, memory, and social cognition (Firth et al., 2019). For Generation Innovate, this isn't a deficit – it's an adaptation to a world where information is abundant and constantly changing. Their brains have evolved to navigate this digital landscape with ease.

For example, while previous generations might see artificial intelligence as a threat, many in Generation Innovate see it as a tool to augment their own capabilities. A survey by Dell Technologies (2023) found that 80% of Gen Z aspire to work with cutting-edge technology, and 91% say technology would influence their job choice among similar employment offers. They're not afraid of being replaced by AI – they're excited about the possibilities of human-AI collaboration.

This comfort with AI and advanced technology isn't just about familiarity – it's about how their brains process information. Generation Innovate has grown up in a world of rapid technological change, and their brains have developed the flexibility to quickly adapt to new interfaces and systems. They're not just using technology – they're co-evolving with it.

But perhaps the most significant difference between Generation Innovate and previous generations lies in their global outlook. Thanks to the internet and social media, Millennials and Gen Z have grown up connected to peers around the world. They're more likely to see themselves as global citizens, concerned with issues that transcend national borders.

A study by Deloitte (2023) found that climate change and environmental protection are the top societal concerns for Millennials and Gen Z globally. This global consciousness influences not just their personal lives, but their career choices and approach to innovation. They're more likely to seek out diverse perspectives and to consider the global implications of their work.

This global mindset is reflected in their brain's neural networks. Exposure to diverse cultures and perspectives can enhance cognitive flexibility and creativity by promoting the formation of novel neural connections (Leung et al., 2008). In essence, Generation Innovate's global outlook isn't just a worldview – it's a cognitive advantage.

Now, it's important to note that these generational differences aren't absolute. There are certainly Baby Boomers who are tech-savvy entrepreneurs and Gen Z individuals who prefer traditional career paths. Human beings are complex, and we can't reduce anyone to just their generational label. The brain's plasticity ensures that we can all adapt and learn throughout our lives.

However, these broad trends do give us valuable insights into the changing landscape of work, creativity, and innovation. They help us understand why traditional approaches to management and innovation may no longer be effective, and point us towards new strategies that can harness the unique strengths of Generation Innovate.

As we move forward, it's crucial for organizations and leaders to understand and adapt to these generational differences. Those who can create environments that align with the values and expectations of Generation Innovate will be best positioned to attract top talent, drive innovation, and thrive in our rapidly changing world.

But here's the real challenge – and opportunity. It's not just about accommodating Generation Innovate. It's about leveraging their unique cognitive strengths to drive innovation across entire organizations. Their digital fluency, global mindset, and comfort with rapid change aren't just personal traits – they're cognitive assets that can transform how we approach problem-solving and creativity.

As we continue to explore the world of Generation Innovate, remember this: we're not just dealing with a new generation of workers. We're witnessing the emergence of a new kind of innovator, with brains that have evolved to thrive in a digital, globalized, rapidly changing world. The future of innovation isn't just about new technologies or business models – it's about harnessing the unique cognitive capabilities of Generation Innovate.

1.3 IMPACT OF DIGITAL TECHNOLOGY

If there's one factor that truly sets Generation Innovate apart, it's their relationship with digital technology. For Millennials and Gen Z, technology isn't just a tool – it's an extension of themselves, a fundamental part of how they interact with the world. This digital fluency isn't just changing how they work; it's reshaping the very nature of creativity and innovation. And here's the kicker: it's literally rewiring their brains.

Let's start with a staggering statistic: according to a report by GlobalWebIndex (2023), the average Gen Z spends 4 hours and 15 minutes per day on their mobile devices. For Millennials, it's not far behind at 3 hours and 45 minutes. They're not just passive consumers of content. They're creators, collaborators, and innovators, using these devices as portals to a world of information and possibility.

Think about it. When I was growing up, if you wanted to learn a new skill, you might take a class or buy a book. Today, Generation Innovate can access world-class instruction on virtually any topic with a few taps on their smartphone. Want to learn 3D modeling? There's a YouTube tutorial for that. Curious about quantum physics? There's a TikTok expert breaking it down in 60-second videos.

This constant exposure to diverse information and rapid learning isn't just convenient – it's transforming their cognitive processes. Research by Small et al. (2020) has shown that internet use can alter brain structure and function, particularly in areas associated with attention, memory, and social cognition. It's as if their brains have developed a new operating system optimized for processing and integrating vast amounts of information quickly. Moreover, recent research by Immordino-Yang et al. (2022) emphasizes the importance of "constructive internal reflection" in the digital age. Their studies suggest that the ability to deeply process information, connect it to personal meaning, and imagine future possibilities is crucial for innovative thinking. This indicates that Generation Innovate's capacity for creativity and problem-solving is not just a function of their digital fluency, but also of their ability to integrate technology use with meaningful internal reflection and social-emotional experiences.

This democratization of knowledge is having a profound impact on innovation. A study by McKinsey (2023) found that companies with digitally savvy leadership teams are 26% more profitable than their industry peers. Why? Because they're able to leverage technology to innovate faster, respond to market changes more quickly, and create more value for their customers. Generation Innovate isn't just using digital tools – they're thinking digitally, and it's giving them a competitive edge.

But it's not just about access to information. Digital technology has fundamentally changed how Generation Innovate collaborates and creates. Take the rise of digital nomads, for instance. A study by MBO Partners (2023) found that 17 million Americans now describe themselves as digital nomads, a 131% increase from 2019. For these individuals, work isn't a place you go – it's something you do, from anywhere in the world with a decent internet connection.

This location-independent, technology-enabled lifestyle is breeding a new kind of innovator. They're global in their outlook, cross-pollinating ideas from different cultures and contexts. They're adaptive, able to pivot quickly in response to changing circumstances. And they're collaborative, leveraging digital tools to work seamlessly with teams spread across the globe.

This constant exposure to diverse environments and ideas is a boon for creativity. Research has shown that multicultural experiences can enhance cognitive flexibility and creative thinking by promoting the formation of novel neural connections (Leung et al., 2008). In essence, the digital nomad lifestyle of many in Generation Innovate isn't just a work preference – it's a creativity enhancer.

The impact of digital technology goes beyond just how Generation Innovate works – it's changing how they think. A fascinating study by Small et al. (2020) used fMRI scans to compare the brain activity of digital natives (people who grew up with the internet) and digital immigrants (those who adopted it later in life) while they performed online tasks. The results? Digital natives showed more efficient neural pathways, suggesting that growing up with technology has literally rewired their brains.

This rewiring has significant implications for creativity and innovation. Digital natives are more comfortable with multitasking, better at filtering large amounts of information, and quicker to adapt to new interfaces and systems. In essence, their brains are optimized for the fast-paced, information-rich environment of the digital age.

Now, I can already hear some of you protesting. "But isn't all this technology making us more distracted? Isn't it hampering deep thinking and creativity?" It's a fair question, and there's certainly research suggesting that excessive screen time can have negative effects on attention and mental health (Twenge, 2017).

Generation Innovate isn't just using technology more, they're using it differently. They've developed strategies to manage the potential downsides of constant connectivity. A study by Google (2023) found that 70% of Gen Z regularly use digital wellbeing features on their devices, compared to just 47% of Baby Boomers. They're not slaves to technology – they're its masters, using it as a tool to enhance their creativity and productivity.

Moreover, their brains may be better equipped to handle the cognitive demands of the digital age. Research has shown that action video game players, for instance, demonstrate enhanced attentional control and cognitive flexibility (Green & Bavelier, 2012). While not all digital activities are equal, this suggests that certain types of digital engagement can actually enhance cognitive skills crucial for innovation.

Let's look at some concrete examples of how digital technology is fueling innovation among Millennials and Gen Z:

1. Collaborative Creativity: Platforms like GitHub for coders or Figma for designers allow real-time collaboration on complex projects. This isn't just about convenience – it's enabling new forms of collective creativity. A study by Harvard Business Review (2023) found that teams using collaborative digital tools were 21% more productive and 32% more innovative than those using traditional methods. These platforms are essentially creating a shared cognitive space, allowing multiple brains to work as one on complex problems.
2. AI-Enhanced Creativity: Generation Innovate isn't afraid of AI – they're embracing it as a creative partner. Tools like

DALL-E for image generation or Chat GPT4o for text are being used not to replace human creativity, but to augment it. A survey by Adobe (2023) found that 68% of Millennial and Gen Z creatives believe AI tools will enhance their creativity rather than replace it. This human-AI collaboration is creating a new kind of hybrid intelligence, combining the pattern recognition capabilities of AI with human intuition and contextual understanding.

3. Rapid Prototyping and Iteration: Digital tools have dramatically reduced the time and cost of prototyping ideas. 3D printing, for instance, allows physical prototypes to be created in hours rather than weeks. This enables a faster, more iterative approach to innovation. A report by Deloitte (2023) found that companies using rapid prototyping techniques were able to bring products to market 28% faster than their competitors. This rapid iteration isn't just about speed – it's about accelerating the learning process, allowing for more experimentation and refinement of ideas.
4. Data-Driven Innovation: Generation Innovate is comfortable with big data and analytics in a way that previous generations simply weren't. They're using data to inform creative decisions, spot trends, and predict market needs. A study by MIT Sloan Management Review (2023) found that companies with a data-driven culture were 58% more likely to exceed their business goals. This isn't just about number crunching – it's about using data as a tool for creative insight, spotting patterns and connections that might not be visible to the naked eye.

5. Virtual and Augmented Reality: VR and AR are opening up entirely new realms for creativity and innovation. From virtual art galleries to AR-enhanced product design, these technologies are allowing Generation Innovate to create immersive experiences that blur the line between digital and physical realities. This isn't just a new medium – it's a new way of thinking about space, interaction, and experience design.

But perhaps the most profound impact of digital technology on Generation Innovate is how it's enabling them to tackle global challenges. Climate change, social inequality, public health crises – these complex, interconnected problems require innovative, collaborative solutions. Digital technology is providing the tools to coordinate efforts across borders, share knowledge instantly, and mobilize resources on a global scale.

Take the example of Boyan Slat, a young Dutch inventor who founded The Ocean Cleanup at the age of 18. Using advanced computer modeling and crowd-sourced data, Slat and his team developed innovative technologies to rid the world's oceans of plastic waste. This kind of tech-enabled, globally coordinated innovation is becoming increasingly common among Generation Innovate.

What's fascinating is how this global, digital approach to problem-solving may be shaping their cognitive processes. Research has shown that exposure to diverse cultures and ideas can enhance cognitive flexibility and creativity by promoting the formation of novel neural connections (Leung et al., 2008). In essence, the global, interconnected nature of digital innovation isn't just changing what Generation Innovate creates – it's changing how their brains work.

The digital revolution has also democratized entrepreneurship in unprecedented ways. Platforms like Shopify, Etsy, and Kickstarter have made it possible for anyone with an idea to start a business or launch a product. This has led to an explosion of niche markets and innovative products that might never have seen the light of day in a pre-digital world.

Consider the case of Melanie Perkins, who co-founded Canva at the age of 22. Frustrated by the complexity of traditional design software, Perkins created a user-friendly platform that made graphic design accessible to everyone. Today, Canva is valued at over $40 billion (May, 2024) and used by 180 million users worldwide. This is a prime example of how Generation Innovate is using technology not just to create new products, but to democratize creativity itself.

This democratization of tools and platforms is significant. It's providing opportunities for a much wider range of individuals to engage in creative and entrepreneurial activities. This increased engagement, in turn, is likely fostering the development of creative problem-solving skills across a broader swath of the population. We're not just seeing more innovation – we're potentially cultivating a more innovative society as a whole.

Of course, the relationship between digital technology and innovation isn't without its challenges. Issues of data privacy, digital addiction, and the digital divide are very real concerns that need to be addressed. The constant connectivity enabled by digital technology can lead to information overload and burnout if not managed carefully.

However, Generation Innovate is showing a remarkable ability to adapt to these challenges. They're developing strategies to manage digital overwhelm, creating new norms around online privacy, and using technology itself to bridge digital divides. A study by the Pew Research Center (2023) found that 73% of Gen Z and Millennials actively manage their digital footprint, compared to only 49% of Baby Boomers.

Moreover, their brains may be better equipped to handle the cognitive demands of the digital age. Research has shown that individuals who engage in complex digital activities demonstrate enhanced cognitive control and multitasking abilities (Cardoso-Leite et al., 2015). While not all digital activities are created equal, this suggests that certain types of digital engagement may actually be enhancing cognitive skills crucial for innovation.

As we look to the future, it's clear that the impact of digital technology on innovation will only grow. Emerging technologies like artificial intelligence, blockchain, and quantum computing promise to open up entirely new frontiers for creativity and problem-solving. Generation Innovate, with their digital fluency and adaptive mindsets, are poised to lead the way in harnessing these technologies for innovation.

But perhaps the most exciting aspect of this digital revolution is how it's enabling new forms of collective intelligence. Platforms like Wikipedia, open-source software communities, and citizen science projects are demonstrating the power of large-scale collaboration.

These initiatives are not just producing impressive results – they're changing our very conception of how knowledge is created and innovation occurs.

For Generation Innovate, this collaborative, networked approach to innovation feels natural. They've grown up in a world where information is abundant and constantly changing, where the best ideas often emerge from the collective wisdom of diverse groups. Their brains have developed in this networked environment, potentially enhancing their ability to synthesize diverse inputs and spot novel connections.

As we move forward, it's crucial for organizations and leaders to understand and harness this digital fluency. Those who can create environments that leverage the technological strengths of Generation Innovate will be best positioned to drive innovation and tackle the complex challenges of our time.

In the next chapter, we'll explore another key aspect of Generation Innovate's approach to creativity and innovation: the rise of the creator economy. We'll look at how digital platforms are enabling new forms of entrepreneurship and changing our very conception of work and value creation. But remember, as we delve into these new paradigms, we're not just observing changes in behavior or business models. We're witnessing the emergence of a new kind of innovator, with brains that have evolved to thrive in a digital, globalized, rapidly changing world. The future of innovation isn't just about new technologies – it's about harnessing the unique cognitive capabilities of Generation Innovate.

KEY INSIGHTS

- Millennials and Gen Z are reshaping the landscape of creativity and innovation
- Digital fluency is a key characteristic of these generations, influencing their approach to work and innovation
- These generations value purpose, flexibility, and continuous learning

INNOVATION CHALLENGE

Spend a week observing and documenting the work styles and communication preferences of different generations in your workplace. How might you adapt your own approach to better collaborate across generational lines?

REFLECTION QUESTIONS

1. How do your own work preferences and values align with or differ from those typically associated with Millennials and Gen Z?

2. In what ways might generational differences in your workplace be hindering or enhancing innovation?

3. How could you leverage the strengths of different generations to create a more innovative work environment?

CHAPTER 2

THE CREATOR ECONOMY REVOLUTION

Imagine a world where your passion isn't just a hobby, but a thriving career. A world where a teenager can build a million-dollar business from their bedroom, where artists can reach global audiences without gatekeepers, and where knowledge shared becomes a currency more valuable than gold. This isn't a utopian fantasy – it's the Creator Economy, and it's revolutionizing how we work, create, and innovate.

At the heart of this revolution is Generation Innovate – the Millennials and Gen-Z who are not just participating in this new economy, but actively shaping its contours. With their digital fluency, global outlook, and entrepreneurial spirit, they're transforming the very nature of work and value creation in the 21st century.

In this chapter, we'll dive deep into the Creator Economy, exploring its origins, its current state, and its exciting future. We'll see how it's reshaping industries, challenging traditional notions of employment, and opening up new avenues for innovation and entrepreneurship. From the bustling virtual marketplaces of digital content to the cutting-edge applications of AI and blockchain, we'll uncover how Generation Innovate is leveraging technology to turn their passions into professions.

But this isn't just a story of individual success – it's a tale of systemic change. We'll examine how the Creator Economy is influencing education, policy-making, and even our understanding of what it means to create value in society. We'll also confront the challenges this new paradigm brings, from issues of digital well-being to questions of equity and sustainability.

As we journey through this new economic landscape, we'll see how it exemplifies the principles of Complex Adaptive Systems we explored in Chapter 1. The Creator Economy isn't just a new business model – it's a dynamic, evolving ecosystem where innovation emerges from the complex interactions of millions of creators, consumers, and technologies.

So, fasten your seatbelts, fellow innovators. We're about to embark on a thrilling exploration of the Creator Economy – a revolution that's redefining the future of work, creativity, and innovation. Welcome to the new world of Generation Innovate.

2.1 The Genesis of the Creator Economy

In the heart of Silicon Valley, a young software engineer streams herself coding late into the night, building a loyal following of aspiring developers. Halfway across the world in Lagos, a fashion designer leverages Instagram to showcase his Afrofuturistic creations, catching the eye of global brands. Meanwhile, in a small town in India, a teacher's simple math explanations on YouTube transform into a thriving online academy.

These aren't isolated success stories – they're snapshots of a seismic shift in our economic landscape. Welcome to the Creator Economy, a paradigm where individual creators can monetize their skills, knowledge, and creativity directly through digital platforms. But how did we get here? Let's trace the fascinating evolution of this revolutionary economic model.

The seeds of the Creator Economy were sown in the early days of the internet. The rise of blogging platforms in the late 1990s and early 2000s gave individuals a voice in the digital sphere. Suddenly, anyone with an internet connection could share their thoughts with the world. As Li Jin, a prominent investor and thought leader in the Creator Economy, notes, "The internet fundamentally changed the economics of content creation and distribution" (Jin, 2020).

But it was the advent of social media platforms in the mid-2000s that truly set the stage for the Creator Economy. Platforms like YouTube (founded in 2005) and Twitter (2006) democratized content creation on a scale never seen before. No longer did you need expensive equipment or industry connections to reach an audience – a smartphone and a good idea were enough.

The smartphone revolution, kickstarted by the iPhone's launch in 2007, further accelerated this trend. Suddenly, powerful creation tools were in everyone's pocket. As Kevin Kelly presciently wrote in his 2008 essay "1,000 True Fans," the internet was making it possible for creators to make a living by connecting directly with a relatively small, dedicated audience (Kelly, 2008).

But the real explosion of the Creator Economy came with the rise of platforms specifically designed to help creators monetize their work. Patreon, launched in 2013, pioneered a model where fans could directly support creators through recurring payments. Substack, founded in 2017, did the same for writers, allowing them to turn newsletters into subscription businesses.

Meanwhile, the evolution of e-commerce platforms like Shopify (founded in 2006) made it easier than ever for individual creators to sell physical products. This blurred the lines between content creator and entrepreneur, giving rise to what's often called the "passion economy" (Brynjolfsson et al., 2019).

The COVID-19 pandemic acted as a massive accelerant to these trends. As people worldwide found themselves stuck at home, online content consumption skyrocketed. A report by SignalFire (2023) found that the number of people identifying as full-time creators grew by over 48% during the pandemic years of 2020-2022.

Today, the Creator Economy is a formidable force. According to a study by Adobe (2023), the global creator economy is valued at more than $250 billion, with over 200 million people worldwide considering themselves creators. This isn't just a niche phenomenon – it's a fundamental reshaping of how value is created and distributed in the digital age.

What makes the Creator Economy particularly fascinating is how it embodies the principles of Complex Adaptive Systems that we explored in Chapter 1. It's a decentralized, self-organizing system where millions of individual actors (creators and consumers) interact in complex ways, leading to emergent phenomena that couldn't be predicted from individual behaviors alone.

Take the viral nature of content on platforms like TikTok, for instance. A single creative idea can spawn thousands of iterations, each adding its own twist, rapidly evolving the original concept. This is emergence in action – collective creativity that arises from the complex interactions of many individuals.

Moreover, the Creator Economy exemplifies the non-linear nature of Complex Adaptive Systems. Small inputs can lead to outsized effects – a single video can launch a career, a tweet can start a movement. This unpredictability is both thrilling and challenging, reshaping how we think about success and opportunity in the digital age.

As we move forward in this chapter, we'll explore how Generation Innovate – our Millennials and Gen-Z changemakers – are not just participating in this new economy, but actively shaping its evolution. We'll see how they're leveraging their unique skills and perspectives to push the boundaries of what's possible in the Creator Economy, and in doing so, redefining the very nature of work and innovation for the 21st century.

The Creator Economy isn't just a new way of making money – it's a revolution in how we create, share, and value human creativity. And we're only at the beginning of this exciting journey.

2.2 GENERATION INNOVATE: ARCHITECTS OF THE NEW ECONOMY

In a world where change is the only constant, Generation Innovate – our Millennials and Gen-Z changemakers – aren't just adapting; they're architecting an entirely new economic paradigm. The Creator Economy isn't just a playground for these digital natives; it's their canvas, their laboratory, and increasingly, their livelihood. Let's explore how Generation Innovate is leveraging their unique characteristics to reshape the economic landscape.

At the core of Generation Innovate's approach to the Creator Economy is their innate digital fluency. For them, technology isn't a tool to be learned; it's an extension of their creative process. This seamless integration of digital skills allows them to push the boundaries of what's possible in content creation and distribution.

Take Zach King, for instance, a Millennial filmmaker who rose to fame with his "Digital sleight of hand" videos. King's mastery of visual effects, combined with his understanding of platform algorithms, allowed him to amass over 70 million followers across social media platforms (King, 2023). His success isn't just about technical skill – it's about understanding the digital ecosystem as a native language.

This digital fluency extends beyond content creation to platform development. Gen-Z entrepreneurs like Dylan Field, co-founder of Figma, are creating tools that are reshaping how creators collaborate and work. Figma's browser-based design tool embodies the collaborative, cloud-native approach that characterizes Generation Innovate's mindset (Konrad, 2022).

Another defining characteristic of Generation Innovate in the Creator Economy is their entrepreneurial spirit. A study by Deloitte (2023) found that 54% of Gen-Z respondents want to start their own business. In the Creator Economy, this entrepreneurial drive manifests in innovative ways of monetizing creativity.

Consider Emma Chamberlain, who parlayed her YouTube success into a coffee company, Chamberlain Coffee. By leveraging her personal brand and deep understanding of her audience, Chamberlain created a business that extends beyond content creation into physical products (Ramaswamy, 2023). This blurring of lines between creator and entrepreneur is a hallmark of how Generation Innovate approaches the Creator Economy.

Perhaps most significantly, Generation Innovate brings a purpose-driven approach to the Creator Economy. For many, it's not just about making money – it's about making a difference. A report by Bloomberg (2023) found that 67% of Millennial and Gen-Z creators consider social impact a key factor in their work.

This purpose-driven approach is exemplified by creators like Isra Hirsi, daughter of U.S. Representative Ilhan Omar. At just 20, Hirsi has leveraged social media to become a prominent climate activist, co-founding the U.S. Youth Climate Strike. Her work demonstrates how Generation Innovate is using the Creator Economy not just for personal gain, but as a platform for social change (Hirsi, 2023).

The global perspective of Generation Innovate is another key factor shaping the Creator Economy. Having grown up in an interconnected world, these creators naturally think beyond geographical boundaries. This global mindset is leading to innovative collaborations and cross-cultural content that enriches the Creator Economy.

For instance, the rise of virtual YouTubers (VTubers) – animated avatars operated by real people – has created a new form of global entertainment. Gawr Gura, a VTuber managed by Hololive Production, has amassed over 4 million subscribers with content that blends Japanese and Western pop culture, showcasing the borderless nature of Generation Innovate's approach (Cover Corp, 2023).

Generation Innovate's comfort with emerging technologies is also pushing the Creator Economy into new frontiers. From leveraging artificial intelligence in content creation to exploring blockchain for new monetization models, these young innovators are at the forefront of technological integration in the creative process.

Take Beeple (Mike Winkelmann), a millennial artist who sold an NFT of his work for $69 million, ushering in a new era of digital art ownership and valuation (Christie's, 2021). Or consider the rise of AI-assisted music production, with tools like AIVA allowing creators to compose with the help of artificial intelligence (AIVA Technologies, 2023).

However, it's important to note that Generation Innovate's approach to the Creator Economy isn't without challenges. Issues of burnout, platform dependency, and income instability are very real concerns. A study by The Tilt (2023) found that 68% of content creators feel burned out at least occasionally.

Yet, true to form, Generation Innovate is finding innovative ways to address these challenges. They're forming creator collectives to share resources and support, advocating for better platform policies, and diversifying their income streams. The rise of "poly-working" – maintaining multiple income streams – is a direct response to the uncertainties of the Creator Economy (Geyser, 2023).

As we look to the future, it's clear that Generation Innovate will continue to be the driving force shaping the Creator Economy. Their unique blend of digital fluency, entrepreneurial spirit, global perspective, and purpose-driven approach is not just changing how content is created and consumed – it's fundamentally reshaping our understanding of work, value creation, and economic participation.

The Creator Economy, as architected by Generation Innovate, is more than just a new business model. It's a Complex Adaptive System that reflects the values, skills, and aspirations of a generation coming into its own. As we move forward, understanding and harnessing the innovative potential of these digital natives will be crucial for anyone looking to thrive in this new economic paradigm.

In the next section, we'll explore how this Generation Innovate-led Creator Economy is reshaping industries and societies on a global scale, creating ripple effects that extend far beyond the digital realm.

2.3 The Global Impact: Reshaping Industries and Societies

The Creator Economy, driven by Generation Innovate, isn't just changing how individuals make a living—it's sending shockwaves through entire industries and reshaping societies worldwide. From entertainment to education, marketing to manufacturing, the ripple effects of this new economic paradigm are being felt across the globe. Let's explore how this revolution is transforming our world.

In the entertainment industry, the Creator Economy has turned the traditional model on its head. No longer do aspiring artists need to court record labels or movie studios to reach an audience. Take the music industry, for example. Billie Eilish, a Gen-Z icon, recorded her Grammy-winning debut album in her brother's bedroom studio (Savage, 2021). This DIY approach, enabled by digital tools and platforms, is democratizing the industry and challenging the dominance of major labels.

The impact extends beyond individual success stories. Streaming platforms like Spotify and YouTube have fundamentally altered how music is consumed and monetized. A study by the International Federation of the Phonographic Industry (IFPI, 2023) found that streaming now accounts for 65% of global recorded music revenue, with user-generated content on platforms like TikTok becoming a major driver of music discovery.

In the world of video entertainment, the rise of YouTubers and Twitch streamers is reshaping the landscape. These creators are not just competing with traditional media—they're often outperforming them, especially among younger audiences. A report by Tubular Labs (2023) revealed that user-generated content now accounts for over 40% of video viewing time among Gen-Z viewers.

The marketing industry has undergone a seismic shift due to the Creator Economy. Influencer marketing, once a niche strategy, has become a cornerstone of many brands' marketing efforts. According to a report by Influencer Marketing Hub (2023), the global influencer marketing market size has more than doubled since 2019, reaching $16.4 billion in 2023.

This shift has profound implications. It's not just changing where advertising dollars are spent—it's transforming how brands communicate with consumers. The authenticity and direct connection offered by creators often resonate more deeply with audiences than traditional advertising. As a result, we're seeing a move towards more personalized, community-driven marketing strategies.

Education is another sector being radically reshaped by the Creator Economy. Online learning platforms like Coursera, edX, and Udemy have democratized access to education, allowing experts to share their knowledge directly with learners worldwide. The global e-learning market is projected to reach $1 trillion by 2028 (Global Market Insights, 2023), driven largely by individual creators and subject matter experts turning their expertise into online courses.

This trend is challenging traditional educational institutions. Universities are being forced to rethink their value proposition in a world where quality educational content is freely available online. Some are adapting by partnering with online platforms or individual creators to offer more flexible, accessible learning options.

The Creator Economy is also having a significant impact on the job market and workforce development. Traditional career paths are being supplemented—and in some cases, replaced—by opportunities in content creation and digital entrepreneurship. A survey by Deloitte (2023) found that 54% of Gen-Z respondents aspire to become entrepreneurs, with many citing the Creator Economy as their preferred route.

This shift is prompting a reevaluation of skills valued in the job market. Creativity, digital literacy, and personal branding are becoming increasingly important alongside traditional qualifications. As a result, we're seeing changes in how companies recruit and develop talent, with some actively seeking out creators and influencers for their marketing and innovation teams.

On a broader societal level, the Creator Economy is influencing how we think about work-life balance and personal fulfillment. The idea of turning one's passion into a profession, long a pipe dream for many, is becoming increasingly attainable. This is leading to a cultural shift in how we view work and success, particularly among younger generations.

However, it's important to note that the global impact of the Creator Economy isn't uniformly positive. Issues of income inequality, digital divide, and cultural homogenization are very real concerns. A study by Patreon (2023) found that while the top 1% of creators on their platform earn substantial incomes, the majority struggle to make a living wage.

Moreover, the Creator Economy's reliance on digital platforms raises questions about data privacy, algorithmic bias, and the concentration of power in the hands of a few tech giants. These issues are prompting discussions about regulation and digital rights on a global scale.

Despite these challenges, the Creator Economy continues to grow and evolve, driven by the innovative spirit of Generation Innovate.

Its impact is being felt not just in economic terms, but in how we create, consume, learn, and connect as a global society.

As we look to the future, it's clear that understanding and engaging with the Creator Economy will be crucial for businesses, educators, policymakers, and individuals alike. It's not just a new economic model—it's a fundamental shift in how value is created and distributed in our increasingly digital world.

In the next section, we'll delve deeper into the challenges and opportunities presented by this new ecosystem, exploring how we can harness its potential while addressing its pitfalls.

2.4 Challenges and Opportunities in the Creator Ecosystem

The Creator Economy, while brimming with potential, is not without its complexities. Like any Complex Adaptive System, it presents a unique set of challenges and opportunities that are constantly evolving. For Generation Innovate, navigating this landscape requires not just creativity and digital savvy, but also resilience, adaptability, and a keen awareness of the ecosystem's dynamics.

One of the most significant challenges in the Creator Economy is the issue of oversaturation and discoverability. With the barriers to entry lower than ever, millions of creators are vying for attention in an increasingly crowded digital space. A study by SignalFire (2023) found that over 50 million people worldwide consider themselves creators, but only a small fraction manage to build a substantial audience.

This saturation creates a 'winner-takes-most' dynamic, where a small percentage of creators capture a disproportionate share of audience attention and revenue. According to a report by Patreon (2023), the top 1% of creators on their platform earn about 33% of the total revenue. This stark inequality poses challenges for aspiring creators and raises questions about the long-term sustainability of the ecosystem.

However, this challenge also presents opportunities for innovation. We're seeing the rise of niche platforms and communities catering to specific interests or demographics. For instance, Twitch has become a hub for gaming content, while Skillshare focuses on educational material. This specialization allows creators to find and nurture more dedicated, engaged audiences.

Another major challenge is the issue of platform dependency. Most creators rely heavily on large tech platforms like YouTube, Instagram, or TikTok to reach their audiences. These platforms can change their algorithms or monetization policies at any time, potentially upending a creator's livelihood overnight. A survey by The Tilt (2023) found that 76% of creators are concerned about their dependence on third-party platforms.

This challenge has sparked a movement towards greater creator independence. We're seeing the emergence of tools and platforms that allow creators to own their audience relationships more directly. Substack, for instance, enables writers to build email lists and monetize through subscriptions, reducing their reliance on social media algorithms.

The issue of burnout and mental health is another significant challenge in the Creator Economy. The pressure to constantly produce content, coupled with the public nature of the work, can take a severe toll. A study by Vibely (2023) revealed that 90% of content creators have experienced burnout, with many citing the relentless pace and public scrutiny as major stressors.

Yet, this challenge has also led to opportunities for innovation in the wellness space. We're seeing the rise of digital wellness tools specifically designed for creators, as well as creator-focused mental health resources and communities. Platforms like Shine, co-founded by Millennial entrepreneurs Marah Lidey and Naomi Hirabayashi, are pioneering personalized self-care for the digital age (Shine, 2023).

The Creator Economy also grapples with issues of diversity and inclusion. While the democratization of content creation has opened doors for underrepresented voices, systemic biases still persist. A report by MSL Group (2022) found a 35% pay gap between white and BIPOC influencers, highlighting ongoing inequalities in the ecosystem.

However, this challenge has spurred efforts to create more inclusive spaces within the Creator Economy. Platforms like Snapchat's 523 program, which provides support to small, minority-owned content companies, are working to level the playing field (Snap Inc., 2023). Additionally, creator collectives focused on amplifying diverse voices are emerging, creating new opportunities for collaboration and mutual support.

Another significant challenge — and opportunity — lies in the realm of education and skill development. The Creator Economy requires a unique blend of creative, technical, and entrepreneurial skills that are not typically taught in traditional educational settings. A survey by Adobe (2023) found that 68% of creators feel they lack some of the skills necessary to grow their creative businesses.

This skills gap has led to a boom in creator-focused educational content and programs. Platforms like YouTuber MrBeast's Creator Academy are emerging to fill this need, offering practical guidance on everything from content strategy to financial management for creators (MrBeast, 2023). Traditional educational institutions are also beginning to incorporate creator skills into their curricula, recognizing the growing importance of this sector.

The evolving regulatory landscape presents both challenges and opportunities for the Creator Economy. Issues around content moderation, data privacy, and fair compensation are increasingly coming under scrutiny from regulators worldwide. The European Union's Digital Services Act, for instance, imposes new obligations on platforms regarding content moderation and algorithmic transparency (European Commission, 2023).

While increased regulation poses challenges, it also creates opportunities for innovators to develop tools and services that help creators and platforms navigate this complex landscape. We're seeing the emergence of legal tech startups focused on creator rights, as well as AI-powered content moderation tools designed to help creators stay compliant with platform policies.

Perhaps the most exciting opportunities in the Creator Economy lie in the integration of emerging technologies. Artificial Intelligence, for instance, is opening up new possibilities for content creation and audience engagement. Tools like Runway ML are enabling creators to leverage AI for video editing and special effects, democratizing capabilities once reserved for big-budget productions (Runway, 2023).

Similarly, blockchain technology and NFTs (Non-Fungible Tokens) are creating new avenues for creators to monetize their work and engage with their audiences. The NFT market, while volatile, has opened up new possibilities for digital artists and creators to sell their work directly to collectors.

As we navigate these challenges and opportunities, it's clear that the Creator Economy is not just a static business model, but a dynamic, evolving ecosystem. For Generation Innovate, success in this space requires not just creativity and digital skills, but also adaptability, resilience, and a willingness to continuously learn and evolve.

In our final section, we'll look ahead to the future of the Creator Economy, exploring emerging trends and making some educated predictions about where this exciting field might be headed.

The Future: Evolving Trends and Predictions

As we stand on the cusp of a new era in the Creator Economy, driven by the innovative spirit of Millennials and Gen-Z, the future promises to be as exciting as it is unpredictable. Like any Complex Adaptive System, the Creator Economy will continue to evolve in response to technological advancements, societal shifts, and the changing needs of both creators and consumers. Let's explore some of the key trends and make some informed predictions about where this dynamic ecosystem is headed.

The Rise of the Metaverse and Virtual Worlds

One of the most exciting frontiers for the Creator Economy is the emerging metaverse. As virtual and augmented reality technologies mature, we're likely to see an explosion of new creative opportunities. Creators won't just be making content for screens, but designing immersive experiences, virtual goods, and entire digital worlds.

Epic Games' Fortnite has already given us a glimpse of this future, hosting virtual concerts attended by millions and selling digital skins worth billions. According to a report by Bloomberg Intelligence (2023), the metaverse market could reach $800 billion by 2027. For Generation Innovate, this represents a vast new canvas for creativity and entrepreneurship.

Prediction: By 2030, we'll see the emergence of "metaverse moguls" – creators who have built vast virtual empires spanning games, social spaces, and digital marketplaces.

AI as a Creative Partner

Artificial Intelligence is set to play an increasingly prominent role in the Creator Economy. Rather than replacing human creativity, AI is likely to augment it, serving as a powerful tool for ideation, production, and distribution.

We're already seeing this with tools like OpenAI's Chat GPT4o for writing assistance, and Midjourney for image generation. As these technologies evolve, they'll enable creators to produce higher-quality content more efficiently, potentially democratizing access to professional-grade creative tools.

Prediction: By 2025, AI-human collaborations will become the norm in content creation, with creators using AI for everything from script writing to video editing, while focusing their human creativity on high-level strategy and emotional resonance.

Decentralized Autonomous Organizations (DAOs) and Creator Collectives

The future of the Creator Economy may be less about individual stars and more about collaborative networks. We're likely to see the rise of creator DAOs – decentralized organizations where decisions are made by community consensus rather than a central authority.

Friends With Benefits, a DAO for artists and creators, has already shown the potential of this model. As blockchain technology matures, these decentralized collectives could provide creators with new ways to pool resources, share risks, and collectively bargain with platforms.

Prediction: By 2028, some of the most influential entities in the Creator Economy will be DAOs, challenging traditional media companies and talent agencies.

4. Hyper-Personalization and AI-Driven Content Curation

As AI and machine learning technologies advance, we're likely to see a shift towards hyper-personalized content experiences. Algorithms will become increasingly sophisticated at understanding individual preferences and serving up tailored content.

For creators, this means the potential for dynamic content that adapts to each viewer's preferences in real-time. Netflix's interactive shows like "Bandersnatch" offer an early glimpse of this potential.

Prediction: By 2026, "adaptive content" that changes based on viewer behavior and preferences will become a major trend, with creators designing modular content that can be reassembled for each individual viewer.

The Creator Middle Class

While much attention has been paid to top earners in the Creator Economy, the future may see the rise of a robust "creator middle class." As monetization tools become more sophisticated and diverse, it will become increasingly viable for niche creators to make a stable income.

Platforms like Patreon and Buy Me a Coffee are already facilitating this trend, allowing creators to monetize smaller, dedicated audiences. According to Li Jin, a prominent investor in the Creator Economy, this could lead to a "1000 True Fans 2.0" model, where creators need even fewer dedicated supporters to make a living (Jin, 2023).

Prediction: By 2030, we'll see a significant increase in the number of people able to make a middle-class income solely from content creation, leading to a reshaping of traditional career paths.

Blockchain and Tokenization in the Creator Economy

Blockchain technology and tokenization are set to play a larger role in the Creator Economy, potentially revolutionizing how creators monetize their work and engage with their audiences.

Social tokens, which allow fans to invest directly in a creator's success, are likely to become more prevalent. Platforms like Rally are already pioneering this model. Meanwhile, NFTs will continue to evolve, potentially becoming a standard way for creators to sell limited-edition digital goods.

Prediction: By 2027, most successful creators will have their own tokens, creating new models of fan engagement and monetization that blur the lines between creators, fans, and investors.

Regulation and Digital Rights

As the Creator Economy grows in economic and cultural importance, it's likely to face increased regulatory scrutiny. Issues around data privacy, content moderation, and fair compensation for creators are likely to come to the forefront.

We may see the emergence of a "Creator Bill of Rights," establishing baseline protections for those working in the digital economy. The European Union's recent steps to ensure fair treatment of gig workers could provide a model for this.

Prediction: By 2029, we'll see comprehensive international frameworks governing the Creator Economy, addressing issues from AI content labeling to minimum pay standards for platform workers.

It's clear that the Creator Economy will continue to be a dynamic, rapidly evolving space. For Generation Innovate, this presents both challenges and unprecedented opportunities. Those who can adapt to these changes, leveraging new technologies while maintaining authenticity and creative vision, will be well-positioned to thrive.

The future of the Creator Economy is not just about new tools or platforms – it's about a fundamental shift in how we create, consume, and value content. It's about the democratization of creativity and the empowerment of individual voices. As we move forward, the innovations driven by Millennials and Gen-Z in this space will continue to reshape not just the digital landscape, but our broader economy and society.

The Creator Economy of tomorrow will be more immersive, more personalized, more decentralized, and more integrated into our daily lives than we can perhaps imagine today. It will present new challenges, but also boundless opportunities for those ready to seize them. The future is bright, and it's being created, one post, one video, one digital experience at a time, by the visionary members of Generation Innovate.

KEY INSIGHTS

- The creator economy is enabling individuals to monetize their creativity directly
- Digital platforms are lowering barriers to entry for creative entrepreneurs
- The creator economy is changing how we think about work, value, and innovation

INNOVATION CHALLENGE

Identify a skill or passion you have. Spend the next week exploring how you might monetize it in the creator economy. What platforms could you use? What audience might you target?

REFLECTION QUESTIONS

1. How might the principles of the creator economy be applied to drive innovation within traditional business structures?

2. What opportunities and challenges do you see in the creator economy for your industry or profession?

3. How could embracing aspects of the creator economy enhance your own creative output or career development?

CHAPTER 3

THE DIGITAL LANDSCAPE OF GENERATION INNOVATE

We stand at the cusp of a digital revolution that has fundamentally reshaped how we interact, create, and innovate. This chapter explores the unique digital landscape that Millennials and Gen-Z navigate daily, a terrain as familiar to them as the physical world was to previous generations. However, this new landscape, while rich with opportunities, also presents significant challenges and potential risks that we must carefully consider.

From the evolution of the digital native to the cognitive adaptations brought about by constant connectivity, from the transformation of social dynamics to the explosion of digital tools for creative expression, we'll examine how technology has not just changed what Generation Innovate does, but who they are at their core. Crucially, we'll also address the growing concerns about how this digital immersion may be impacting mental health and well-being.

As we embark on this exploration, we'll uncover both the tremendous opportunities and the significant challenges that this digital immersion presents. We'll see how the ability to process vast amounts of information coexists with struggles for deep focus, how global connectivity can lead to both expanded horizons and echo chambers, and how digital creativity tools offer unprecedented possibilities while potentially reshaping the very nature of innovation. At the same time, we'll confront the rising alarm about increased rates of anxiety, depression, and social isolation among this generation, directly linked to their digital experiences.

Our journey through this digital landscape will provide crucial insights into how we can harness the unique strengths of Generation Innovate while addressing the pitfalls of their digital upbringing. This includes not only leveraging their digital fluency for innovation but also developing strategies to protect and promote their mental health in an increasingly connected world. By understanding this new terrain, we can better prepare to foster a generation of innovators who are not only equally adept in both digital and physical realms but also emotionally resilient and mentally well-equipped to tackle the complex challenges of our rapidly evolving world.

As we proceed, we'll maintain a balanced perspective, acknowledging both the exciting potential and the serious concerns that come with this digital landscape. Our goal is to paint a comprehensive picture that will inform how we approach fostering innovation in Generation Innovate, always keeping in mind the critical importance of their overall well-being.

3.1 THE EVOLUTION OF THE DIGITAL NATIVE

The term "Digital native" has become a ubiquitous descriptor for younger generations, but its meaning has evolved significantly since Marc Prensky first coined it in 2001. Prensky used the term to describe individuals born into the digital age, contrasting them with "Digital immigrants" who adopted technology later in life (Prensky, 2001). But as we've moved from Millennials to Gen-Z, the concept of a digital native has taken on new dimensions.

Millennials, born roughly between 1981 and 1996, were the first generation to come of age alongside the internet. They witnessed the transformation from dial-up connections and clunky desktop computers to high-speed broadband and sleek smartphones. In contrast, Gen-Z, born from 1997 onwards, has never known a world without Wi-Fi, social media, or smartphones. For them, the digital world isn't a separate space to be navigated; it's an integral part of their reality.

This shift is vividly captured in Jean Twenge's research, detailed in her book "iGen." Twenge highlights how Gen-Z's constant connectivity has fundamentally reshaped their experiences and expectations. Unlike previous generations, Gen-Z's social lives, education, and entertainment are deeply intertwined with digital technology (Twenge, 2017). This has led to what Jonathan Haidt calls a "phone-based childhood" in his work "The Anxious Generation," where smartphones have become central to nearly every aspect of young people's lives (Haidt, 2024).

However, it's crucial to understand that being a digital native isn't just about technological proficiency. As Palfrey and Gasser argue in

"Born Digital," it's about a fundamentally different way of processing information and interacting with the world (Palfrey & Gasser, 2008). Gen-Z's digital fluency often translates into unique skills such as rapid information processing, multitasking, and an intuitive understanding of user interfaces. They're not just consumers of digital content; they're creators, curators, and critics, constantly engaging with and shaping the digital landscape.

This digital immersion has led to some remarkable abilities. Many Gen-Zers can navigate complex digital ecosystems with ease, quickly adopting new platforms and technologies. They're often adept at visual communication, having grown up in a world of emojis, memes, and short-form video content. Their ability to quickly assess and filter large amounts of information – a necessity in the age of information overload – is often impressive.

Yet, this digital immersion comes with trade-offs. Haidt's research suggests that the phone-based childhood may be contributing to decreased face-to-face interactions and potentially impacting mental health (Haidt, 2024). The constant connectivity can lead to issues with attention span, sleep quality, and anxiety. There's also concern about the depth of knowledge acquisition when information is always just a Google search away.

The challenge for Generation Innovate lies in leveraging their digital fluency while maintaining a healthy balance with real-world experiences. As educators, parents, and mentors, we need to recognize both the strengths and potential pitfalls of this digital upbringing. We should encourage the innovative use of technology while also fostering skills that may be underdeveloped due to digital immersion – things like sustained focus, face-to-face communication, and comfort with ambiguity and boredom.

As we explore the innovative potential of this generation, it's essential to recognize both the advantages and challenges of their digital upbringing. Their unique perspective, shaped by constant connectivity and access to global information, positions them to approach problems in novel ways. They're often more comfortable with rapid change and iteration, qualities that are invaluable in today's fast-paced innovation landscape.

However, nurturing their creativity and innovation may require strategies that complement their digital skills with offline experiences and interpersonal connections. This might involve creating opportunities for hands-on, tactile learning experiences or encouraging periods of digital detox to allow for deeper reflection and creativity.

The evolution of the digital native from Millennials to Gen-Z represents a profound shift in how we interact with technology and information. As we continue to explore the innovative potential of Generation Innovate, we must remain mindful of this shifting landscape. By understanding and embracing the unique characteristics of these digital natives, while also addressing the challenges their digital upbringing presents, we can help foster a generation of innovators who are equally adept in both digital and physical realms.

3.2 COGNITIVE ADAPTATIONS IN THE DIGITAL AGE

The digital age hasn't just changed what we know; it's fundamentally altered how we think. As Marshall McLuhan famously said, "We shape our tools, and thereafter our tools shape us." This is particularly true for Generation Innovate, whose cognitive processes have developed in tandem with digital technology.

Research by Firth et al. (2019) suggests that internet use is literally reshaping our cognitive processes. Their study, published in World Psychiatry, proposes that the internet may be producing both acute and sustained alterations in specific areas of cognition. For Generation Innovate, who have grown up with this technology, these changes are particularly pronounced.

One of the most significant cognitive adaptations is in the realm of attention and multitasking. Many members of Gen-Z pride themselves on their ability to juggle multiple streams of information simultaneously - texting while watching a video, for instance, or switching between various apps and platforms. However, Uncapher and Wagner's (2018) work on media multitaskers reveals a more complex picture. While Gen-Z often engages in multiple streams of information simultaneously, this doesn't necessarily translate to improved multitasking abilities. Instead, it may lead to a more distributed form of attention, allowing for quick shifts between tasks but potentially at the cost of deep focus.

This distributed attention can be both a strength and a weakness. On one hand, it allows for rapid processing of diverse information sources, which can be valuable in our information-rich world. On the other hand, it may hinder the ability to engage in deep, sustained focus - a crucial skill for complex problem-solving and creative breakthroughs.

The way we remember and process information has also evolved. Sparrow et al.'s (2011) "Google Effects on Memory" study demonstrates that constant access to information is changing how we encode and retrieve memories. Their research, published in Science, found that when people expect to have future access to information, they have lower rates of recall of the information itself and enhanced recall of where to access it. In other words, we're becoming more adept at remembering where to find information rather than remembering the information itself.

This "outsourcing" of memory to digital devices frees up cognitive resources but may also change how we approach problem-solving and creativity. On one hand, it allows us to quickly access a vast array of information, potentially leading to novel connections and ideas. On the other hand, it may reduce our capacity for deep, internalized knowledge, which is often crucial for innovation.

Loh and Kanai's (2016) research further explores how internet use might be altering our neural circuitry. They suggest that the internet's hypertext structure may be promoting non-linear thinking, which could enhance creativity and innovation. The ability to quickly jump between different ideas and information sources might foster more associative thinking, a key component of creativity.

However, this same hypertext structure may also be reducing our capacity for deep reading and sustained concentration. Nicholas Carr, in his book "The Shallows," argues that the internet may be rewiring our brains to be more adept at shallow processing of multiple information streams, at the expense of deep reading and contemplation (Carr, 2010).

For Generation Innovate, these cognitive adaptations present both opportunities and challenges. Their ability to quickly process and synthesize information from multiple sources can be a significant asset in fast-paced, innovative environments. They're often able to make rapid connections between disparate ideas, a skill that's crucial for innovation.

However, cultivating the ability to engage in deep, focused work remains crucial for complex problem-solving and creative breakthroughs. Many groundbreaking innovations come not from rapid idea generation, but from sustained, deep engagement with a problem or idea.

As we consider the innovative potential of this generation, it's important to recognize these cognitive shifts. Strategies for fostering innovation may need to leverage their unique cognitive strengths while also developing their capacity for sustained focus and deep thinking. This might involve designing work environments and processes that accommodate both quick, collaborative ideation and periods of intense, individual concentration.

Educational and professional development programs might need to be adapted to suit these cognitive patterns. For instance, incorporating more interactive, multimedia elements can engage distributed attention, while also including exercises to build sustained focus and deep reading skills.

It's also worth noting that these cognitive adaptations are not set in stone. The brain's neuroplasticity means that we can cultivate different cognitive skills throughout our lives. For Generation Innovate, this might mean consciously developing skills that don't come as naturally in the digital age - like sustained focus or memorization - while also leveraging their strengths in rapid information processing and non-linear thinking.

Ultimately, the goal should be to create a cognitive toolkit that's adaptable to different situations. In some cases, the rapid, multitasking approach of the digital native will be most effective. In others, the ability to shut out distractions and focus deeply will be crucial. By recognizing and working with these cognitive adaptations, we can help Generation Innovate harness their unique strengths while also developing the full range of cognitive skills needed for innovation in the 21st century.

3.3 Social Dynamics and Connectivity

The digital landscape has fundamentally altered how Generation Innovate forms and maintains social connections. To understand this shift, we need to look beyond mere technological changes and examine the profound impact on social structures, relationships, and the very nature of community.

Danah Boyd's seminal work, "It's Complicated," provides crucial insights into how social media has become an integral part of young people's social lives. Boyd argues that social media isn't just a new communication tool; it's a new social context in which teens live their lives (Boyd, 2014). For Generation Innovate, platforms like

Instagram, TikTok, or Discord aren't just apps - they're digital spaces where friendships are formed, identities are shaped, and social norms are negotiated.

One of the most significant changes in social dynamics is the shift towards what sociologist Barry Wellman calls "networked individualism." This concept, explored in Wellman et al.'s (2003) work, describes how digital technology allows individuals to maintain large, diverse networks of weak ties alongside smaller networks of strong ties. For Generation Innovate, this means unprecedented access to diverse perspectives and ideas, potentially fueling innovation through cross-pollination of concepts from different domains.

Consider a young entrepreneur in Generation Innovate. She might have a close-knit group of friends she interacts with daily via group chats, a broader network of acquaintances she keeps up with through social media, and an even wider network of weak ties - perhaps followers of her business account or members of online communities related to her field. Each of these network layers provides different types of social capital and information flow, creating a rich, multifaceted social environment.

However, this hyperconnectivity comes with its own challenges. Sherry Turkle's "Alone Together" highlights the paradox of feeling increasingly isolated despite being more connected than ever (Turkle, 2017). Turkle argues that our constant digital connections can sometimes come at the expense of deeper, more meaningful relationships. This phenomenon could have implications for the collaborative aspects of innovation, potentially impacting the depth and quality of interpersonal relationships that often drive creative partnerships.

Hampton et al.'s (2011) research on core networks and social isolation provides a more nuanced view. Their study found that while digital technology can expand our networks, it doesn't necessarily lead to more diverse or supportive core relationships. For Generation Innovate, this suggests a need to consciously cultivate meaningful connections alongside their expansive digital networks.

The global connectivity afforded by digital technology also plays a crucial role in shaping Generation Innovate's perspective. Exposure to global issues and diverse cultures through social media and online communities can foster a more inclusive and globally-minded approach to innovation. A young innovator today might be inspired by a viral video from halfway across the world, collaborate with team members across multiple time zones, and receive feedback on their ideas from a global audience - all before breakfast.

This global outlook may be particularly valuable in addressing complex, interconnected challenges like climate change or public health crises. Generation Innovate often approaches these issues with a sense of global citizenship, understanding that solutions need to transcend national boundaries.

However, it's important to note that this global connectivity can also lead to echo chambers and filter bubbles. Eli Pariser's work on filter bubbles highlights how algorithmic curation of our online experiences can limit exposure to diverse viewpoints, potentially narrowing our perspective rather than broadening it (Pariser, 2011). For Generation Innovate, being aware of these digital echo chambers and actively seeking out diverse viewpoints is crucial for fostering true innovation.

The impact of these altered social dynamics on innovation is multifaceted. On one hand, the ability to quickly form and leverage diverse networks can accelerate the spread of ideas and facilitate rapid iteration. The collaborative tools that Generation Innovate has grown up with - from Google Docs to GitHub - make it easier than ever to co-create and build upon others' ideas.

On the other hand, the potential lack of depth in digital relationships could impact the kind of trust and understanding that often underlies truly groundbreaking collaborations. There's also the risk of "performative innovation" - where the focus is more on being seen as innovative on social media rather than doing the deep, often unglamorous work of true innovation.

As we consider the innovative potential of this generation, it's important to recognize how these altered social dynamics might influence their approach to collaboration and problem-solving. Their comfort with digital collaboration tools and their ability to tap into global networks of knowledge could be significant assets. However, strategies for fostering innovation may need to include opportunities for deep, in-person collaboration to complement these digital interactions.

Educational and workplace environments might need to be redesigned to accommodate these new social dynamics. This could involve creating spaces that facilitate both digital and face-to-face collaboration, or developing programs that help young innovators build meaningful relationships alongside their expansive networks.

Ultimately, the goal should be to harness the power of Generation Innovate's expanded social networks while also fostering the deep, trusting relationships that often drive true innovation. By understanding and working with these new social dynamics, we can help create an environment where the collaborative potential of the digital age can be fully realized.

3.4 Digital Tools and Creative Expression

The proliferation of digital tools has dramatically expanded the possibilities for creative expression, providing Generation Innovate with unprecedented means to bring their ideas to life. This digital toolkit isn't just changing how creativity is expressed; it's reshaping the very nature of creative processes and products.

Lev Manovich's work on "Cultural Analytics" provides a fascinating lens through which to view these changes. Manovich argues that digital media isn't just a new set of tools, but a new cultural language with its own grammar and aesthetics (Manovich, 2020). For Generation Innovate, this digital language is often their native tongue. They think in terms of pixels and algorithms, memes and remixes, creating new forms of expression that blend technology and art in novel ways.

Consider the rise of digital art forms like generative art, where algorithms are used to create visual or musical pieces. Or think about the complex narratives being woven through interactive media like video games and virtual reality experiences. These aren't just new mediums; they're new ways of thinking about creativity itself.

Peppler and Kafai's research on digital media production in informal learning environments demonstrates how platforms like Scratch are enabling young people to engage in complex creative processes, blending coding with artistic expression (Peppler & Kafai, 2007). This convergence of technical and creative skills is a hallmark of Generation Innovate's approach to creativity. For them, the line between "coder" and "artist" is often blurry, if it exists at all.

Take, for example, a young creator using a tool like Processing to create interactive visual art. They're simultaneously engaging with principles of computer science, visual design, and interactive storytelling. This multidisciplinary approach to creativity is often second nature to Generation Innovate, and it's leading to innovative cross-pollinations between fields that were once considered separate.

The collaborative aspect of digital creativity is another key feature of this landscape. Paulus and Nijstad's work on group creativity explores how digital platforms have made it easier than ever for creators to collaborate across geographical boundaries, leading to new forms of distributed creativity (Paulus & Nijstad, 2003). We see this in action with phenomena like open-source software development, where thousands of contributors around the world can work together on a single project.

Literat and Glăveanu's research on online creative participation further illuminates how digital platforms are fostering new models of collective creativity, where the boundaries between creator and audience become increasingly blurred (Literat & Glăveanu, 2018). Think of platforms like Twitch, where streamers co-create content with their audience in real-time, or crowdsourced art projects where thousands of individuals contribute to a single work.

These digital tools and platforms are not just changing how creativity is expressed, but also how it's learned and developed. Online tutorials, creative communities, and digital mentorship are providing Generation Innovate with diverse pathways for skill acquisition and creative growth outside of traditional educational structures. A young person interested in animation, for instance, might learn through YouTube tutorials, practice with free software, share their work on social media for feedback, and even monetize their creations through platforms like Patreon - all without ever setting foot in a formal classroom.

However, the ubiquity of digital tools also presents challenges. The ease of digital creation can sometimes lead to a focus on quantity over quality, or a reliance on pre-made templates that might stifle true innovation. There's a risk of what we might call "pseudo-creativity" - work that looks creative on the surface but lacks depth or originality.

Additionally, the rapid pace of technological change means that creative skills need to be continually updated and adapted. A digital tool that's cutting-edge today might be obsolete tomorrow, requiring creators to be in a constant state of learning and adaptation. This can be both exhilarating and exhausting for young innovators.

For Generation Innovate, navigating this landscape of digital creativity requires a balance between leveraging the power of digital tools and maintaining a connection to traditional creative practices. The most innovative approaches often emerge from the intersection of digital and analog techniques, combining the flexibility and reach of digital platforms with the tactile engagement and serendipity of physical creation.

Consider, for example, the resurgence of analog technologies like vinyl records or instant cameras among digital natives. These aren't just nostalgic trends; they represent a desire for tangible, physical experiences in a world that's increasingly digital. The most interesting innovations often happen at the intersection of these digital and physical realms - think of augmented reality experiences that overlay digital information on the physical world, or 3D printing technologies that bring digital designs into physical reality.

As we consider how to foster innovation in this generation, it's crucial to provide opportunities that embrace the full spectrum of creative tools, both digital and traditional. This might involve creating hybrid workspaces that combine digital fabrication tools with traditional craft materials, or developing projects that require both online collaboration and physical prototyping.

Educational institutions and workplaces need to adapt to this new creative landscape. This might involve more flexible, project-based learning environments that allow for experimentation with diverse creative tools. It could also mean rethinking how we assess and value creative work, moving beyond traditional metrics to consider factors like community engagement or iterative development.

Ultimately, the goal should be to help Generation Innovate develop a rich, versatile creative toolkit that spans both digital and physical realms. By embracing this holistic approach to creativity, we can help them harness the full potential of their digital fluency while still grounding their innovations in the physical world. This balanced approach will be crucial for addressing the complex, multifaceted challenges of the 21st century, where solutions often need to bridge the digital and physical worlds.

As we conclude our exploration of the digital landscape that shapes Generation Innovate, it's clear that we're witnessing a profound transformation in how creativity and innovation unfold. The digital tools and platforms we've discussed offer unprecedented opportunities for connection, collaboration, and creative expression, reshaping cognitive processes, social dynamics, and the very nature of creative work. However, this digital revolution is not without its challenges. The constant connectivity, information overload, and rapid pace of change can take a toll on individuals navigating this landscape, with the same tools that empower innovation also having the potential to overwhelm and fragment attention.

This brings us to crucial questions: How can Generation Innovate harness the immense potential of this digital landscape while maintaining their well-being and sustaining their creative drive? How do we ensure that the benefits of our digital tools don't come at the cost of mental health and long-term innovative capacity?

In the next chapter, we'll delve deeper into these critical issues, exploring the psychological impact of digital immersion and examining both the opportunities and challenges it presents for mental well-being. We'll investigate strategies for digital wellness, techniques for fostering creativity amid constant distraction, and approaches to building a sustainable innovation mindset. As we transition from understanding the digital landscape to navigating its psychological terrain, we'll seek to equip Generation Innovate with the tools they need not just to survive in this new world, but to thrive and drive meaningful change. The future of innovation depends not just on our technological capabilities, but on our ability to cultivate resilient, balanced, and creatively fulfilled innovators.

KEY INSIGHTS

- Digital natives possess unique skills in rapid information processing and visual communication
- Cognitive adaptations in the digital age affect attention, memory, and problem-solving approaches
- Digital connectivity has transformed social dynamics and creative collaboration possibilities

INNOVATION CHALLENGE

Identify a traditional process in your work or life. Spend a week reimagining how digital tools and platforms could transform this process. How would a digital native approach it differently?

REFLECTION QUESTIONS

1. How has the digital landscape shaped your own cognitive processes and social interactions?

2. What opportunities and challenges do you see in leveraging digital natives' unique skills for innovation?

3. How can organizations balance the benefits of digital connectivity with the need for deep, focused work?

CHAPTER 4

DIGITAL WELL-BEING FOR GENERATION INNOVATE

In the bustling digital landscape of the Creator Economy, Generation Innovate finds itself at an exciting yet challenging crossroads. Armed with unprecedented tools for creativity and global reach, these young innovators are reshaping industries and redefining success. Yet, as they navigate this new frontier, they face unique challenges to their well-being that previous generations could scarcely imagine.

This chapter explores the intricate dance between digital opportunity and personal wellness that defines the experience of Millennial and Gen-Z creators. We'll delve into the cognitive, psychological, and physical impacts of deep digital immersion, uncovering both the pitfalls and the potential for growth. More importantly, we'll explore strategies for thriving in this new ecosystem, ensuring that the creative fire that drives Generation Innovate can burn brightly without burning out.

From mindful technology use to building supportive digital communities, we'll uncover how young creators are pioneering new approaches to well-being that are as innovative as their content. Join us as we explore how Generation Innovate is not just reshaping the digital landscape, but also redefining what it means to live a balanced, fulfilling life in the age of constant connectivity.

4.1 The Creator's Dilemma: Balancing Opportunity and Well-being in the Digital Age

Picture this: A young content creator sits in her room, bathed in the glow of multiple screens. She's simultaneously editing a video, engaging with followers on social media, and brainstorming her next big project. It's 2 AM, but in the world of the Creator Economy, time zones blur and opportunities never sleep. This scene encapsulates both the exhilarating potential and the pressing challenges faced by Generation Innovate in the digital age.

The Creator Economy has opened up unprecedented opportunities for young innovators. A survey by SignalFire (2023) found that over 50 million people worldwide now consider themselves creators, with Millennials and Gen-Z making up the majority. This democratization of creativity has allowed talented individuals to build careers, reach global audiences, and drive change in ways that were unimaginable just a decade ago.

Take Emma Chamberlain, for example. Starting her YouTube channel at 16, she quickly rose to fame with her authentic, relatable content. By 20, she had launched her own coffee company, Chamberlain Coffee, leveraging her online following to build a successful business (Forbes, 2022). Chamberlain's journey exemplifies the potential of the Creator Economy to turn passion into profession at a young age.

However, this new frontier of opportunity comes with its own set of challenges. The same digital tools that empower creators also have the potential to overwhelm them. A study by The Tilt (2023) found that 68% of content creators feel burned out at least occasionally. The pressure to constantly produce content, engage with audiences, and stay ahead of algorithmic changes can take a significant toll on well-being.

The dilemma faced by Generation Innovate is multifaceted. On one hand, digital platforms offer the tools to express creativity, build communities, and even change the world. On the other, the always-on nature of these platforms can lead to stress, anxiety, and a blurring of work-life boundaries.

This double-edged sword is particularly sharp for young creators. Their digital fluency allows them to navigate online spaces with ease, but it also means they're more deeply immersed in the digital world than any generation before them. A report by Common Sense Media (2023) found that teens now spend an average of 7 hours and 22 minutes per day on screens, not including time spent on school or homework.

This level of digital immersion has profound implications for well-being. While it can foster creativity and connection, it also poses risks to mental health, sleep patterns, and physical well-being. A study published in the Journal of Adolescent Health (Chen et al., 2022) found a correlation between high social media use and increased symptoms of depression and anxiety among young adults.

Yet, it's crucial to note that the relationship between digital engagement and well-being isn't straightforward. The same technologies that can contribute to stress and burnout can also be powerful tools for self-expression, learning, and personal growth. Many young creators report that their online activities provide a sense of purpose, community, and creative fulfillment.

The key lies in finding balance. Successful creators in Generation Innovate are those who can harness the opportunities of the digital age while maintaining their physical and mental well-being. They're pioneering new approaches to work-life balance that reflect the realities of the Creator Economy.

For instance, many are adopting flexible work schedules that align with their natural rhythms rather than traditional 9-to-5 structures. Others are incorporating digital detoxes into their routines, setting boundaries around device use to ensure time for offline activities and relationships.

Moreover, there's a growing recognition among young creators of the importance of diversifying both their income streams and their sources of personal fulfillment. Many are exploring hybrid careers that combine online content creation with offline pursuits, reducing their dependence on any single platform or revenue source.

The Creator Economy is also fostering new conversations about mental health and well-being. Influential creators like Zoe Sugg and Tyler Oakley have used their platforms to openly discuss mental health challenges, helping to destigmatize these issues among their young audiences.

As we move forward, it's clear that navigating the Creator's Dilemma will be crucial for the long-term success and well-being of Generation Innovate. The challenge isn't to choose between digital opportunity and personal wellness, but to find ways to pursue both simultaneously.

In the sections that follow, we'll explore specific strategies for maintaining cognitive, psychological, and physical health in the digital age. We'll uncover how young creators are leveraging technology not just for content creation, but for wellness and personal growth. And we'll examine how the principles of innovation that drive the Creator Economy can also be applied to revolutionize our approach to digital well-being.

The Creator's Dilemma isn't just a personal challenge—it's a frontier for innovation in its own right. As Generation Innovate navigates this complex landscape, they're not just creating content; they're pioneering new models of work, creativity, and well-being that could shape the future for generations to come.

4.2 Mind and Body: The Holistic Impact of Digital Immersion on Young Innovators

The digital world that Generation Innovate inhabits isn't just a space for creativity and commerce—it's an environment that profoundly shapes their cognitive processes, emotional landscapes, and physical well-being. To truly understand the impact of the Creator Economy on young innovators, we need to take a holistic view of how deep digital immersion affects both mind and body.

Cognitively, the constant stream of information and stimuli that creators navigate is reshaping how their brains process information. A study by Firth et al. (2019) suggests that internet use can alter brain structure and function, particularly in areas associated with attention, memory, and social cognition. For young creators, this translates into an enhanced ability to multitask and quickly shift between different types of information—skills that are crucial in the fast-paced world of content creation.

However, this cognitive agility comes at a cost. The same study found that heavy internet users often struggle with sustained attention and deep, focused work. This presents a unique challenge for creators who need to balance quick, reactive content creation (like social media posts) with more in-depth, thoughtful projects.

Take the case of Alex, a 24-year-old YouTuber and podcaster. "I can shoot and edit a TikTok video in minutes," he says, "but when it comes to scripting my long-form content, I find myself constantly distracted by notifications and the urge to check analytics." Alex's experience is common among young creators, highlighting the need for strategies to cultivate deep focus in a hyper-connected world.

Psychologically, the impact of digital immersion is equally profound. The Creator Economy often blurs the lines between personal and professional life, leading to what psychologists call "context collapse" (Davis & Jurgenson, 2014). When your personal brand is your business, it becomes increasingly difficult to separate work from life, leading to heightened stress and potential burnout.

Moreover, the public nature of content creation exposes young innovators to unprecedented levels of feedback—both positive and negative. While recognition and engagement can be incredibly rewarding, the flip side is increased vulnerability to criticism and online harassment. A survey by the Pew Research Center (2023) found that 64% of young adults have experienced some form of online harassment, with content creators being particularly vulnerable.

This psychological toll can manifest in various ways. Anxiety, depression, and imposter syndrome are common challenges faced by young creators. The pressure to constantly produce engaging content, coupled with the unpredictable nature of online success, can create a perfect storm of stress and self-doubt.

Physically, the sedentary nature of much digital work poses its own set of challenges. Prolonged screen time can lead to issues like digital eye strain, poor posture, and disrupted sleep patterns. A study published in the International Journal of Environmental Research and Public Health (Lee et al., 2022) found that content creators reported higher rates of musculoskeletal problems, particularly in the neck, shoulders, and wrists, compared to the general population.

Sleep disruption is another significant concern. The blue light emitted by screens can interfere with the body's natural circadian rhythms, making it harder to fall asleep and reducing sleep quality. For creators who often work late into the night to meet deadlines or engage with global audiences, this can lead to a chronic sleep deficit, impacting both their health and their creative output.

However, it's important to note that Generation Innovate isn't passively accepting these challenges. Many young creators are at the forefront of developing innovative solutions to maintain their well-being in the digital age.

For instance, some creators are incorporating movement into their content creation process. Standing desks, treadmill desks, and regular stretching breaks are becoming common in home studios.

Others are leveraging technology to protect their health, using apps that remind them to take screen breaks or adjusting their devices' color temperature to reduce blue light exposure.

Mindfulness and meditation practices are also gaining traction among young creators as ways to manage stress and improve focus. Apps like Headspace and Calm have seen a surge in popularity, with many creators integrating short meditation sessions into their daily routines.

Moreover, the Creator Economy itself is spawning new wellness-focused content and products. From fitness influencers promoting active lifestyles to mental health advocates sharing coping strategies, creators are using their platforms to foster healthier digital habits among their audiences.

The rise of the "slow content" movement is another interesting development. Pioneered by creators like YouTuber Ali Abdaal, this approach emphasizes quality over quantity, encouraging creators to take their time with projects and prioritize their well-being over rapid content production.

As we look to the future, it's clear that addressing the holistic impact of digital immersion will be crucial for the sustainability of the Creator Economy. Platforms and tools that support creator well-being are likely to gain prominence. We're already seeing this with features like Instagram's "Take a Break" reminder and YouTube's bedtime reminders.

Education will also play a key role. As digital creativity becomes an increasingly viable career path, schools and universities may need to incorporate digital well-being into their curricula, teaching future creators how to thrive in online environments while protecting their health.

Ultimately, the challenge for Generation Innovate is to harness the immense potential of the digital world without being consumed by it. By understanding the holistic impact of their digital immersion—cognitive, psychological, and physical—young creators can develop strategies to maintain their well-being while pushing the boundaries of innovation.

As we move forward, we'll explore specific digital wellness strategies that young creators are employing to navigate these challenges. The goal isn't to disconnect from the digital world, but to engage with it in a way that's sustainable, fulfilling, and conducive to long-term creative success.

4.3 DIGITAL WELLNESS STRATEGIES FOR THE CREATOR ECONOMY

In the fast-paced world of the Creator Economy, maintaining digital wellness isn't just about personal health—it's a crucial component of sustainable success. Generation Innovate is at the forefront of developing and implementing strategies that allow them to thrive in the digital landscape while safeguarding their well-being. Let's explore some of the most effective approaches young creators are using to strike this delicate balance.

Intentional Disconnection and Digital Detox

One of the most powerful strategies employed by successful creators is the practice of intentional disconnection. This doesn't mean abandoning the digital world entirely, but rather creating structured periods of offline time to recharge and refocus.

Take the case of Amber, a 26-year-old lifestyle vlogger with over a million subscribers. "I used to be online 24/7," she shares. "But I found my creativity suffering. Now, I have a strict 'no screens after 9 PM' rule, and I take a full day offline every week. It's been game-changing for my content quality and my mental health."

Research supports Amber's approach. A study by the University of East Anglia (Wilson et al., 2023) found that regular digital detox periods can lead to reduced anxiety, improved sleep quality, and enhanced creative thinking among content creators.

Many creators are now building these offline periods into their content calendars, treating them as non-negotiable parts of their creative process. Some even turn their digital detox into content, sharing their experiences and insights with their audiences, thus normalizing the practice of intentional disconnection.

Mindful Technology Use

Beyond periodic disconnection, creators are becoming more mindful about how they engage with technology on a day-to-day basis. This involves being intentional about when, how, and why they use digital tools.

One popular approach is the "batch processing" of social media interactions. Instead of responding to comments and messages in real-time throughout the day, creators set aside specific time blocks for engagement. This allows for deeper focus during creative work while still maintaining audience connection.

Tools like Freedom, Forest, and RescueTime are gaining popularity among creators, helping them block distracting websites during work hours and track their digital habits. By becoming more aware of their online behaviors, creators can make informed decisions about their technology use.

Ergonomics and Physical Well-being

Recognizing the physical toll of digital work, many young innovators are investing in ergonomic setups and incorporating movement into their routines. Standing desks, ergonomic chairs, and proper lighting are becoming standard in home studios.

Riley, a 23-year-old graphic designer and content creator, shares her approach: "I use a Pomodoro timer app. For every 25 minutes of work, I take a 5-minute break to stretch or do a quick yoga flow. It keeps me energized and helps prevent back pain."

Some creators are even turning their wellness routines into content. Fitness influencers like Blogilates founder Cassey Ho have built entire brands around integrating physical activity into desk-bound lifestyles, resonating strongly with their fellow creators and digital professionals.

Mental Health and Emotional Resilience

The Creator Economy can be an emotional rollercoaster, with viral successes and crushing disappointments often separated by mere days or even hours. Building emotional resilience is therefore crucial for long-term success and well-being.

Many creators are turning to meditation and mindfulness practices. Apps like Headspace and Calm report a significant uptick in usage among content creators and digital entrepreneurs. Some platforms, recognizing this trend, are partnering with wellness apps to offer subscriptions as part of their creator support packages.

Therapy and coaching are also becoming more normalized in the creator community. Platforms like BetterHelp and Talkspace, which offer online therapy sessions, are increasingly marketing to creators and digital professionals. Some successful creators are even building therapy costs into their business budgets, recognizing it as an essential investment in their most important asset—themselves.

Community Building and Support Networks

Perhaps one of the most powerful wellness strategies emerging in the Creator Economy is the formation of strong support networks. Recognizing that the challenges they face are unique, many young creators are building communities to share experiences, offer support, and collaborate.

Creator collectives, both online and offline, are on the rise. These groups provide not just professional networking opportunities, but also emotional support and a sense of belonging. For instance, the Women in Tech SEO community, founded by Areej AbuAli, has become a powerful support network for women in the digital marketing space, combining professional development with mental health support.

Platforms themselves are starting to recognize the importance of these communities. YouTube's Creator Connect events and Instagram's Creator Week are examples of how platforms are facilitating community building among creators.

Sustainable Content Strategies

Lastly, creators are rethinking their content strategies with sustainability in mind. The "always-on" approach is giving way to more measured, quality-focused strategies.

The "slow content" movement, mentioned earlier, is gaining traction. Creators are prioritizing depth over frequency, giving themselves permission to take the time needed to produce high-quality content without burning out.

Moreover, creators are becoming more strategic about repurposing content across platforms, reducing the pressure to create entirely new content for each channel. This approach not only eases the creative burden but often results in a more cohesive brand presence across platforms.

As the Creator Economy matures, these digital wellness strategies are likely to become increasingly sophisticated and integrated into the fabric of creator culture. Platforms and tools that support these practices will likely gain prominence, and we may see digital wellness becoming a key differentiator in the competitive creator landscape.

The most successful creators of the future will likely be those who can not only produce great content but also maintain their well-being in the face of digital pressures. As one young creator put it, "In this game, longevity is the real measure of success. And you can't have longevity without wellness."

As we move forward, we'll explore how these wellness strategies feed into the broader goal of fostering sustainable creativity and innovation in the digital age. The Creator Economy isn't just changing how we work—it's revolutionizing our approach to work-life balance and well-being in the digital era.

4.4 Fostering Sustainable Creativity and Innovation

In the dynamic world of the Creator Economy, sustaining creativity and innovation over the long term is both a challenge and a necessity. For Generation Innovate, the goal isn't just to create viral content or launch the next big app—it's to build a lasting creative career that continues to evolve and thrive. Let's explore how young creators are fostering sustainable creativity and innovation in the digital age.

Embracing the Creative Cycle

Successful creators understand that creativity isn't a constant state—it ebbs and flows. They're learning to work with these natural cycles rather than fighting against them.

Take the case of Samantha, a 28-year-old podcast host and writer. "I used to panic during creative lulls," she shares. "Now, I see them as part of the process. I use these periods for research, reflection, and recharging. It's made my creative bursts so much more powerful."

This approach aligns with scientific understanding of the creative process. According to the work of Dr. R. Keith Sawyer, author of "Zig Zag: The Surprising Path to Greater Creativity," creativity involves a cyclical process of generation and evaluation, with periods of incubation in between (Sawyer, 2021).

Many creators are now deliberately building these cycles into their work schedules, allowing for periods of intense production followed by time for rest and inspiration-gathering. This cyclical approach not only leads to more sustainable creativity but often results in higher-quality output.

Continuous Learning and Skill Diversification

In the rapidly evolving digital landscape, continuous learning isn't just beneficial—it's essential for survival. Generation Innovate is taking this to heart, constantly expanding their skill sets and exploring new areas.

Platforms like Skillshare and Coursera report that content creators are among their most active users. Many creators are using these platforms not just to refine their core skills, but to explore complementary areas. A YouTuber might take a course on data analytics to better understand their audience metrics, or a graphic designer might learn basic coding to expand their service offerings.

This approach to continuous learning serves multiple purposes. It keeps creators intellectually stimulated, preventing creative stagnation. It also provides a hedge against platform or industry changes, giving creators more flexibility in their career paths.

Cross-Pollination and Collaboration

Innovation often happens at the intersection of different fields and perspectives. Generation Innovate is leveraging the interconnected nature of the digital world to foster cross-pollination of ideas and collaborative innovation.

Creator collaborations, once mostly about cross-promotion, are evolving into genuine creative partnerships. We're seeing fashion vloggers partnering with coders to create AR try-on experiences, or educators teaming up with game designers to create interactive learning content.

These collaborations not only result in innovative content but also help creators stay inspired and expand their creative horizons. As Jake, a 25-year-old animator, puts it: "Every collaboration teaches me something new. It's like getting a fresh pair of eyes on my creative process."

Mindful Technology Adoption

While Generation Innovate is known for their tech-savviness, the most successful creators are becoming more discerning about which technologies they adopt. Rather than chasing every new platform or tool, they're focusing on technologies that genuinely enhance their creative process or offer new ways to connect with their audience.

For instance, many creators are exploring how AI can augment their work rather than replace it. Tools like Chat GPT4o for writing assistance or AI-powered video editing software are being integrated into workflows not to reduce creative input, but to handle routine tasks and free up more time for high-level creative thinking.

This mindful approach to technology helps prevent overwhelm and ensures that creators' energy is focused on what truly matters—their unique creative vision.

Purpose-Driven Creation

Increasingly, young creators are finding that aligning their work with a larger purpose helps sustain their creativity and motivation over the long term. This doesn't necessarily mean every piece of content needs to tackle world issues, but rather that creators are considering the broader impact of their work.

Lisa, a 30-year-old lifestyle content creator, explains: "When I started tying my content to my values—like sustainability and mental health awareness—I found a whole new level of creative energy. It's not just about views anymore; it's about making a difference."

This purpose-driven approach not only provides deeper motivation but often results in more meaningful connections with audiences, leading to more sustainable success in the Creator Economy.

Redefining Success and Growth

Perhaps one of the most important shifts for sustainable creativity is how Generation Innovate is redefining success. Moving away from vanity metrics like follower counts or viral hits, many creators are focusing on more meaningful measures of growth.

These might include the depth of audience engagement, the impact of their work on individuals, or their personal creative growth. Some creators are even incorporating well-being metrics into their definition of success, considering factors like work-life balance and personal fulfillment alongside more traditional success markers.

This redefinition of success allows for a more sustainable approach to growth. Instead of chasing trends or burning out trying to game algorithms, creators can focus on steady, meaningful progress that aligns with their personal and professional goals.

As the Creator Economy matures, these approaches to sustainable creativity and innovation are likely to become increasingly important. The future leaders of this space will be those who can not only capture attention but maintain creative momentum over the long haul.

By embracing creative cycles, committing to continuous learning, fostering collaboration, adopting technology mindfully, aligning with purpose, and redefining success, Generation Innovate is pioneering a more sustainable model of digital creativity. This approach not only benefits individual creators but has the potential to shape a more resilient and innovative Creator Economy for years to come.

As we look to the future, it's clear that sustainable creativity isn't just about individual practices—it's about building supportive ecosystems. In our final section, we'll explore how Generation Innovate is creating communities and support systems to foster resilience in the digital age.

4.5 Building Resilience: Community and Support in the Digital Age

In the often-solitary world of digital creation, building resilience isn't just an individual endeavor—it's a community effort. Generation Innovate is pioneering new ways of creating support systems that foster resilience, creativity, and long-term success in the Creator Economy. Let's explore how these digital natives are reimagining community and support for the digital age.

The Rise of Creator Collectives

One of the most significant trends in the Creator Economy is the emergence of creator collectives. These groups bring together creators, often across different niches, to share resources, collaborate, and provide mutual support.

Take the example of VRSUS, a collective of visual artists and designers. Founded by Millenials Jun Inoue and Max Berger, VRSUS isn't just a networking group—it's a supportive community where members share skills, critique each other's work, and even collaborate on projects. "It's like having a team in a solo career," says Inoue. "We push each other creatively and catch each other during the low points" (VRSUS, 2023).

These collectives serve multiple purposes. They provide emotional support, combating the isolation many creators feel. They foster creative growth through peer learning and collaboration. And they often lead to business opportunities, as members refer work to each other or team up on larger projects.

Mental Health Initiatives

Recognizing the unique mental health challenges faced by creators, many platforms and communities are launching targeted mental health initiatives. YouTube's Creator Academy, for instance, now includes courses on managing stress and avoiding burnout. Meanwhile, creator-focused mental health organizations like Silence the Shame are gaining prominence, offering resources tailored to the specific pressures of the Creator Economy.

Twitch streamer Dr. Alok Kanojia, known online as Dr. K, has built a community around mental health for creators and gamers. His organization, Healthy Gamer, offers coaching, support groups, and educational content specifically designed for digital natives navigating the stresses of online creation and competition (Healthy Gamer, 2023).

Peer Mentorship Programs

Formal mentorship programs are becoming increasingly common in the Creator Economy. These programs pair experienced creators with newcomers, providing guidance, support, and insider knowledge of the industry.

The Adobe Creator Residency program is a prime example. It offers emerging creators financial support, mentorship, and access to Adobe's creative tools. But beyond these official programs, informal peer mentorship is flourishing within creator communities. Platforms like Discord and Slack host numerous creator groups where knowledge sharing and mentorship happen organically.

Financial Wellness Communities

Given the often unpredictable nature of creator income, financial wellness has become a key focus for many support communities. Groups like Supercharge, founded by Gen-Z entrepreneur Coco Breedan, offer financial education and support specifically tailored to young creators and entrepreneurs.

These communities go beyond just offering financial advice. They provide spaces for creators to discuss the unique financial challenges of the Creator Economy, from managing irregular income to planning for taxes as a self-employed individual. "Understanding your finances is key to sustainable creativity," says Breedan. "It's hard to innovate when you're stressed about money" (Supercharge, 2023).

Digital Co-working Spaces

To combat isolation and foster productivity, many creators are turning to digital co-working spaces. Platforms like Focusmate pair creators for virtual co-working sessions, while others like Cosmos offer persistent virtual offices where creators can "work alongside" each other.

These digital spaces provide the accountability and ambient social connection of a physical office, without the need for creators to be in the same location. They've proven particularly popular among Gen-Z creators, who are comfortable with digital-first social interactions.

Cross-Industry Support Networks

Recognizing that innovation often happens at the intersection of different fields, some communities are fostering connections between creators and professionals from other industries. The Creator Science community, for instance, brings together content creators, data scientists, and researchers to explore the science behind creative success in the digital age.

These cross-industry networks not only provide fresh perspectives for creators but also help legitimize and professionalize the Creator Economy, building bridges between traditional industries and the new digital landscape.

Platform-Initiated Communities

Recognizing the value of community in creator retention and success, many platforms are now actively fostering creator communities. TikTok's Creator Portal and Instagram's Creator Week are examples of how platforms are bringing creators together for learning, networking, and mutual support.

These platform-initiated communities offer valuable resources and connections. However, many creators are careful to also maintain platform-independent communities, ensuring they have support systems that aren't tied to any single platform's success.

As the Creator Economy continues to evolve, these community-based approaches to resilience are likely to become increasingly sophisticated and integral to creator success. They represent a shift from the myth of the lone creative genius to a more collaborative, supportive model of innovation.

Moreover, these communities are not just supporting individual creators—they're shaping the future of the Creator Economy itself. By fostering connections, sharing knowledge, and advocating for creators' needs, these communities are helping to create a more sustainable, equitable, and innovative digital creative landscape.

For Generation Innovate, building resilience through community isn't just about surviving in the digital age—it's about thriving and driving positive change. As one young creator put it, "In the Creator Economy, we're all competitors, but we're also all in this together. Our collective success will define the future of digital creativity."

As we conclude this chapter, it's clear that navigating well-being in the digital age is a complex but crucial task for Generation Innovate. By addressing the holistic impact of digital immersion, implementing effective wellness strategies, fostering sustainable creativity, and building strong support communities, these young innovators are not just adapting to the digital landscape—they're actively shaping it to be more human-centered, sustainable, and creatively fulfilling.

The future of the Creator Economy, and indeed of work itself, may well be defined by how successfully we can integrate these lessons of digital well-being into our broader economic and social structures. As we move forward, the innovations in well-being pioneered by Generation Innovate may prove to be just as impactful as their digital creations.

KEY INSIGHTS

- The digital age presents both opportunities and challenges for mental well-being
- Digital wellness and productive technology use are crucial for sustainable innovation
- Balancing digital engagement with offline activities is key to fostering creativity and preventing burnout

INNOVATION CHALLENGE

Create and implement a personal "Digital wellness Plan" for one week. Include strategies for managing screen time, fostering deep work, and maintaining work-life balance. Reflect on how it impacts your creativity and well-being.

Reflection Questions

1. How do you currently balance digital connectivity with your mental health and creative needs?

2. What strategies have you found effective for maintaining focus and creativity in the face of digital distractions?

3. How can organizations promote a culture of digital wellness while still driving innovation?

CHAPTER 5

PRO-C CREATIVITY IN THE DIGITAL AGE

In the bustling digital marketplace of ideas, where content is currency and innovation is the gold standard, a new breed of creators is emerging. Generation Innovate - our Millennials and Gen-Z changemakers - are redefining what it means to be a professional creator. They're not just participating in the Creator Economy; they're architecting a new paradigm of creativity that blends professional expertise with the dynamic, adaptive spirit of the digital age.

This chapter delves into the world of professional creator with Pro-C Creativity - a level of creative achievement that sits at the intersection of professional skill and innovative thinking. We'll explore how this concept, first introduced in the Kaufman-Beghetto Model of Creativity, is taking on new dimensions in the hands of digital natives.

From viral TikTok creators pushing the boundaries of short-form storytelling to indie game developers crafting immersive digital worlds, we'll see how Generation Innovate is leveraging Pro-C

Creativity to carve out unique niches in the crowded digital landscape. We'll examine how the democratization of creative tools, the global reach of digital platforms, and the collaborative nature of online communities are reshaping what it means to be a professional creator.

Moreover, we'll explore how the principles of Pro-C Creativity are being applied beyond content creation, influencing fields as diverse as tech entrepreneurship, digital marketing, and online education. We'll see how the innovative approaches of Millennial and Gen-Z creators are not just changing the Creator Economy, but potentially reshaping our understanding of professional creativity across industries.

Join us as we unpack the nuances of Pro-C Creativity in the digital age, examining its characteristics, its manifestations in the work of Generation Innovate, and strategies for nurturing this level of creativity in our evolving innovation ecosystem. Welcome to the new frontier of professional creativity in the digital era.

5.1 The Definition of Pro-C and Understanding Professional Creativity

To understand the creative revolution led by Millennials and Gen-Z, we must first grasp the concept of Pro-C creativity and its evolution in the digital age.

Pro-C creativity, as defined by Kaufman and Beghetto (2009) in their Four C Model of Creativity, represents professional-level creative contributions. These are the innovations of skilled individuals who consistently produce creative work in their fields but haven't (or haven't yet) achieved eminent status. In the pre-digital era, Pro-C creators might have been respected jazz musicians known within the industry, or innovative designers whose work influenced their peers but didn't necessarily reach the mainstream (Sawyer, 2012).

The Four C Model provides a nuanced framework for understanding different levels of creative achievement:

1. Mini-c: Personal and interpretive creativity involved in the learning process.
2. Little-c: Everyday problem-solving and creative expression.
3. Pro-C: Professional-level creativity that hasn't yet had a field-changing impact.
4. Big-C: Eminent creativity that transforms a field or domain.

This model helps us appreciate the developmental nature of creativity and recognize the significant contributions made at each level (Kaufman & Beghetto, 2013).

In the hands of digital natives, Pro-C creativity has taken on new dimensions. The democratization of creative tools has dramatically lowered the barriers to entry for professional-level creativity (Jenkins et al., 2016). A smartphone with a high-quality camera and editing apps can turn anyone into a potential filmmaker. Platforms like Canva have made graphic design accessible to all. This accessibility has accelerated the journey from little-c (everyday creativity) to Pro-C, allowing creators to hone their skills and reach professional levels of quality at unprecedented speeds (Shirky, 2010).

The path to Pro-C creativity in the digital age is marked by several key characteristics:

1. Multidisciplinary Approach: Millennial and Gen-Z creators often blur the lines between different creative disciplines. A YouTuber might be simultaneously a videographer, a writer, a performer, and a marketing strategist (Burgess & Green, 2018). This multidisciplinary approach is not just a necessity of digital creation but a reflection of these generations' adaptability and willingness to learn new skills.
2. Personal Branding: For these generations, separating the creator from the creation is often neither possible nor desirable. They build personal brands around their creative identities, turning their authentic selves into part of their creative output (Marwick, 2013). This integration of personal and professional identities aligns with the concept of self-actualization in Maslow's hierarchy of needs, suggesting that Pro-C creativity for these generations isn't just about making a living – it's about self-expression and personal fulfillment (Koltko-Rivera, 2006).
3. Entrepreneurial Mindset: Many young Pro-C creators are not just artists but entrepreneurs, building businesses around their creativity. They're not waiting to be discovered – they're actively creating opportunities for themselves (Duffy & Hund, 2015). This entrepreneurial approach to creativity aligns with the growth mindset theory proposed by Carol Dweck (2006), which posits that abilities can be developed through dedication and hard work.
4. Global Reach and Networked Creativity: Digital platforms allow Pro-C creators to reach global audiences instantly. Moreover, they're part of vast, interconnected creative ecosystems, participating in remix culture and collaborative

creation on a scale never before possible (Jenkins et al., 2013). This networked creativity enhances cognitive flexibility and creative thinking by exposing creators to diverse ideas and perspectives (Leung et al., 2008).

The digital age has also transformed the economics of Pro-C creativity. The "long tail" theory proposed by Chris Anderson (2006) suggests that the internet enables niche products (or in this case, niche creative content) to be economically viable. This has allowed Pro-C creators to find and serve specific audiences, no matter how niche their creative focus might be.

Moreover, the rise of crowdfunding platforms like Kickstarter and Patreon has provided new funding models for Pro-C creators. These platforms allow creators to bypass traditional gatekeepers and fund their projects directly through their audiences (Gerber & Hui, 2013). This direct creator-audience relationship is reshaping the power dynamics in creative industries.

However, the digital age also presents unique challenges for Pro-C creators. The constant pressure to produce content, the fickleness of algorithms, and the blurring of work-life boundaries can lead to burnout. A study by The Tilt (2021) found that 68% of content creators feel burned out at least occasionally. This highlights the need for sustainable creative practices and self-care strategies among Pro-C creators.

The concept of "context collapse" (Marwick & Boyd, 2011) is another challenge faced by digital Pro-C creators. As they share their work across various platforms with different audiences, maintaining consistent self-presentation while catering to diverse audience expectations can be challenging.

Despite these challenges, Pro-C creativity in the digital age offers unprecedented opportunities for Millennials and Gen-Z. It allows for rapid skill development through immediate feedback and iterative creation. The ability to reach global audiences and collaborate across borders opens up new possibilities for cultural exchange and hybrid creativity (Jenkins et al., 2013).

Furthermore, Pro-C creativity in the digital age is reshaping our understanding of expertise and professional development. The traditional model of spending years honing a craft before "going pro" is being challenged by a new paradigm of learning-by-doing in the public eye. This aligns with the concept of "legitimate peripheral participation" proposed by Lave and Wenger (1991), where learners become part of a "community of practice" by participating in simple and low-risk tasks that are nonetheless productive and necessary.

This new paradigm of Pro-C creativity leverages the brain's neuroplasticity – its ability to form new neural connections throughout life. The varied experiences and rapid feedback loops characteristic of digital creation provide the kind of stimulating environment that promotes neural growth and cognitive flexibility (Cotman & Berchtold, 2002).

The impact of Pro-C creativity extends beyond individual creators to shape entire industries and cultural landscapes. The rise of influencer marketing, for instance, is a direct result of the Pro-C creativity of social media content creators. According to a report by Influencer Marketing Hub (2021), the influencer marketing industry was set to grow to approximately $13.8 billion in 2021, demonstrating the economic impact of this new form of Pro-C creativity.

In education, the rise of Pro-C creativity in the digital age is challenging traditional curricula and teaching methods. There's a growing recognition of the need to foster not just technical skills, but also the soft skills required for Pro-C creativity – things like adaptability, self-directed learning, and entrepreneurial thinking (World Economic Forum, 2020).

As we move forward, understanding and nurturing Pro-C creativity will be crucial for harnessing the full innovative potential of Millennials and Gen-Z. It represents a new paradigm of professional creativity – one that's more accessible, more entrepreneurial, more networked, and more intertwined with personal identity than ever before.

In the following sections, we'll explore how Millennials and Gen-Z are leveraging Pro-C creativity to reshape industries, challenge traditional notions of work, and drive innovation in the digital age. We'll also examine the challenges they face and the strategies they're developing to thrive in this new creative landscape.

5.2 The Kaufman-Beghetto Model: A Deeper Dive

Now that we've dipped our toes into the waters of Pro-C creativity, let's dive deeper into the model that gave us this concept. The Four C Model of Creativity, developed by James C. Kaufman and Ronald A. Beghetto, is like a map of the creative landscape. It helps us understand not just where we are in our creative journey, but where we might be headed.

Think of creativity as a vast continent. For a long time, we only had maps of the coastline – the everyday creativity we all experience and the world-changing breakthroughs of eminent creators. But Kaufman and Beghetto's model is like a detailed topographic map, showing us the hills, valleys, and rivers in between. It gives us a more nuanced understanding of how creativity develops and manifests at different levels.

Let's start our expedition at the beginning, with mini-c creativity.

Think back to when you first learned something new – maybe the thrill of cracking a recipe or solving a problem at work. That's mini-c creativity in action. It's defined as the "novel and personally meaningful interpretation of experiences, actions, and events" (Kaufman & Beghetto, 2009, p. 3). This is the kind of creativity we engage in when we're learning something new, making connections, and constructing personal knowledge.

Mini-c creativity is closely tied to the process of forming new neural connections. When we learn something new or make a novel (to us) connection, our brains are literally rewiring themselves. This process, known as neuroplasticity, is the foundation of all learning and creativity (Costandi, 2016).

As we gain more experience and confidence, we start to venture into the realm of little-c creativity. This is the creativity of everyday problem-solving and self-expression. It's coming up with a new recipe for dinner, finding an innovative solution to a workplace challenge, or crafting a witty tweet.

Little-c creativity is where most of us spend most of our creative time. It's accessible to everyone and doesn't require any special training or expertise. But don't let its "everyday" nature fool you – little-c creativity is incredibly important. It's the creativity that helps us navigate our daily lives, adapt to new situations, and express ourselves.

Little-c creativity often involves what psychologists call "divergent thinking" – the ability to generate multiple ideas or solutions to a problem (Guilford, 1967). It's about making unexpected connections and thinking outside the box.

For a long time, creativity researchers focused mainly on Big-C creativity – the eminent creativity that changes entire fields or cultures. Think Einstein's theory of relativity, Picasso's cubism, or Steve Jobs' iPhone. Big-C creativity is rare and often only recognized in hindsight.

But Kaufman and Beghetto realized there was a vast creative territory between little-c and Big-C that wasn't being adequately explored. That's where Pro-C creativity comes in.

Pro-C creativity represents professional-level creative contributions. These are people who are experts in their fields, consistently producing creative work, but who haven't (or haven't yet) had a revolutionary, field-changing impact.

Think of a respected jazz musician who's known in the industry but isn't a household name. Or a user experience designer who's consistently creating innovative interfaces but hasn't fundamentally changed how we interact with technology. These are Pro-C creators.

What sets Pro-C creativity apart is the combination of domain expertise and creative thinking. Pro-C creators have put in the hours to master their craft (remember the 10,000-hour rule?), but they're not content to simply replicate what's been done before. They're constantly pushing boundaries, trying new approaches, and solving complex problems in innovative ways.

Neuroscience research gives us some fascinating insights into what might be happening in the brains of Pro-C creators. Studies have shown that expertise is associated with more efficient neural processing in domain-specific areas of the brain (Neumann et al., 2016). At the same time, creative thinking involves the dynamic interaction of several large-scale brain networks, including the default mode network (associated with spontaneous thought) and the executive control network (involved in focused attention and evaluation) (Beaty et al., 2018).

In other words, Pro-C creators have brains that are highly efficient at processing domain-specific information, freeing up cognitive resources for creative thinking. They're able to seamlessly switch between generating new ideas and critically evaluating them – a cognitive flexibility that's crucial for professional-level creativity.

But here's the thing: while the Four C Model often follows a trajectory, creativity can develop in many ways. Some may jump between categories, while others might stay at one level – and that's okay. The model isn't just a static categorization. It's a way of understanding the different manifestations of creativity and how they might develop over time.

This developmental aspect is crucial for understanding how we can nurture creativity at all levels. It suggests that Big-C creativity doesn't just emerge out of nowhere – it's often the result of years of mini-c learning experiences, little-c problem-solving, and Pro-C professional development.

Think about it this way: Before Pablo Picasso revolutionized art with cubism (Big-C), he spent years learning the fundamentals of painting (mini-c), experimenting with different styles (little-c), and establishing himself as a professional artist (Pro-C). The Four C Model helps us understand this journey.

But it's important to note that not all creativity follows this linear path. Some people might engage in Pro-C creativity in one domain while still being at the mini-c level in another. And not all Pro-C creators will go on to achieve Big-C status – nor do they need to. Pro-C creativity is valuable and impactful in its own right.

So why does this model matter? Why should we care about these different levels of creativity?

First, it helps us recognize and value creativity at all levels. In a world that often celebrates only breakthrough innovations, the Four C Model reminds us that creativity is a much broader and more inclusive concept. It's not just about world-changing ideas; it's about personal growth, everyday problem-solving, and professional excellence.

Second, it provides a framework for nurturing creativity. By understanding these different levels, we can create environments and practices that support creative development. For example, in education, we might focus on fostering mini-c and little-c creativity in younger students, gradually introducing more Pro-C elements as they advance.

Third, it helps us understand our own creative journeys. Maybe you've always thought of yourself as "not creative" because you haven't painted a masterpiece or written a bestseller. But the Four C Model shows us that we're all creative in different ways and at different levels. It's a more inclusive and empowering way of thinking about creativity.

For Generation Innovate, the Four C Model is particularly relevant. In a world where traditional career paths are increasingly obsolete, the ability to navigate between different levels of creativity is becoming a crucial skill. Millennials and Gen-Z are often juggling multiple creative identities – maybe they're engaging in Pro-C creativity in their day job, little-c creativity in their side hustle, and mini-c creativity as they learn new skills for the future.

The model also aligns with the entrepreneurial spirit that characterizes much of Generation Innovate. The journey from mini-c to Pro-C (and potentially Big-C) creativity mirrors the journey of many startups – from initial idea to professional execution to (in some cases) industry-changing innovation.

As we move forward in our exploration of creativity and innovation, the Four C Model will serve as a valuable map. It will help us understand the different manifestations of creativity we encounter, and it will guide our thinking about how to nurture and develop creative potential at all levels.

5.3 PRO-C CREATIVITY IN THE DIGITAL AGE: MILLENNIALS AND GEN-Z

In the hands of Generation Innovate, Pro-C Creativity is undergoing a transformation as profound as the digital revolution itself. Millennials and Gen-Z are not just adapting the concept to the digital age - they're reinventing it, infusing it with the fluidity, interconnectedness, and rapid iteration that characterize the online world.

One of the most striking aspects of Pro-C Creativity in the digital age is the speed at which creators can reach professional-level skills. The abundance of online learning resources, coupled with platforms for immediate feedback and audience building, has compressed the traditional timeline for developing expertise.

Take the case of Emma Chamberlain, who started her YouTube channel at 16 and within two years had amassed millions of subscribers, won a Streamy Award, and launched her own coffee company. Chamberlain's rapid rise exemplifies how digital platforms can accelerate the journey from novice to professional-level creator (Chamberlain Coffee, 2023).

This accelerated skill development is facilitated by what might be called "public learning." Unlike previous generations who might have honed their craft in private before presenting it to the world, digital creators often learn in full view of their audience. This transparency in the creative process not only speeds up learning through constant feedback but also builds a deeply engaged audience invested in the creator's journey.

Another key characteristic of Pro-C Creativity in the digital age is its interdisciplinary nature. Generation Innovate creators rarely confine themselves to a single medium or skill set. Instead, they fluidly move between different creative domains, combining skills in novel ways.

Consider the work of Karen X. Cheng, a Millennial creator known for her innovative video content. Cheng combines skills in videography, dance, visual effects, and marketing to create viral content that defies easy categorization. Her "Girl Learns to Dance in a Year" video, which seamlessly blended storytelling, time-lapse photography, and dance, exemplifies this interdisciplinary approach to Pro-C Creativity (Cheng, 2023).

The collaborative nature of digital creativity is another defining feature of how Generation Innovate approaches Pro-C Creativity. Online communities and social platforms have made co-creation and remixing central to the creative process. This networked creativity allows for rapid iteration and the cross-pollination of ideas across different creative communities.

The rise of creator collectives like VRSUS or High'R Collective showcases this trend. These groups bring together creators from various disciplines to collaborate, share resources, and push each other creatively. This collective approach to Pro-C Creativity is reshaping our understanding of what it means to be a professional creator, emphasizing community and collaboration alongside individual skill (VRSUS, 2023).

Moreover, Pro-C Creativity in the digital age is characterized by its global reach and cultural fluidity. Generation Innovate creators are not bound by geographic or cultural boundaries in the same way as previous generations. They draw inspiration from and contribute to global creative trends, often blending diverse cultural influences in their work.

The phenomenon of "virtual YouTubers" or VTubers, which originated in Japan but has gained global popularity, illustrates this trend. Creators like Gawr Gura, who has amassed over 4 million subscribers, represent a fusion of anime-inspired aesthetics, gaming culture, and global pop culture references, creating content that resonates across cultural boundaries (Cover Corp, 2023).

Another crucial aspect of Pro-C Creativity in the digital age is the integration of data and analytics into the creative process. Generation Innovate creators are often as fluent in analyzing engagement metrics as they are in their primary creative skills. This data-driven approach allows for rapid iteration and optimization of content, blending creativity with strategic thinking in unprecedented ways.

However, it's important to note that Pro-C Creativity in the digital age also comes with unique challenges. The pressure to constantly produce content, the fickleness of algorithms, and the public nature of online creation can lead to burnout and creative blocks. Successful digital creators are those who can balance the demands of consistent content creation with the need for creative renewal and personal well-being.

As we look to the future, it's clear that Pro-C Creativity in the digital age will continue to evolve. The integration of emerging technologies like AI and virtual reality into the creative process, the growing importance of community-driven creativity, and the increasing overlap between creativity and entrepreneurship are all likely to shape how Generation Innovate approaches professional-level creativity.

In our next section, we'll explore strategies for nurturing Pro-C Creativity in this dynamic, digital-first innovation ecosystem. From educational approaches to platform design, we'll examine how we can support and amplify the creative potential of Generation Innovate.

5.4 Nurturing Pro-C Creativity in the Innovation Ecosystem

As we've seen, Pro-C Creativity in the digital age is a dynamic, multifaceted phenomenon that's reshaping our understanding of professional creativity. But how can we nurture and amplify this creative potential? How can we create an innovation ecosystem that supports the unique approach to Pro-C Creativity exemplified by Generation Innovate? Let's explore some key strategies.

Reimagining Education for Digital Creators

Traditional educational models often struggle to keep pace with the rapidly evolving needs of digital creators. To nurture Pro-C Creativity, we need educational approaches that are as dynamic and interdisciplinary as the Creator Economy itself.

Some institutions are rising to this challenge. For instance, the New York University Tisch School of the Arts now offers a course on "The Business of Being a YouTuber," blending creative skills with entrepreneurship and digital marketing (NYU Tisch, 2023). Similarly, online learning platforms like Skillshare and MasterClass are providing targeted, flexible education for aspiring creators, taught by successful professionals in the field.

But nurturing Pro-C Creativity goes beyond just teaching skills. It requires fostering an entrepreneurial mindset, encouraging cross-disciplinary thinking, and developing resilience in the face of rapid change. Educational programs that incorporate real-world projects, internships with digital creators, and exposure to diverse creative disciplines are likely to be most effective in preparing the next generation of digital creators.

Developing Supportive Platforms and Tools

The platforms and tools available to creators play a crucial role in nurturing Pro-C Creativity. Platforms that balance creative freedom with useful structure, provide meaningful analytics, and facilitate community building are more likely to foster professional-level creativity.

Take Patreon, for example. By providing a direct connection between creators and their audience, along with tools for managing subscriptions and analyzing supporter data, Patreon enables creators to focus on their craft while building sustainable businesses (Patreon, 2023).

Similarly, tools that lower the technical barriers to high-quality creation are crucial. Adobe's Creative Cloud Express, for instance, brings professional-grade design capabilities to creators who may not have formal design training, democratizing access to Pro-C level creative tools (Adobe, 2023).

Fostering Collaborative Communities

Given the importance of networked creativity in the digital age, nurturing Pro-C Creativity requires fostering strong, supportive creative communities. This goes beyond just providing forums or comment sections - it's about creating spaces for meaningful collaboration, mentorship, and peer learning.

Discord servers dedicated to specific creative niches, LinkedIn groups for digital professionals, and in-person creator meetups all play a role in building these communities. Platforms and institutions that actively facilitate these connections - like YouTube's Creator Academy or Twitch's Creator Camp - are contributing significantly to the development of Pro-C Creativity in the digital space.

Promoting Digital Wellness and Sustainable Creativity

As we discussed in the previous chapter, maintaining well-being is crucial for sustainable creativity in the digital age. Nurturing Pro-C Creativity means not just focusing on skill development, but also on strategies for managing the unique stresses of online creation.

This could involve platforms building in features that encourage breaks and set healthy boundaries like Instagram's "Take a Break" reminders. It could also mean incorporating digital wellness education into creator training programs, teaching strategies for managing online feedback, balancing productivity with rest, and maintaining creativity over the long term.

Encouraging Ethical and Responsible Creativity

As digital creators gain increasing influence, nurturing Pro-C Creativity must also involve fostering a sense of ethical responsibility. This includes understanding the impact of one's work, respecting intellectual property, and considering the well-being of one's audience.

Platforms can play a role here by providing clear guidelines and educational resources on ethical creation. For instance, TikTok's Creator Portal includes sections on creating responsibly and understanding content policies (TikTok, 2023). Educational programs for creators should also incorporate modules on digital ethics and the social impact of online content.

Facilitating Cross-Industry Connections

Pro-C Creativity in the digital age often involves applying creative skills to diverse fields. Nurturing this creativity means facilitating connections between the Creator Economy and other industries.

Initiatives like Adobe's Creative Residency, which places creators in professional settings to work on real-world projects, exemplify this approach (Adobe Creative Residency, 2023). Similarly, hackathons that bring together creators, technologists, and industry professionals can spark innovative applications of creative skills.

Supporting Research and Innovation in Digital Creativity

Finally, nurturing Pro-C Creativity requires ongoing research into the nature of creativity in the digital age. This involves not just studying successful creators, but also experimenting with new models of creative work, exploring the impact of emerging technologies on creativity, and investigating the long-term effects of digital creation on cognitive and social development.

Institutions like the MIT Media Lab, with its focus on the intersection of technology, media, and creativity, play a crucial role in this research (MIT Media Lab, 2023). But platforms and creator communities can also contribute by sharing data, participating in studies, and funding research initiatives.

As we nurture Pro-C Creativity in the digital age, we're not just supporting individual creators - we're shaping the future of creative work. By building an ecosystem that supports the unique needs and potentials of digital creators, we can unlock new realms of innovation, drive economic growth in the Creator Economy, and enrich our cultural landscape.

The Pro-C Creativity of Generation Innovate represents a new frontier in human creative potential. By understanding and nurturing this creativity, we can help ensure that the digital age is not just an era of technological advancement, but a renaissance of human creativity and innovation.

KEY INSIGHTS

- Pro-C creativity represents professional-level creative contributions
- It involves a balance of domain expertise and creative thinking
- Pro-C creativity can be developed and enhanced over time

INNOVATION CHALLENGE:

Choose an area where you have expertise. Over the next month, commit to exploring a new approach or technique in this area. Document your process and any creative insights that emerge.

Reflection Questions

1. How might you create more opportunities for Pro-C creativity in your current role or organization?

2. What barriers to Pro-C creativity do you encounter in your work, and how might you overcome them?

3. How could developing your Pro-C creativity impact your professional growth and contributions to your field?

PART II

THE CREATIVE PROCESS AND FLOW

CHAPTER 6

WHAT IS CREATIVITY?

As we've explored in the previous chapter, Pro-C creativity represents a fascinating category of creative expression, particularly relevant to Millennials and Gen-Z in our digital age. We've seen how these generations are redefining professional creativity, leveraging technology and global connectivity to push creative boundaries in unprecedented ways. But to truly understand and harness the power of Pro-C creativity - or any form of creative expression - we need to dive deeper into the very nature of creativity itself.

What exactly is this force we call creativity? How does it work, and what drives it? These questions have intrigued philosophers, scientists, and artists for centuries, and they're particularly pertinent in our rapidly evolving world. As we navigate the challenges of the 21st century, from technological disruption to global crises, creativity isn't just a luxury - it's a necessity.

In this chapter, we'll embark on a journey to unravel the mysteries of creativity. We'll explore it not as a fixed trait possessed by a gifted few, but as a multifaceted capacity that can be understood, developed, and enhanced by anyone willing to engage in the process.

Imagine creativity as a vibrant, ever-shifting kaleidoscope. With each turn, new patterns emerge, blending colors and shapes in unexpected ways. This kaleidoscopic nature of creativity is at the heart of Scott Barry Kaufman's groundbreaking work in "Wired to Create" (2015), and it serves as a fitting metaphor for our exploration. Just as a kaleidoscope creates complex patterns from simple elements, creativity emerges from the intricate interplay of cognitive processes, personality traits, and environmental factors.

We'll begin by defining creativity, examining its various facets and the sometimes paradoxical attributes of creative individuals. Drawing on cutting-edge research from psychology and neuroscience, we'll delve into the cognitive processes that underlie creative thinking. We'll explore how our environment - both physical and digital - shapes our creative expressions, a consideration particularly relevant for our digitally native generations.

But understanding creativity is only half the journey. The real power lies in knowing how to foster and enhance it. In the latter part of this chapter, we'll translate theory into practice, offering strategies and techniques for cultivating creativity. These aren't one-size-fits-all solutions, but a toolkit from which you can select and adapt approaches that resonate with your unique creative style and goals.

For Millennials and Gen-Z, who are navigating a world of unprecedented change and opportunity, this exploration of creativity is more than academic - it's a roadmap for thriving in an innovation-driven economy. Whether you're a budding entrepreneur, a digital artist, a social media influencer, or simply someone looking to infuse more creativity into your daily life, the insights in this chapter will provide you with the understanding and tools to expand your creative horizons.

As we embark on this exploration, remember that creativity isn't just about producing art or coming up with breakthrough innovations. It's a fundamental human capacity that allows us to adapt, solve problems, express ourselves, and imagine new possibilities. By understanding and fostering our creativity, we're not just enhancing our personal and professional lives - we're equipping ourselves to shape the future.

So, let's turn the kaleidoscope and see what patterns emerge. Welcome to the fascinating world of creativity - in all its complex, paradoxical, and infinitely inspiring glory.

6.1 THE KALEIDOSCOPE OF CREATIVITY: A MULTIFACETED PERSPECTIVE

Imagine creativity as a vibrant, ever-shifting kaleidoscope. With each turn, new patterns emerge, blending colors and shapes in unexpected ways. This kaleidoscopic nature of creativity is at the heart of Scott Barry Kaufman's groundbreaking work in "Wired to Create" (2015). Kaufman, along with other leading researchers, paints a picture of creativity that is as complex and multifaceted as the human mind itself.

At its core, creativity is the ability to generate ideas, solutions, or expressions that are both novel and valuable. But this simple definition belies the intricate dance of cognitive processes, personality traits, and environmental factors that give rise to creative thought and action.

David Eagleman and Anthony Brandt (2017) offer another lens through which to view this kaleidoscope of creativity. In their book "The Runaway Species," they propose that creative thinking involves three fundamental cognitive processes: bending, breaking, and blending. These processes, which we'll explore in depth later, offer a framework for understanding how our minds manipulate and recombine ideas to create something new.

Kaufman's research, complemented by the work of other leading creativity scholars, suggests that creative individuals possess a constellation of attributes that often seem paradoxical. Like a kaleidoscope, these attributes shift and combine in unique ways, creating the conditions for creative insight and expression.

Consider the interplay between dreaming and doing in the creative process. Creative individuals often embody a fascinating duality - they are both dreamers and doers. On one hand, they possess a rich inner world, characterized by vivid imagination and a tendency towards mind-wandering. Jonathan Schooler's research (2011) has shown that mind-wandering can lead to creative insights by allowing for unconscious processing of information. It's those moments when you're in the shower or taking a walk, and suddenly an idea strikes - your mind has been quietly working in the background.

Yet, creative people are also driven by passion and the desire to bring their ideas to life. Teresa Amabile's work on intrinsic motivation (1996) underscores this, showing that creative individuals are often deeply motivated by the work itself, rather than external rewards. It's not just about having great ideas; it's about having the drive to turn those ideas into reality.

This dance between dreaming and doing creates a fertile ground for creativity. The dreamer aspect allows for the generation of novel ideas, while the doer aspect provides the drive to turn those ideas into tangible creations. It's a balance that many Millennials and Gen-Z creators intuitively understand as they navigate between ideation and execution in their creative projects.

But the paradoxes don't stop there. Creative individuals often display a unique combination of sensitivity and resilience. They tend to be highly attuned to their environment and experiences, what Elaine Aron (1997) calls "high sensitivity." This sensitivity allows them to pick up on subtle cues and patterns that others might miss, fueling their creative insights.

At the same time, creative people often show remarkable resilience in the face of adversity. Kaufman's emphasis on "turning adversity into advantage" echoes the concept of post-traumatic growth studied by psychologists like Richard Tedeschi and Lawrence Calhoun (2004). This ability to find meaning and opportunity in challenging experiences can be a powerful driver of creativity.

For many young creators, this combination of sensitivity and resilience is crucial. In a world of constant feedback and potential criticism, especially online, being able to stay open to experiences while bouncing back from setbacks is a valuable skill.

Another intriguing paradox in creative individuals is the balance between openness and focus. Openness to experience is consistently associated with creativity across numerous studies (McCrae, 1987). Creative individuals tend to be curious, imaginative, and willing to entertain unusual ideas. This openness aligns well with Eagleman and Brandt's concept of "bending" - the ability to take an existing idea and transform it, asking "What if?" and imagining new possibilities.

Yet, creativity also requires focus and persistence. Mihaly Csikszentmihalyi's research on flow states (1996) highlights the importance of deep, concentrated work in the creative process. This seeming contradiction between openness and focus is resolved in the creative process itself - periods of open exploration are balanced with periods of focused execution.

The playful and disciplined nature of creative individuals presents another fascinating duality. Kaufman emphasizes the importance of imaginative play in the creative process, which aligns with the work of Sandra Russ (1993) on pretend play and creativity in children. This playfulness allows for the kind of free association and "breaking" of ideas that Eagleman and Brandt describe - taking things apart and reassembling them in new ways.

Yet, this playful approach is often coupled with a disciplined work ethic. Dean Keith Simonton's (1997) historiometric studies of eminent creators show that prolific output - which requires discipline and persistence - is often a key factor in creative achievement. This interplay between playfulness and discipline allows creative individuals to generate numerous ideas through playful exploration, while also having the persistence to develop and refine these ideas.

The kaleidoscopic nature of creativity, with its shifting patterns of seemingly contradictory attributes, helps explain why creativity can be so challenging to pin down and cultivate. It's not about possessing a single "creative personality," but rather about developing a dynamic, flexible cognitive and behavioral repertoire that can adapt to different creative challenges.

For Millennials and Gen Z, understanding this multifaceted nature of creativity offers both validation and inspiration. It suggests that their diverse interests, experiences, and sometimes contradictory traits aren't hindrances to creativity, but potentially valuable assets. By embracing and integrating these various aspects of themselves, they can create their own unique creative kaleidoscopes.

Moreover, this perspective on creativity aligns well with the rapidly changing, complex world that Millennials and Gen Z navigate. In a world where adaptability and innovation are increasingly prized, the ability to shift between different modes of thinking and being - to turn the kaleidoscope and see new patterns - is a valuable skill indeed.

As we continue to explore the landscape of creativity in the following sections, we'll delve deeper into how these various attributes interact with cognitive processes, environmental factors, and modern technologies to shape the creative process. We'll explore Eagleman and Brandt's concepts of bending, breaking, and blending in more depth, seeing how they manifest in the creative work of Millennials and Gen Z. We'll also examine practical strategies for nurturing and enhancing creativity, drawing on both traditional wisdom and cutting-edge research.

Remember, creativity isn't a fixed trait, but a dynamic process that can be developed and enhanced. By understanding the complex interplay of factors that contribute to creativity, we can all learn to turn our own creative kaleidoscopes, revealing new patterns of thought and innovation. For Millennials and Gen Z, this kaleidoscopic view of creativity offers a framework for understanding and harnessing their unique creative potential in an ever-changing world.

6.2 The Cognitive Dance: Understanding the Minds of Creators

Just as a kaleidoscope creates intricate patterns through the interaction of multiple elements, creativity emerges from the complex interplay of various cognitive processes. Understanding this cognitive dance can help us not only appreciate the depth of creative thinking but also find ways to enhance our own creative abilities.

At the heart of creative cognition lies the interplay between two fundamental types of thinking: divergent and convergent. J.P. Guilford (1967) was one of the first to highlight the importance of divergent thinking in creativity. It's the ability to generate multiple ideas or solutions to a problem - the mental equivalent of a brainstorming session, where ideas flow freely and judgment is suspended.

Imagine you're tasked with redesigning a coffee cup. Divergent thinking might lead you to consider a cup that changes color with temperature, a cup that folds flat for easy storage, or even a cup that doubles as a mini-planter. It's about exploring possibilities, no matter how wild or impractical they might seem at first glance.

This is where David Eagleman and Anthony Brandt's framework of bending, breaking, and blending (2017) comes into play, offering specific strategies for divergent thinking:

1. Bending involves taking an existing idea and transforming it in some way. In our coffee cup example, bending might lead to a cup with a flexible, squeezable body that can fit into any bag.
2. Breaking is about deconstructing ideas and reassembling them in new ways. Applied to our coffee cup, breaking might result in a modular cup design where different sections serve different purposes - one for the drink, one for snacks, and one for utensils.
3. Blending combines two or more existing ideas to create something new. For our coffee cup, blending might produce a cup that incorporates elements of a thermos and a smart device, regulating temperature and tracking hydration.

These strategies align well with the cognitive flexibility that characterizes many Millennial and Gen-Z creators. Growing up in a rapidly changing digital landscape has primed these generations for the kind of mental agility required to bend, break, and blend ideas effectively.

However, creativity isn't just about generating ideas - it's also about evaluating and refining them. This is where convergent thinking comes into play. It's the process of analyzing and selecting the most promising ideas, the ones worth pursuing further. In our coffee cup example, convergent thinking would help you assess which ideas are feasible, which align with user needs, and which have the potential for commercial success.

Recent neuroscience research has given us fascinating insights into how these processes play out in the brain. Roger Beaty and colleagues (2018) found that creative thought involves the dynamic interaction of three large-scale brain networks:

1. The Default Mode Network, associated with spontaneous thinking and mind-wandering
2. The Executive Control Network, involved in focusing attention and evaluating ideas
3. The Salience Network, which helps determine what we pay attention to

This research paints a picture of creativity as a whole-brain process, requiring the coordination of multiple cognitive systems. It's not just about being "right-brained" or "left-brained" - it's about how effectively these different parts of the brain work together.

For Millennials and Gen Z, who have grown up in an era of multitasking and rapid context-switching, this cognitive flexibility might come more naturally. The ability to quickly shift between different modes of thinking - from brainstorming to critical analysis, from focused work to open-ended exploration - is a valuable asset in the creative process.

Another crucial element in the cognitive dance of creativity is what psychologists call "cognitive disinhibition." This is the ability to consider ideas that might otherwise be filtered out by our conscious minds. In other words, it's about being open to seemingly irrelevant or "weird" thoughts.

Shelley Carson's research (2011) suggests that highly creative individuals often have lower levels of cognitive inhibition. This doesn't mean they're impulsive or unable to focus. Rather, it means they're more likely to entertain unconventional ideas and make unexpected connections. This lowered inhibition facilitates the kind of bending, breaking, and blending that Eagleman and Brandt describe.

Think about how often great ideas seem to come "out of nowhere" - when you're in the shower, or just about to fall asleep. These moments of insight often occur when our minds are relaxed and our cognitive filters are lowered. For young creators navigating a world of information overload, learning to create space for this kind of open, associative thinking can be crucial.

The concept of analogical thinking is another key player in the cognitive dance of creativity. This is the ability to see connections between seemingly unrelated concepts, which aligns closely with Eagleman and Brandt's notion of blending. Analogical thinking allows us to apply solutions from one domain to problems in another. For instance, the invention of Velcro was inspired by the way burrs stick to dog fur. The inventor, George de Mestral, made an analogy between this natural mechanism and the need for a new type of fastener.

For Millennials and Gen Z, who often have diverse interests and exposure to a wide range of ideas through digital media, analogical thinking can be a powerful creative tool. The challenge is in making these connections deliberately and productively.

The role of memory in creativity is also worth considering. While we often think of creativity as being about generating something entirely new, in reality, much of creative thinking involves recombining existing elements in novel ways. This is where Eagleman and Brandt's concept of breaking becomes particularly relevant.

Recent research by Beaty and colleagues (2020) has shown that creative thinking involves a process they call "episodic memory retrieval and recombination." This means that when we're being creative, we're often retrieving memories or knowledge and recombining them in new ways. This process aligns well with the breaking and blending strategies in Eagleman and Brandt's framework.

For Millennials and Gen Z, who have grown up with unprecedented access to information, this aspect of creativity presents both opportunities and challenges. On one hand, they have a vast repository of knowledge to draw from. On the other hand, the sheer volume of information can be overwhelming. Learning to effectively retrieve and recombine knowledge is a crucial skill for young creators.

It's also important to consider the role of expertise in creativity. While we often associate creativity with "thinking outside the box," research shows that domain-specific knowledge is crucial for high-level creative achievement. As psychologist Robert Weisberg (1999) puts it, "You can't think outside the box unless you have a box in the first place."

This ties into the concept of "adaptive expertise" proposed by Hatano and Inagaki (1986). Adaptive experts not only have deep knowledge in their field but also the ability to apply this knowledge flexibly to new situations. This kind of expertise facilitates the bending, breaking, and blending processes that Eagleman and Brandt describe.

For Millennials and Gen Z, who often value breadth of knowledge and experience, finding a balance between developing deep expertise and maintaining the flexibility to apply knowledge creatively can be a key challenge.

Finally, it's crucial to recognize that creativity isn't just an individual cognitive process - it's also inherently social and cultural. As Keith Sawyer (2007) argues, many of our most important creative achievements are the result of collaboration and collective effort. This social dimension of creativity aligns well with the connected, collaborative ethos of many Millennial and Gen-Z creators.

In the digital age, this social aspect of creativity has taken on new dimensions. Online communities, collaborative digital tools, and social media platforms have created new opportunities for collective creativity. Ideas can be bent, broken, and blended not just within individual minds, but across vast networks of creators.

Understanding these cognitive processes isn't just academic - it has practical implications for how we approach creative work. By recognizing the different cognitive strategies involved in creativity, we can more deliberately structure our creative processes. We can create opportunities for both divergent and convergent thinking, practice bending, breaking, and blending ideas, and cultivate the kind of cognitive flexibility that underlies creative thought.

For Millennials and Gen Z navigating an increasingly complex and rapidly changing world, understanding these cognitive aspects of creativity can be empowering. It provides a framework for consciously developing and applying creative thinking skills, leveraging their unique strengths, and continually refining their creative processes.

As we move forward, we'll explore how these cognitive processes interact with environmental factors and modern technologies to shape the creative landscape. We'll also delve into practical strategies for fostering creativity, drawing on this understanding of creative cognition to provide actionable insights for enhancing creative potential.

6.3 The Creative Ecosystem: How Environment Shapes Innovation

While our cognitive processes form the core of creativity, the environment we inhabit acts as a powerful lens, focusing and shaping our creative efforts. Just as a kaleidoscope's patterns are influenced by the light shining through it, our creative expressions are profoundly shaped by the world around us. For Millennials and Gen-Z, who have grown up in a rapidly changing, highly connected world, understanding this interplay between environment and creativity is crucial.

Teresa Amabile's componential theory of creativity (1983) emphasizes the crucial role of the environment in fostering or hindering creative expression. This theory suggests that creativity emerges from the intersection of domain-relevant skills, creativity-relevant processes, and task motivation – all of which are influenced by the social environment. For young creators navigating the complexities of the digital age, this means that the environments they choose to inhabit – both physical and virtual – can significantly impact their creative output.

Let's start by considering physical environments. The spaces we occupy can have a surprising influence on our thought processes and creative abilities. A fascinating study by Joan Meyers-Levy and Rui Zhu (2007) found that ceiling height can affect the way we think, with higher ceilings promoting more abstract and creative thinking. This research suggests that the very architecture of our surroundings can nudge us towards more expansive, creative thought patterns.

But it's not just about grand architectural features. Even the ambient conditions of our immediate environment can play a role. Research by Ravi Mehta and Rui Zhu (2009) suggests that moderate levels of ambient noise, like what you might find in a bustling café, can enhance creative performance. This might explain why so many writers and artists throughout history have found cafés to be fertile ground for creativity – and why many Millennials and Gen-Z creators gravitate towards co-working spaces and coffee shops.

The color of our surroundings can also impact creativity. A study by Ravi Mehta and Rui Zhu (2009) found that exposure to the color blue can enhance performance on creative tasks, while exposure to red can improve performance on detail-oriented tasks. For young creators designing their work spaces or choosing environments for different phases of the creative process, these findings could inform more intentional choices.

However, in our digital age, the concept of "environment" extends far beyond physical spaces. For Millennials and Gen-Z, the digital realm is an integral part of their creative ecosystem. Online platforms, social media, and digital tools form a significant part of the environment that shapes their creative processes.

This digital environment offers unprecedented access to information and inspiration. At any moment, a young creator can access a vast repository of knowledge, view works by artists from around the world, or connect with like-minded individuals across the globe. This wealth of stimuli can fuel the kind of cognitive processes we discussed earlier – the bending, breaking, and blending of ideas that Eagleman and Brandt (2017) describe as fundamental to creativity.

However, this digital abundance also presents challenges. The constant stream of information and stimuli can lead to what psychologist David Levy (2007) calls "information overload" or

"Digital overwhelm." For creative individuals, who often rely on periods of focused attention and deep work, managing this digital deluge becomes a crucial skill.

This is where the concept of "Digital hygiene" becomes relevant for Millennial and Gen-Z creators. Creating boundaries around digital consumption, cultivating periods of digital silence, and curating one's online environment can all contribute to a more conducive creative ecosystem. As Newport (2016) argues in his book "Deep Work," the ability to focus without distraction on a cognitively demanding task is becoming increasingly rare and increasingly valuable in our hyper-connected world.

The social environment is another crucial factor in shaping creativity. Keith Sawyer's (2007) research on group creativity highlights how collaborative environments can spark ideas and innovations that no individual could have conceived alone. This aligns well with the collaborative, connected ethos of many Millennials and Gen-Z individuals.

In the digital age, this social dimension of creativity has taken on new forms. Online communities, from subreddits to Discord servers, have become incubators for creative ideas and collaborative projects. Platforms like GitHub for coders or Behance for designers allow creators to share works-in-progress, receive feedback, and collaborate across geographical boundaries.

These digital collaborations can lead to what Pierre Lévy (1997) calls "collective intelligence" – the idea that by pooling our intellectual resources, we can achieve creative outcomes that surpass what any individual could accomplish alone. For Millennials and Gen-Z, who have grown up with these collaborative platforms, navigating and leveraging these collective creative spaces often comes naturally.

However, as Scott Barry Kaufman reminds us, solitude is also crucial for creativity. In our hyper-connected world, finding time for quiet reflection can be challenging but essential. For young creatives, this might mean consciously creating "Digital detox" periods to allow for deep, focused work. It's about striking a balance between the stimulation and collaboration offered by connected environments, and the deep focus and introspection facilitated by solitude.

The cultural context we inhabit also plays a significant role in shaping our creative expressions. Mihaly Csikszentmihalyi's systems model of creativity (1988) emphasizes that creativity doesn't happen in a vacuum, but within a cultural context that determines what is considered novel and valuable.

Recent cross-cultural research by Vlad Glăveanu (2010) has shown how different cultures conceptualize and value creativity differently. For instance, Western cultures often emphasize individual creativity and breakthrough innovations, while many Eastern cultures place more value on collective creativity and incremental improvements.

For Millennials and Gen-Z, who are often characterized by their global outlook and cultural fluency, this cultural dimension of creativity presents both challenges and opportunities. On one hand, navigating different cultural expectations around creativity can be complex. On the other hand, exposure to diverse cultural perspectives can enrich the creative process, providing new lenses through which to view problems and solutions.

The economic environment also plays a crucial role in shaping creative expression. The rise of the gig economy and the increasing value placed on innovation in the business world have created new opportunities for creative work. At the same time, economic pressures and job insecurity can impact creative risk-taking.

For many Millennial and Gen-Z creators, this has led to a blending of creative and entrepreneurial pursuits. The rise of the "creator economy" – where individuals can monetize their creative output directly through platforms like Patreon, Substack, or Etsy – has opened up new avenues for creative careers. This shift aligns well with the desire for autonomy and meaningful work that characterizes many in these generations.

However, this new creative landscape also presents challenges. The pressure to constantly produce content, navigate algorithm changes, and manage parasocial relationships with audiences can be overwhelming. A study by The Tilt (2021) found that 68% of content creators feel burned out at least occasionally, highlighting the need for sustainable creative practices in this new environment.

The technological environment is another crucial factor shaping creativity for Millennials and Gen-Z. Digital tools have dramatically lowered the barriers to entry for many forms of creative expression. Software for music production, video editing, or graphic design – once prohibitively expensive – is now accessible to anyone with a computer or even a smartphone.

These tools don't just make creation easier – they can fundamentally shape the creative process itself. The constraints and affordances of digital tools influence the kind of work we produce. For instance, the rise of social media has given birth to entirely new art forms, from Twitter threads to TikTok dances.

However, as media theorist Marshall McLuhan famously said, "We shape our tools, and thereafter our tools shape us." For young creators, developing a critical awareness of how their tools influence their creative processes is crucial. It's about leveraging technology as a powerful creative ally while maintaining the ability to think beyond its constraints.

Looking ahead, emerging technologies like artificial intelligence and virtual reality promise to reshape the creative landscape once again. AI tools like Chat GPT4o for text generation or DALL-E for image creation are already being integrated into creative workflows. For Millennials and Gen-Z, learning to collaborate with these AI tools – to bend, break, and blend ideas in conjunction with artificial intelligence – may become a key creative skill.

In conclusion, the environment we inhabit – physical, digital, social, cultural, economic, and technological – plays a crucial role in shaping our creative expressions. For Millennials and Gen-Z navigating this complex creative ecosystem, understanding these environmental influences can be empowering. It provides a framework for consciously shaping their creative environments, leveraging the unique opportunities of the digital age while mitigating its challenges.

As we move forward, we'll explore practical strategies for fostering creativity, drawing on this understanding of environmental factors to provide actionable insights for enhancing creative potential. Remember, creativity isn't just about what happens inside our heads – it's about how we interact with the world around us. By consciously shaping our creative ecosystems, we can create the conditions for our most innovative and fulfilling work.

6.4 Calibrating Your Creative Kaleidoscope: Strategies for Fostering Creativity

Creativity isn't a fixed trait bestowed upon a lucky few; it's a skill that can be cultivated and enhanced through deliberate practice and targeted strategies. Just as a kaleidoscope can be turned to reveal new patterns, your creative potential can be unlocked and expanded with the right approaches. In this section, we'll explore practical strategies for fostering creativity, tailored to the unique challenges and opportunities faced by Millennials and Gen-Z in today's rapidly evolving creative landscape.

Cognitive Calisthenics: Exercises for Your Creative Mind

Let's start by focusing on cognitive strategies that can enhance your creative thinking abilities. One powerful approach is to practice divergent thinking - the ability to generate multiple ideas or solutions to a problem. Alex Osborn's classic brainstorming technique (1953) remains a valuable tool, but with a modern twist. Instead of traditional group brainstorming, which can sometimes lead to groupthink, try "brainwriting" (Paulus & Yang, 2000). In this technique, participants write down their ideas individually before sharing and building on each other's thoughts. This approach can be particularly effective in digital collaborations, using shared documents or virtual whiteboards.

To practice Eagleman and Brandt's (2017) concepts of bending, breaking, and blending, try the "SCAMPER" technique developed by Bob Eberle (1996). This acronym stands for Substitute, Combine, Adapt, Modify, Put to another use, Eliminate, and Reverse. Take an existing idea or object and systematically apply each of these operations to it. For instance, if you're redesigning a smartphone, you might ask: What if we substitute the screen with holographic projections? How could we combine it with wearable technology? How could we adapt it for underwater use?

Enhancing cognitive flexibility - the ability to switch between different modes of thinking - is crucial for creativity. Mindfulness meditation has been shown to improve cognitive flexibility (Moore & Malinowski, 2009). For Millennials and Gen-Z who might find traditional meditation challenging, apps like Headspace or Calm offer guided sessions tailored to busy lifestyles. Even a few minutes of mindfulness practice each day can yield benefits for your creative thinking.

Designing Your Creative Environment

Your environment plays a crucial role in shaping your creativity. While you might not be able to raise your ceilings for more abstract thinking (Meyers-Levy & Zhu, 2007), you can make intentional choices about your workspace. Create a dedicated area for creative work, filled with objects that inspire you. Research by McCoy and Evans (2002) suggests that visual complexity and natural elements can enhance creativity, so consider adding plants, artwork, or a view of nature to your space.

In our digital age, managing your virtual environment is equally important. Practice digital curation by carefully selecting the content you consume. Use tools like Pinterest or Are.na to create inspiration boards that fuel your creative thinking. However, be mindful of digital overwhelm. Implement regular "Digital detox" periods where you disconnect from screens and allow your mind to wander. This can create space for the kind of incubation period that often leads to creative insights (Ritter & Dijksterhuis, 2014).

Habits and Routines: Structuring for Creativity

Establishing a regular creative practice can significantly boost your creative output. Julia Cameron's (1992) concept of "Morning Pages" - three pages of stream-of-consciousness writing done first thing in the morning - can help clear your mind and tap into your creativity. For those who find writing challenging, consider adapting this to "Morning Sketches" or even "Morning Code" - the key is consistent, low-stakes creative expression.

Balancing structure and spontaneity is crucial for sustained creativity. Try timeboxing your creative work using techniques like the Pomodoro method (Cirillo, 1980s) - work intensely for 25 minutes, then take a 5-minute break. This can help maintain focus while also allowing for regular cognitive breaks that can spark new ideas.

When facing creative blocks, change your environment or activity. Physical movement, in particular, has been shown to enhance creative thinking (Oppezzo & Schwartz, 2014). For Millennials and Gen-Z accustomed to sedentary, screen-based work, even a short walk or a quick yoga session can help shift your perspective and overcome creative hurdles.

Leveraging Technology for Creativity

While technology can sometimes be a distraction, it can also be a powerful creative ally when used intentionally. Experiment with AI tools like Chat GPT4o for writing or DALL-E for image creation, not as replacements for human creativity, but as collaborators that can spark new ideas or help overcome creative blocks.

For collaborative projects, leverage digital platforms that align with your creative process. Tools like Miro for visual collaboration or Notion for project management can help structure your creative work and facilitate seamless collaboration with team members across different locations.

Building Resilience and Embracing Growth

Creativity inherently involves risk and potential failure. Developing resilience is crucial for sustained creative practice. Try reframing "failures" as experiments or learning opportunities. Keep a "failure resume" where you document your setbacks and what you learned from them. This practice, advocated by Stanford professor Tina Seelig (2015), can help build resilience and a growth mindset.

Seek out feedback on your creative work, but be strategic about it. Research by Sheila Heen and Douglas Stone (2014) suggests that asking for specific feedback (e.g., "What's one thing I could improve in this design?") tends to yield more useful insights than general feedback requests.

Interdisciplinary Exploration and Collaboration

Creativity often thrives at the intersection of different domains. Practice "cross-pollination" by regularly exploring fields outside your primary area of expertise. If you're a designer, read about biology. If you're a programmer, study poetry. These seemingly unrelated pursuits can spark unexpected connections and innovative ideas.

Collaboration can significantly enhance creativity, but it requires skill to navigate effectively. When engaging in group creative work, practice "yes, and" thinking from improvisational theatre (Vera & Crossan, 2005). This approach encourages building on others' ideas rather than shutting them down, fostering a more generative creative process.

For Millennials and Gen-Z navigating the creator economy, building a supportive creative community is crucial. Engage with other creators through online platforms, virtual meetups, or local events. Share your work-in-progress, offer feedback to others, and create accountability partnerships to help maintain creative momentum.

Remember, fostering creativity is a personal journey. What works for one person may not work for another. Experiment with these strategies, reflect on what resonates with you, and gradually build a creative practice that aligns with your unique strengths and goals. By consistently calibrating your creative kaleidoscope - adjusting your cognitive approaches, environment, habits, and collaborations - you can unlock new patterns of innovation and expression.

In our rapidly changing world, the ability to think creatively and adapt to new challenges is more valuable than ever. By intentionally fostering your creativity, you're not just enhancing your personal expression - you're developing a crucial skill for thriving in the 21st-century landscape. So turn that kaleidoscope, embrace the unexpected patterns that emerge, and let your creativity flourish.

Key Insights

- Creativity involves both novelty and usefulness
- It's a cognitive process that can be understood and enhanced
- Creativity is influenced by various factors, including personality, motivation, and environment

Innovation Challenge:

For one week, practice divergent thinking daily. Spend 10 minutes each day generating as many uses as possible for a common object (e.g., a paperclip). Note how your ideas evolve over the week.

REFLECTION QUESTIONS

1. How do you typically define creativity in your work? How might broadening this definition open up new possibilities for innovation?

2. Which factors discussed in this chapter do you think most influence your own creativity? How could you leverage or enhance these factors?

3. In what ways might your current work environment be supporting or inhibiting creativity? How could you influence this environment to better foster creativity?

CHAPTER 7

HOW FLOW TURBOCHARGES CREATIVITY

Imagine being so engrossed in a task that time seems to melt away, your focus is laser-sharp, and everything just clicks. You're operating at the peak of your abilities, yet it feels almost effortless. This is the state of "flow" - a concept that holds the key to unlocking unprecedented levels of creativity and innovation. As we delve into this fascinating phenomenon, we'll discover how it can revolutionize the way Millennials and Gen-Z approach creative work in our rapidly evolving digital landscape.

In the previous chapter, we explored the multifaceted nature of creativity, unraveling its cognitive processes and environmental influences. Now, we're about to embark on a journey into flow - a state of optimal experience that acts as a powerful catalyst for creative expression. First introduced by psychologist Mihaly Csikszentmihalyii, flow represents the sweet spot where challenge meets skill, where we're pushing our abilities to their limit without quite overwhelming them.

But what makes flow so crucial for our generation of innovators? In a world of constant distractions and information overload, the ability to achieve deep, focused states of creativity is becoming increasingly rare and valuable. For Millennials and Gen-Z navigating the complexities of the digital age, mastering flow could be the differentiator that sets truly groundbreaking creators apart.

Throughout this chapter, we'll explore the neuroscience behind flow, uncovering how it alters our brain chemistry to enhance focus, pattern recognition, and creative problem-solving. We'll examine how flow acts as a turbocharger for creativity, allowing us to tap into levels of performance and innovation that might otherwise remain out of reach.

But understanding flow is only half the journey. We'll also delve into practical strategies for achieving flow in our distraction-filled digital world. From designing flow-friendly environments to cultivating flow-inducing habits, you'll gain a toolkit for creating more opportunities for this optimal state in your creative work.

We'll explore how flow operates not just on an individual level, but also in group settings. In an era where collaboration and collective creativity are increasingly important, understanding and fostering group flow could be a game-changer for teams and organizations.

As we navigate this exploration, we'll draw on cutting-edge research, real-world examples, and practical insights tailored to the unique challenges and opportunities faced by Millennials and Gen-Z creators. Whether you're a digital artist, an entrepreneur, a content creator, or simply someone looking to infuse more creativity into your daily life, the concepts and strategies in this chapter will provide you with a roadmap for leveraging the power of flow.

So, are you ready to dive into the world of flow and discover how it can revolutionize your creative process? Let's begin our journey into this optimal state of creativity - where time seems to stand still, self-consciousness fades away, and innovation flourishes. Welcome to the power of flow.

7.1 UNDERSTANDING FLOW STATES

Have you ever been so engrossed in a task that time seemed to fly by, your focus was laser-sharp, and everything just clicked? If so, you've experienced what psychologist Mihaly Csikszentmihalyi calls "flow" - a state of optimal experience that can supercharge your creativity and productivity. In this chapter, we'll explore the fascinating world of flow and how it can revolutionize your creative process.

Csikszentmihalyi first introduced the concept of flow in his seminal work "Flow: The Psychology of Optimal Experience" (1990). He described it as a state of complete absorption in an activity, where you're so focused that everything else fades into the background. It's that sweet spot where challenge meets skill, where you're pushing your abilities to their limit but not quite overwhelming them.

But what's happening in your brain during these magical moments of flow? Neuroscientists have discovered some intriguing answers. When you're in flow, your brain undergoes a unique shift in activity. Arne Dietrich's research on the neurocognitive mechanisms of flow (2004) revealed a phenomenon called "transient hypofrontality." In simple terms, parts of your prefrontal cortex - the area responsible for self-reflection and impulse control - become less active. It's as if your inner critic takes a coffee break, allowing your raw creativity to shine through unfiltered.

At the same time, your brain releases a cocktail of feel-good neurochemicals. Dopamine, the reward chemical, sharpens your focus and helps you see connections between ideas. Norepinephrine keeps you alert and engaged, while anandamide (nicknamed the "bliss molecule") promotes lateral thinking and elevates your mood. This neurochemical party in your brain doesn't just make you feel good - it's a powerhouse for creative thinking and innovation.

The key components of flow are directly tied to creativity. First, there's intense and focused concentration on the present moment. When you're in flow, you're not worrying about the past or future - you're fully immersed in the task at hand. This laser focus allows for deeper exploration of ideas and more nuanced problem-solving.

Second, flow is intrinsically rewarding. The experience itself is so enjoyable that you're motivated to keep going, even when faced with challenges. This intrinsic motivation is crucial for creativity, as it fuels persistence and the willingness to explore multiple solutions.

Third, flow alters your sense of time. Hours can pass in what feels like minutes, allowing for extended periods of creative work. This time dilation effect often leads to more thorough exploration of ideas and more innovative solutions.

Lastly, flow reduces self-consciousness. The voice of self-doubt quiets down, allowing for freer thinking and more willingness to take creative risks. It's like turning off the strict teacher in your head and letting your inner creative child run wild.

But how do we actually get into this magical state of flow? Csikszentmihalyi's research identified several conditions that make flow more likely to occur. One key factor is the balance between challenge and skill. If a task is too easy, you'll get bored. If it's too difficult, you'll feel anxious or frustrated. But when the challenge level is just right - pushing you to the edge of your abilities but still within reach - that's when flow is most likely to happen.

Another important factor is clear goals and immediate feedback. When you know exactly what you're trying to achieve and can see your progress in real time, it's easier to stay focused and engaged. This is why activities like playing a musical instrument or coding can be so conducive to flow - you can hear or see the results of your efforts immediately.

It's also worth noting that while flow often feels effortless once you're in it, getting there usually requires some initial effort. Many people experience a period of struggle or frustration before entering a flow state. This is normal and even necessary - it's your brain gearing up for the intense focus that flow requires.

Understanding these conditions can help you create environments and choose activities that are more likely to induce flow. For instance, you might break a large project into smaller, manageable tasks with clear endpoints. Or you might deliberately seek out challenges that stretch your skills just beyond your current comfort zone.

The benefits of experiencing flow regularly are numerous and profound. Beyond the obvious boost to creativity and productivity, flow experiences can increase overall life satisfaction and well-being. Csikszentmihalyi's research found that people who experience flow regularly report higher levels of happiness and fulfillment in their lives.

Moreover, the skills you develop through flow experiences can transfer to other areas of your life. The ability to focus intensely, persist through challenges, and find intrinsic enjoyment in difficult tasks can be invaluable in both personal and professional contexts.

As we continue to explore flow throughout this chapter, we'll delve deeper into its relationship with creativity, discuss strategies for achieving flow in our distraction-filled digital age, and look at how flow operates in group settings. We'll also explore practical ways to integrate flow into your daily creative practice and work environment.

By understanding and harnessing the power of flow, you're not just optimizing your creative output - you're opening the door to a more engaging, fulfilling way of working and living. So let's dive in and discover how you can ride the wave of flow to new heights of creativity and innovation.

7.2 Flow as a Catalyst for Creativity

Now that we've dipped our toes into the concept of flow, let's dive deeper into how it supercharges our creative abilities. The relationship between flow and creativity isn't just a feel-good theory - it's backed by solid scientific research and countless real-world examples.

Csikszentmihalyi and LeFevre's groundbreaking study "Optimal Experience in Work and Leisure" (1989) found that people report being up to five times more productive when in flow compared to their normal state. But it's not just about working faster - it's about working smarter, more creatively, and with greater enjoyment.

Flow enhances creativity in several key ways. First, it provides enhanced focus and attention. When you're in flow, your attention is laser-focused on the task at hand. This intense focus allows for a deeper exploration of ideas and more nuanced problem-solving. It's like having a high-powered microscope for your thoughts.

Consider the experience of J.K. Rowling when she first conceived the idea for Harry Potter. She describes being in a state of flow on a delayed train journey, where the idea for the boy wizard "fell into her head" fully formed. The noisy, crowded train carriage faded away as her mind exploded with ideas for characters, plots, and the intricate wizarding world. This intense focus and flood of ideas is characteristic of the creative benefits of flow.

Second, flow reduces self-consciousness. It quiets the self-critical voice in our heads, allowing for freer thinking and more willingness to take creative risks. Think of it as turning off the strict teacher in your head and letting your inner creative child run wild. This reduced self-consciousness can lead to more original and daring ideas.

The famous painter Salvador Dali often spoke about entering trance-like states while painting, where he felt disconnected from his surroundings and even his own body. This detachment from self-consciousness allowed him to create surreal, boundary-pushing art that defied conventional norms and expectations.

Third, flow alters our sense of time, often allowing for extended periods of creative work. This can lead to more thorough exploration of ideas and more innovative solutions. Many creatives report losing track of time during their most productive sessions.

The renowned author Stephen King describes entering a state of "hypnosis" while writing, where hours pass like minutes. In his memoir "On Writing," he recounts writing entire chapters of his novels in single sittings, only realizing how much time had passed when he finally looked up from his work.

Fourth, flow is intrinsically rewarding, which can lead to greater persistence in tackling creative challenges. When you're enjoying the process, you're more likely to push through obstacles and explore multiple solutions. This persistence is crucial for creativity, as groundbreaking ideas often come after prolonged engagement with a problem.

Research by Keith Sawyer, author of "Explaining Creativity: The Science of Human Innovation" (2006), supports this idea. Sawyer found that creative breakthroughs often occur not in sudden "Eureka!" moments, but after periods of sustained, focused work - exactly the kind of work facilitated by flow states.

The neuroscience behind these creativity-enhancing effects of flow is fascinating. Remember the "transient hypofrontality" we mentioned earlier? This temporary quieting of the prefrontal cortex might explain why we feel less self-conscious and more creative during flow. It's as if your brain's overly cautious editor takes a break, allowing your raw, unfiltered creativity to shine through.

At the same time, there's increased activity in brain networks associated with implicit information processing and procedural memory. This shift may allow us to access knowledge and skills more fluently, contributing to that sense of effortless expertise that characterizes flow. It's as if your brain is accessing its entire database of knowledge and skills without the usual access restrictions, allowing for unique combinations and applications of what you know.

A study by De Manzano et al. (2010) on "The Psychophysiology of Flow During Piano Playing" provides empirical evidence linking flow to physiological responses that support creative performance. They found that during flow states, pianists showed decreased heart rate, increased respiratory depth, and activation of the zygomaticus major facial muscle (associated with positive emotions). These physiological changes support the focused attention and positive emotional state conducive to creative performance.

For our generation of innovators, understanding these neurological underpinnings of flow and creativity isn't just interesting - it's empowering. It means we can actively work to create conditions that foster these brain states and supercharge our creative output.

As we move forward in this chapter, we'll explore how to achieve flow in our distraction-filled digital age, how to harness the power of group flow, and how to integrate flow into our daily creative practices. By mastering the art of flow, you'll be setting yourself up for unprecedented levels of creativity and innovation. The next world-changing idea could be just a flow state away!

7.3 ACHIEVING FLOW IN THE DIGITAL AGE

In our hyper-connected world, achieving flow can feel like swimming upstream. Constant notifications, the lure of social media, and the pressure to always be "on" can make it challenging to find the deep focus necessary for flow. But fear not - with the right strategies, it's entirely possible to cultivate flow states even in our digital age.

First, let's understand the barriers. A study by Killingsworth and Gilbert (2010) titled "Wandering Mind Is an Unhappy Mind" found that people spend almost 47% of their waking hours thinking about something other than what they're currently doing. This mind-wandering, often exacerbated by digital distractions, is the antithesis of flow. Every notification ping or quick glance at your phone can pull you out of a potential flow state, resetting the clock on your focused attention.

Moreover, our digital devices have trained us to expect constant novelty and instant gratification. This can make it harder to persist through the initial struggle phase that often precedes flow. We might give up on a challenging task too quickly, reaching for our phones for a quick dopamine hit instead of pushing through to achieve flow.

But don't despair - there are effective strategies to overcome these barriers and achieve flow in our digital age:

1. Create a distraction-free environment: This might seem obvious, but it's crucial. Turn off notifications on your devices, use apps that block distracting websites, or even consider working in airplane mode. Remember, flow requires uninterrupted focus.
2. Practice digital mindfulness: Be intentional about your technology use. Set specific times for checking emails or social media, rather than constantly dipping in and out. This helps train your brain to focus for longer periods.
3. Use technology to your advantage: Paradoxically, technology can also help induce flow. Apps like Forest or Focus@Will use various techniques (like gamification or specially designed music) to help you maintain focus.
4. Embrace the struggle: Remember, flow often follows a period of struggle. Don't get discouraged if you're not

immediately in the zone. Push through the initial difficulty - it's setting the stage for flow.

5. Create clear goals and feedback loops: Flow thrives on clear objectives and immediate feedback. Break your work into manageable chunks with definite endpoints. Use productivity techniques like the Pomodoro method to create built-in feedback loops.
6. Balance challenge and skill: Csikszentmihalyi's research shows that flow occurs when the task at hand is just challenging enough to stretch your skills without overwhelming them. Regularly assess and adjust the difficulty of your tasks to maintain this balance.
7. Cultivate intrinsic motivation: Flow is closely tied to intrinsic motivation - doing something for its own sake rather than for external rewards. Reconnect with why you love what you do. Find ways to make your tasks more inherently enjoyable.
8. Practice mindfulness meditation: Regular mindfulness practice can enhance your ability to focus and enter flow states. Even just 10 minutes a day can make a significant difference.

Implementing these strategies might feel challenging at first, but remember - it's a skill you can develop over time. Start small, perhaps with 25-minute focused work sessions, and gradually build up your "flow stamina."

As you work on cultivating flow, you might find it helpful to track your experiences. Keep a "flow journal" where you note the conditions that led to flow states - the time of day, the type of task, your environment, your mental state. Over time, you'll start to see patterns that can help you create more opportunities for flow.

It's also worth noting that sometimes, stepping away from technology entirely can be the best way to achieve flow. Many creatives find that their best ideas come when they're taking a walk in nature, sketching in a notebook, or engaging in hands-on work. Don't underestimate the power of occasional "Digital detoxes" to reset your ability to focus and enter flow.

Remember, the goal isn't to be in a constant state of flow. That's neither possible nor desirable. Instead, aim to create more opportunities for flow in your work and life. By doing so, you'll not only boost your creativity and productivity but also experience more enjoyment and fulfillment in your tasks.

As we continue our exploration of flow, we'll look at how it operates in group settings and how you can integrate flow habits into your daily creative work. The digital age presents challenges, but it also offers unprecedented opportunities for creativity and innovation. By mastering flow, you'll be well-equipped to seize these opportunities and push the boundaries of what's possible in your chosen field.

7.4 Flow in Group Settings

While we often think of flow as a solitary experience, it can also occur in group settings. This phenomenon, known as "group flow," can lead to extraordinary levels of collective creativity and innovation. Understanding and fostering group flow can be a game-changer for teams working on creative projects.

Keith Sawyer, in his book "*Group Genius: The Creative Power of Collaboration*" (2007), describes group flow as a collective state of peak performance. It's what happens when a team is so in sync that their collective output far exceeds the sum of their individual contributions. Think of a jazz ensemble improvising a breathtaking performance, or a software development team working seamlessly to solve a complex problem.

But what makes group flow different from individual flow? While many of the core elements are the same - such as clear goals, immediate feedback, and a balance between challenge and skill - group flow has some unique characteristics:

1. Shared goals: The group must have a common understanding of what they're trying to achieve. This shared purpose aligns everyone's efforts and creates a sense of collective motivation.
2. Close listening: In group flow, team members are intensely attuned to each other. They're not just waiting for their turn to speak, but actively listening and building on each other's ideas.
3. Complete concentration: Just like in individual flow, the group is fully focused on the task at hand. Distractions fall away as the team becomes immersed in their collective work.
4. Blending egos: In group flow, individual egos take a backseat to the collective goal. There's less concern about who gets credit for an idea and more focus on how to build on each other's contributions.

5. Equal participation: While there may be differences in experience or expertise, in group flow, everyone has the opportunity to contribute. Ideas are evaluated on their merit, not on who suggested them.
6. Familiarity: Groups that have worked together and developed a shared language and understanding are more likely to achieve flow. However, this familiarity needs to be balanced with a degree of novelty to prevent stagnation.
7. Communication: Clear, open communication is crucial for group flow. This doesn't necessarily mean constant talking - in fact, groups in flow often develop a kind of shorthand, communicating complex ideas with minimal words.
8. Moving it forward: In group flow, there's a sense of constant progress. Each contribution builds on the last, moving the project forward in a seamless flow of ideas and action.

A fascinating example of group flow in action comes from the world of improvisational theater. In her research on collaborative creativity, R. Keith Sawyer studied improv groups and found that they frequently entered states of group flow during performances. The actors were so attuned to each other that they could seamlessly build complex narratives without any pre-planning. This same principle can apply to business teams, research groups, or any collective engaged in creative work.

Another compelling example comes from the tech world. The development of the first Macintosh computer at Apple is often cited as an instance of sustained group flow. The team, led by Steve Jobs, worked in an intense, collaborative environment where ideas flowed freely and the collective vision of creating a revolutionary product drove them forward. The result was a product that changed the course of personal computing.

So how can we foster conditions for group flow in our teams and organizations? Here are some strategies:

1. Create a shared vision: Ensure that everyone on the team understands and is committed to the collective goal. This shared purpose is the foundation for group flow.
2. Foster psychological safety: Team members need to feel safe to share ideas without fear of ridicule or retribution. This psychological safety allows for the free exchange of ideas necessary for group flow.
3. Encourage diversity of thought: While familiarity is important for group flow, so is novelty. Bring together team members with diverse backgrounds and perspectives to spark creative friction.
4. Design for collaboration: Create physical and digital spaces that facilitate easy communication and collaboration. This could mean open office layouts, digital whiteboards, or collaborative software tools.
5. Balance structure and flexibility: Provide enough structure to guide the team's efforts, but allow flexibility for creativity to flourish. Too much rigidity can stifle flow, while too little can lead to chaos.
6. Practice, practice, practice: Like individual flow, group flow becomes easier with practice. Engage in regular

collaborative exercises or brainstorming sessions to help the team develop their collective flow muscles.

7. Reflect and iterate: After group sessions, take time to reflect on what worked well and what could be improved. Use these insights to refine your approach to group work over time.

By fostering conditions for group flow, you can unlock extraordinary levels of collective creativity and innovation in your team or organization. In the next section, we'll explore how to integrate flow habits into your daily creative work, helping you make flow a consistent part of your creative process.

7.5 Flow Habits: Integrating Flow into Creative Work

Now that we understand what flow is and how it enhances creativity, let's explore how to make it a regular part of your creative process. Developing flow habits isn't just about boosting productivity – it's about crafting a more engaging, fulfilling approach to your work.

One of the key insights from flow research is that while flow states themselves feel effortless, getting into flow often requires deliberate effort. It's like surfing – catching the perfect wave might seem effortless, but it requires skill, practice, and the right conditions. Let's look at some strategies for cultivating these conditions in your daily work:

1. Ritualize your creative process: Creating a consistent routine can help signal to your brain that it's time to enter

a flow state. This could be as simple as brewing a special cup of tea, putting on noise-canceling headphones, or lighting a specific candle before you start work. Over time, these cues can become powerful triggers for flow.

2. Start with the right challenge level: Remember, flow occurs when the challenge of a task is well-matched to your skill level. Start your work sessions with tasks that are just beyond your comfort zone. As Angela Duckworth discusses in her book "Grit: The Power of Passion and Perseverance" (2016), this kind of deliberate practice – pushing yourself to improve specific aspects of your performance – is key to developing expertise and finding flow more consistently.
3. Break down big projects: Large, amorphous tasks can be overwhelming and make flow difficult to achieve. Instead, break your projects into smaller, concrete tasks with clear endpoints. This creates natural opportunities for the immediate feedback that flow thrives on.
4. Create a flow-friendly environment: Minimize potential distractions in your workspace. This might mean turning off notifications, using noise-canceling headphones, or even rearranging your physical space to reduce visual clutter. Remember, flow requires sustained attention, so anything that might interrupt your focus is a potential barrier.
5. Harness your peak hours: Pay attention to when you naturally feel most focused and creative. For many people, this is in the morning, but it varies from person to person. Schedule your most important creative work

during these peak hours to maximize your chances of achieving flow.

6. Practice mindfulness: Regular mindfulness meditation can enhance your ability to focus and enter flow states. Even just 10 minutes a day can make a significant difference. Mindfulness trains your brain to stay present and focused, key skills for achieving flow.
7. Embrace deep work: Cal Newport's concept of "deep work" aligns closely with flow states. In his book "Deep Work: Rules for Focused Success in a Distracted World" (2016), Newport advocates for scheduling extended periods of uninterrupted, focused work. This approach can help create the conditions necessary for flow.
8. Use the "20-minute rule": When you're struggling to get started, commit to working on the task for just 20 minutes. Often, this is enough time to overcome initial resistance and start to enter a flow state. If after 20 minutes you're still not feeling it, take a break and try again later.
9. Cultivate intrinsic motivation: Flow is closely tied to intrinsic motivation – doing something for its own sake rather than for external rewards. Regularly reconnect with why you love what you do. Find ways to make your tasks more inherently enjoyable or meaningful to you.
10. Practice active recovery: Flow states are intense and can be mentally draining. Make sure to balance periods of deep focus with adequate rest and recovery. This might include physical exercise, socializing, or engaging in hobbies unrelated to your primary creative work.

It's important to note that developing these flow habits takes time and patience. You're essentially rewiring your brain to focus more deeply and enter flow states more easily. Be patient with yourself and celebrate small victories along the way.

One effective way to reinforce these habits is to keep a "flow journal." After each work session, take a few minutes to note:

- Whether you experienced flow
- What you were working on
- Environmental factors (time of day, location, noise level, etc.)
- Your mental and physical state
- Any strategies you used to induce flow

Over time, you'll start to see patterns emerge. Maybe you consistently achieve flow when working on challenging design problems in the morning, or perhaps you find it easier to enter flow after a brief meditation session. Use these insights to fine-tune your approach and create more opportunities for flow.

Remember, the goal isn't to be in a constant state of flow. That's neither possible nor desirable. Instead, aim to create more opportunities for flow in your work and life. By doing so, you'll not only boost your creativity and productivity but also experience more enjoyment and fulfillment in your tasks.

As psychologist Mihaly Csikszentmihalyi notes in his book "Flow: The Psychology of Optimal Experience" (1990), people who learn to control their inner experience will be able to determine the quality of their lives. By cultivating flow habits, you're not just optimizing your creative output – you're taking control of your inner experience and crafting a more engaging, satisfying approach to your work and life.

7.6 Flow-Driven Innovation in Organizations

While we've primarily focused on individual experiences of flow, the concept has profound implications for organizations as well. Companies that can foster flow states among their employees are likely to see significant boosts in creativity, innovation, and overall productivity.

Let's explore how organizations can create environments conducive to flow and harness its power for innovation:

1. Autonomy and trust: Self-Determination Theory, developed by psychologists Edward Deci and Richard Ryan (2000), identifies autonomy as a key factor in intrinsic motivation. Organizations that give employees more control over their work – including what they work on, when they work, and how they approach tasks – are more likely to foster flow states. This doesn't mean a free-for-all; rather, it's about providing clear objectives and then trusting employees to find the best way to achieve them.
2. Skill-challenge balance: Remember, flow occurs when the challenge of a task is well-matched to an individual's skill level. Organizations can support this by providing opportunities for continuous learning and growth, and by

carefully matching employees with projects that stretch their abilities without overwhelming them.

3. Clear goals and feedback: Flow thrives on clear objectives and immediate feedback. Organizations can support this by setting clear, meaningful goals at both the individual and team level, and by creating systems for regular, constructive feedback.
4. Minimize interruptions: Constant meetings, emails, and other interruptions can make it difficult for employees to achieve the deep focus necessary for flow. Organizations might consider implementing "no meeting" days, quiet spaces for focused work, or policies around email response times to create more opportunities for uninterrupted work.
5. Foster a growth mindset: Carol Dweck's research on mindset shows that individuals who believe their abilities can be developed (a growth mindset) are more likely to embrace challenges and persist in the face of setbacks – both key elements of achieving flow. Organizations can foster this mindset through their approach to learning, feedback, and even how they frame failures.
6. Create flow-friendly spaces: The physical environment can have a significant impact on an individual's ability to achieve flow. This might involve creating a variety of workspaces to suit different tasks and working styles – from quiet, private areas for deep focus to collaborative spaces for group work.
7. Encourage intrinsic motivation: While extrinsic rewards like bonuses have their place, research shows that

intrinsic motivation is more conducive to flow and creativity. Organizations can support this by helping employees connect their work to their personal values and to the broader mission of the company.

8. Support work-life balance: While it might seem counterintuitive, allowing for adequate rest and recovery can actually increase opportunities for flow. Burned-out employees are less likely to achieve the deep focus and engagement characteristic of flow states.

A compelling example of a flow-driven approach to innovation comes from Google's famous "20% time" policy. This policy, which allowed employees to spend 20% of their time on projects of their own choosing, led to the development of some of Google's most innovative products, including Gmail and Google News. While the specific implementation of this policy has evolved over time, the underlying principle – giving employees autonomy and space for deep, focused work on projects they're passionate about – is a textbook example of creating conditions for flow.

Another interesting case study is Patagonia, the outdoor clothing company. Patagonia has long embraced a culture that supports flow states. They encourage employees to pursue their passions both inside and outside of work, believing that this leads to more creativity and innovation. For instance, they have a policy where employees can take surf breaks when the waves are good. This might seem counterintuitive, but it aligns perfectly with flow theory – employees return from these breaks refreshed and often with new insights and ideas.

It's worth noting that implementing flow-friendly policies isn't always straightforward. It requires a shift in organizational culture and mindset. Many companies are used to equating time spent at a desk with productivity, but flow theory suggests that short bursts of intense, focused work can be far more productive than long hours of distracted effort.

Moreover, what works for one organization or team might not work for another. The key is to experiment, gather feedback, and iterate. Some teams might thrive with daily stand-up meetings that provide clear goals and feedback, while others might benefit more from longer periods of uninterrupted work.

As Teresa Amabile and Steven Kramer discuss in their book "The Progress Principle: Using Small Wins to Ignite Joy, Engagement, and Creativity at Work" (2011), one of the most powerful motivators is the sense of making progress in meaningful work. By creating conditions that support flow states, organizations can help employees experience this sense of progress more frequently, leading to higher levels of engagement, creativity, and innovation.

In conclusion, flow isn't just a tool for individual creativity – it's a powerful framework for driving innovation at the organizational level. By understanding and applying the principles of flow, leaders can create environments where creativity thrives, employees are more engaged and fulfilled, and breakthrough innovations are more likely to emerge.

As we wrap up this chapter, remember that mastering flow – whether as an individual or an organization – is an ongoing journey. It requires patience, experimentation, and a willingness to challenge conventional ways of working. But the potential rewards – in terms of creativity, innovation, and overall well-being – make it a journey well worth taking.

So, whether you're an individual creator looking to boost your creative output, or a leader aiming to foster a more innovative organization, embracing the power of flow could be your key to unlocking new levels of creativity and success. The flow is out there – are you ready to catch the wave?

KEY INSIGHTS

- Flow is a state of optimal experience that enhances creativity and performance.
- Achieving flow requires a balance between skill and challenge, clear goals, and immediate feedback.
- The digital age presents both challenges and opportunities for achieving flow states.
- Group flow can lead to extraordinary levels of collective creativity and innovation.
- Organizations can drive innovation by creating environments that support flow states.

INNOVATION CHALLENGE:

For one week, implement daily 30-minute "flow sessions" in your creative work. Minimize distractions, set clear goals, and choose tasks that challenge you but are within your abilities. After each session, briefly note your experience and any creative insights gained.

Reflection Questions

1. Think about a time when you experienced flow in your creative work. What conditions facilitated this state, and how might you recreate them more often?

2. How do your digital habits impact your ability to achieve flow? What changes could you make to create more opportunities for deep, focused work?

3. How might you apply the concept of group flow to enhance collaboration and innovation in your team or organization?

PART III

INNOVATING IN THE MODERN ERA

CHAPTER 8
LEADERSHIP IN INNOVATION

In the fast-paced world of innovation, leadership isn't just about having a fancy title or making top-down decisions. It's about creating an environment where creativity thrives, where ideas collide, and where the next big breakthrough can emerge from anywhere. For Generation Innovate - our tech-savvy Millennials and Gen Z changemakers - this new paradigm of leadership is not just appealing; it's essential.

In this chapter, we'll dive into the evolving landscape of leadership in innovation. We'll explore how emerging theories like Complexity Leadership and Adaptive Leadership are reshaping our understanding of what it means to lead in uncertain and rapidly changing environments. We'll unpack the characteristics that define innovative leaders, from their comfort with ambiguity to their insatiable curiosity and their willingness to embrace failure as a learning opportunity.

But we won't stop at theory. We'll bring these concepts to life with real-world examples of Millennial and Gen Z leaders who are already putting these principles into practice, revolutionizing industries, and tackling global challenges head-on.

Whether you're an aspiring leader looking to make your mark, or a seasoned professional seeking to adapt to the new realities of innovation, this chapter will provide you with insights and strategies to thrive in the dynamic world of innovation leadership.

Are you ready to reimagine what leadership looks like in the age of rapid innovation? Let's dive in and explore the future of leadership - a future that Generation Innovate is already shaping.

8.1 THE EVOLVING ROLE OF LEADERSHIP IN INNOVATION

Remember the days when innovation was the sole purview of R&D departments, locked away in their ivory towers? Well, those days are long gone. In today's rapidly evolving digital landscape, innovation is no longer a separate function but a core competency that permeates every aspect of an organization. And at the heart of this transformation is a new breed of leaders who are redefining what it means to drive innovation in the 21st century.

Gone are the days of the autocratic leader barking orders from the corner office. Today's innovation leaders are more akin to orchestra conductors, skillfully orchestrating a symphony of diverse talents and ideas. They understand that in our complex, interconnected world, breakthrough innovations often emerge from unexpected collaborations and cross-pollination of ideas.

This shift in leadership style is not just a matter of preference; it's a necessity born out of the changing nature of innovation itself. As Harvard Business School professor Amy Edmondson notes,

"Today's business challenges are too complex for any one leader to solve" (Edmondson, 2019). The problems we face – from climate change to cybersecurity – require multidisciplinary approaches and collective intelligence.

Enter the concept of "adaptive leadership," pioneered by Ronald Heifetz and Marty Linsky at Harvard Kennedy School. This approach recognizes that many of today's challenges are adaptive problems – issues with no easy answers, where even the definition of the problem might be unclear. Adaptive leaders don't provide ready-made solutions; instead, they create environments where people can tackle tough problems, experiment with solutions, and learn from both successes and failures (Heifetz & Linsky, 2017).

This new paradigm of leadership aligns perfectly with the values and expectations of Generation Innovate – our Millennials and Gen-Z changemakers. A study by Deloitte found that 76% of Millennials and Gen Z believe innovation is essential for business growth and societal progress (Deloitte, 2021). These digital natives have grown up in a world where change is the only constant, and they expect their leaders to not just keep up but to actively drive positive change.

But here's the kicker: being an innovation leader in the digital age isn't just about embracing new technologies or jumping on the latest trends. It's about creating a culture where innovation can thrive. As Ed Catmull, co-founder of Pixar, puts it, "The role of the leader is to create an environment where people can come up with ideas and solve problems" (Catmull, 2014).

This culture-building aspect of leadership is crucial because innovation doesn't happen in a vacuum. It requires psychological safety – an environment where people feel safe to take risks, voice their ideas, and even fail without fear of negative consequences. Google's Project Aristotle, a comprehensive study of team effectiveness, found that psychological safety was the most important factor in building successful teams (Duhigg, 2016).

Moreover, innovation leaders in the digital age need to be masters of ambidexterity – the ability to balance exploitation of existing capabilities with exploration of new possibilities. As Harvard Business School professor Michael Tushman explains, "The most successful organizations are ambidextrous – aligned and efficient in their management of today's business while also adaptive enough to changes in the environment that they're able to survive tomorrow" (O'Reilly & Tushman, 2016).

This balancing act is no easy feat. It requires leaders to cultivate what author and consultant Margaret Heffernan calls "constructive dissent" – the ability to encourage and manage productive disagreement. As Heffernan argues, "The capacity to manage conflict is critical for high-performing teams and organizations" (Heffernan, 2019).

But perhaps the most significant shift in innovation leadership is the move towards a more distributed model of leadership. In today's fast-paced, complex business environment, waiting for decisions to trickle down from the top is often too slow. Instead, innovation leaders are empowering their teams to make decisions and take calculated risks.

This distributed leadership model aligns with what complexity leadership theorists like Mary Uhl-Bien call "enabling leadership" – creating the conditions for adaptive, creative problem-solving to emerge (Uhl-Bien & Arena, 2018). It's about setting the stage for innovation rather than trying to control every aspect of the process.

As we look to the future, it's clear that the role of innovation leadership will continue to evolve. The leaders who will thrive are those who can create environments where creativity flourishes, where diverse perspectives are valued, and where failure is seen as a stepping stone to success. They'll be the ones who can navigate the complex, interconnected challenges of our digital age, harnessing the collective intelligence of their teams to drive meaningful innovation.

In essence, the innovation leaders of tomorrow won't just be visionaries or strategists. They'll be culture-builders, enablers, and orchestrators of collective creativity. And in doing so, they'll be shaping not just the future of their organizations, but the future of innovation itself.

8.2 Characteristics of Innovative Leaders in the Digital Age

Picture this: a leader who's as comfortable discussing quantum computing as they are exploring the nuances of human psychology. Someone who can navigate the complexities of global supply chains while also fostering a culture of creativity and risk-taking. This might sound like a tall order, but it's increasingly the reality for innovative leaders in our digital age.

So, what sets these leaders apart? What characteristics enable them to thrive in an environment of constant change and disruption? Let's dive in and explore the unique traits that define innovative leaders in the digital era.

First and foremost, innovative leaders in the digital age are masters of ambiguity. They don't just tolerate uncertainty; they embrace it as a source of opportunity. As INSEAD professor Nathan Furr puts it, "Uncertainty is not something to be feared, but rather something to be leveraged" (Furr & Dyer, 2014). These leaders understand that in a world of rapid technological change, the ability to navigate ambiguity is not just a nice-to-have skill – it's a survival trait.

This comfort with ambiguity often manifests as a high tolerance for risk. But make no mistake – we're not talking about reckless gambling here. Innovative leaders take calculated risks, understanding that in the digital age, the biggest risk is often not taking any risk at all. As Amazon founder Jeff Bezos famously said, "If you decide that you're going to do only the things you know are going to work, you're going to leave a lot of opportunity on the table" (Bezos, 2016).

Hand in hand with this risk tolerance is a profound resilience. Innovative leaders understand that failure is an inevitable part of the innovation process. But rather than being deterred by setbacks, they view them as learning opportunities. This aligns with what Stanford psychologist Carol Dweck calls a "growth mindset" – the belief that abilities can be developed through dedication and hard work (Dweck, 2006).

Another crucial characteristic of innovative leaders in the digital age is their insatiable curiosity. They're not content with surface-level understanding; they dive deep into new technologies, business models, and social trends. This curiosity isn't just about staying informed – it's about connecting dots that others might miss. As Steve Jobs once said, "Creativity is just connecting things" (Isaacson, 2011).

But here's where it gets really interesting: the most innovative leaders aren't just tech-savvy – they're people-savvy too. They understand that at its core, innovation is a deeply human endeavor. As such, they possess high emotional intelligence, able to read and respond to the needs and motivations of their team members. Daniel Goleman's research has shown that emotional intelligence is twice as important as IQ or technical skills in determining outstanding leadership (Goleman, 2004).

This emotional intelligence often manifests as empathy – the ability to understand and share the feelings of others. Empathetic leaders can create psychological safety, fostering environments where people feel comfortable taking risks and sharing ideas. As Microsoft CEO Satya Nadella puts it, "Empathy makes you a better innovator" (Nadella, 2017).

Innovative leaders in the digital age are also master communicators. They can articulate complex visions in simple, compelling terms, inspiring their teams to reach for ambitious goals. But it's not just about top-down communication. These leaders are also excellent listeners, able to pick up on weak signals and emerging trends from all levels of their organization and beyond.

Another key characteristic is adaptability. In a world where the half-life of skills is shrinking rapidly, innovative leaders are committed to continuous learning and reinvention. They model this adaptability for their teams, creating cultures of lifelong learning. As Alvin Toffler presciently noted, "The illiterate of the 21st century will not be those who cannot read and write, but those who cannot learn, unlearn, and relearn" (Toffler, 1970).

Innovative leaders in the digital age also possess a global mindset. They understand that in our interconnected world, innovation can come from anywhere. They actively seek out diverse perspectives, recognizing that the collision of different viewpoints often sparks creative breakthroughs. Research by McKinsey has shown that companies with more diverse leadership teams are 33% more likely to outperform their competitors (Hunt et al., 2018).

But perhaps one of the most crucial characteristics of innovative leaders in the digital age is their ability to balance different, often competing, priorities. They can think both short-term and long-term, balancing the need for quarterly results with investments in disruptive innovations that may take years to pay off. As Harvard Business School professor Linda Hill puts it, "Innovation requires leaders who can build organizations that are consistently able to transform ideas into solutions" (Hill et al., 2014).

This balancing act extends to how these leaders approach technology itself. While they're often early adopters and enthusiastic proponents of new technologies, they're not tech-obsessed. They understand that technology is a means to an end, not an end in itself. As MIT professor Erik Brynjolfsson notes, "The key to winning the race is not to compete against machines but to compete with machines" (Brynjolfsson & McAfee, 2014).

Lastly, innovative leaders in the digital age possess a strong sense of purpose. They're driven not just by profit, but by a desire to make a positive impact on the world. This sense of purpose is particularly important for engaging Millennial and Gen-Z talent, who often prioritize meaningful work over traditional markers of success.

In essence, innovative leaders in the digital age are a unique breed. They combine technological savvy with deep human insight, risk-taking with thoughtful analysis, and visionary thinking with pragmatic execution. They're comfortable with complexity and ambiguity, yet able to provide clarity and direction. They're lifelong learners, empathetic listeners, and inspiring communicators.

As we navigate the challenges and opportunities of our digital age, these leaders will be the ones guiding us into new frontiers of innovation. They're not just adapting to the future – they're actively shaping it, one bold idea at a time.

8.3 FOSTERING A CULTURE OF INNOVATION

Picture a workplace where wild ideas are welcomed, failure is viewed as a stepping stone to success, and everyone from the intern to the CEO feels empowered to challenge the status quo. This isn't a utopian fantasy – it's what a true culture of innovation looks like. And in today's rapidly evolving digital landscape, fostering such a culture isn't just nice to have; it's essential for survival and success.

But here's the million-dollar question: How do you create this kind of innovation-friendly environment? It's not as simple as installing a ping pong table or hosting the occasional hackathon. Building a culture of innovation requires a deliberate, sustained effort that touches every aspect of an organization.

Let's start with the foundation: psychological safety. This term, coined by Harvard Business School professor Amy Edmondson, refers to a shared belief that the team is safe for interpersonal risk-taking. In other words, it's an environment where people feel comfortable speaking up, sharing ideas, and yes, even failing.

Google's Project Aristotle, a comprehensive study of team effectiveness, found that psychological safety was the most important factor in building successful teams (Duhigg, 2016). When people feel safe to take risks without fear of negative consequences, innovation flourishes. As Edmondson puts it, "In a psychologically safe workplace, people are not hindered by interpersonal fear. They feel willing and able to take the risks of learning and collaboration" (Edmondson, 2018).

But psychological safety is just the beginning. To truly foster a culture of innovation, leaders need to actively encourage and reward creative thinking and risk-taking. This means moving beyond traditional metrics of success and recognizing the value of experimentation and learning.

Take Intuit, for example. The financial software company has built innovation into its DNA through programs like "Innovation Time Off," which allows employees to spend 10% of their time pursuing new ideas. But what's really innovative about Intuit's approach is how they measure success. Instead of focusing solely on outcomes, they track metrics like the number of customer interviews conducted or experiments run. As Intuit's founder Scott Cook explains, "The key to innovation is testing many ideas quickly and cheaply, and killing the bad ones" (Rao, 2011).

This approach aligns perfectly with the mindset of Generation Innovate. Millennials and Gen Z have grown up in a world of rapid iteration and constant feedback. They're comfortable with the idea of "failing fast" and learning from mistakes. By creating systems that encourage and reward this kind of iterative approach, organizations can tap into the natural tendencies of these younger innovators.

Another crucial element in fostering a culture of innovation is diversity and inclusion. Innovation thrives on the collision of different perspectives and ideas. Research by Boston Consulting Group found that companies with above-average diversity on their management teams reported innovation revenue 19 percentage points higher than companies with below-average leadership diversity (Lorenzo et al., 2018).

But it's not enough to just have diverse teams – you need to create an environment where diverse voices are heard and valued. This is where inclusive leadership comes into play. Inclusive leaders actively seek out different perspectives, create opportunities for all team members to contribute, and show openness to new ideas.

For Generation Innovate, this inclusive approach to innovation is particularly important. As the most diverse generation in history, they expect workplaces that not only tolerate but celebrate differences. As a study by Deloitte found, 69% of Millennials and Gen Z believe diversity and inclusion are critical to fostering innovation (Deloitte, 2021).

But fostering a culture of innovation isn't just about internal dynamics – it's also about how an organization interacts with the outside world. In today's interconnected digital landscape, the most innovative companies are those that can tap into broader ecosystems of talent and ideas.

This is where the concept of open innovation comes into play. Coined by Henry Chesbrough, open innovation is the use of purposive inflows and outflows of knowledge to accelerate internal innovation and expand the markets for external use of innovation (Chesbrough, 2003). It's about recognizing that in a world of widely distributed knowledge, companies can't rely entirely on their own research but should instead buy or license processes or inventions from other companies.

Generation Innovate, with their digital fluency and global outlook, are natural adopters of open innovation principles. They're comfortable collaborating across organizational boundaries and leveraging digital platforms to tap into global talent pools. Companies that can harness this tendency and create structures for open innovation will have a significant advantage.

Take Procter & Gamble's Connect + Develop program, for example. This open innovation initiative has allowed P&G to source ideas from inventors, suppliers, and academics around the world, significantly accelerating their innovation process. As former P&G CEO A.G. Lafley put it, "Half the company's new products should come from outside" (Huston & Sakkab, 2006).

But perhaps the most crucial element in fostering a culture of innovation is leadership. Leaders set the tone for the entire organization. They need to model the behaviors they want to see – taking risks, embracing failure as a learning opportunity, and actively seeking out diverse perspectives.

This kind of innovation leadership aligns well with the expectations of Generation Innovate. They're looking for leaders who can provide vision and direction while also empowering their teams to take ownership and drive innovation. As a study by Deloitte found, 76% of Millennials and Gen Z believe business leaders should drive societal and economic progress through innovation (Deloitte, 2021).

Fostering a culture of innovation also requires rethinking traditional organizational structures. Rigid hierarchies and siloed departments can stifle creativity and slow down innovation. Instead, innovative organizations are adopting more flexible, network-based structures that allow for rapid formation of cross-functional teams and easy flow of ideas.

Spotify's "squad" model is a prime example of this approach. The music streaming company organizes its workforce into small, cross-functional teams (squads) that operate with a high degree of autonomy. This structure allows for rapid experimentation and innovation, with ideas flowing freely across traditional departmental boundaries (Mankins & Garton, 2017).

Finally, it's crucial to recognize that fostering a culture of innovation is not a one-time effort but an ongoing process. The most innovative organizations are those that have built-in mechanisms for continuous learning and adaptation. They regularly assess their innovation culture, gather feedback from employees, and make adjustments as needed.

As we navigate the complexities of the digital age, fostering a culture of innovation isn't just about staying competitive – it's about creating environments where Generation Innovate can thrive. By building psychological safety, encouraging risk-taking, embracing diversity, adopting open innovation principles, and modeling innovative leadership, organizations can create cultures where breakthrough ideas flourish and where the full creative potential of Millennials and Gen Z can be realized.

In essence, fostering a culture of innovation is about creating the conditions where innovation can emerge organically. It's about building an ecosystem where creative ideas can take root, grow, and ultimately transform industries and societies. As we look to the future, the organizations that can cultivate these innovation-friendly cultures will be the ones leading the charge into new frontiers of creativity and problem-solving.

8.4 Case Studies: Millennial and Gen-Z Innovation Leaders

As we've explored the evolving nature of innovation leadership and the characteristics that define innovative leaders in the digital age, it's time to bring these concepts to life through real-world examples. Let's dive into some inspiring case studies of Millennial and Gen-Z leaders who are redefining innovation leadership for the 21st century.

First up, let's talk about Whitney Wolfe Herd, the founder and CEO of Bumble. At just 31 years old, Wolfe Herd became the youngest woman to take a company public in the United States. But it's not just her age that makes her story remarkable – it's how she's innovating in the often-problematic world of online dating.

Wolfe Herd's leadership style exemplifies many of the characteristics we've discussed. She saw an opportunity in the ambiguity and challenges of online dating, particularly for women. Her empathy for this user base led her to create a platform where women make the first move, flipping the script on traditional dating dynamics. As she puts it, "We're not trying to be sexist, that's not the goal. The goal is to recalibrate gender norms and create a more equal environment" (Solk, 2021).

This focus on empathy and purpose-driven innovation has paid off. Bumble has grown to over 100 million users worldwide and expanded into friendship and business networking. Wolfe Herd's ability to balance innovation with social impact demonstrates the kind of multifaceted leadership that thrives in the digital age.

Next, let's turn our attention to Boyan Slat, the Dutch inventor and entrepreneur who founded The Ocean Cleanup at the age of 18. Slat's story is a masterclass in turning curiosity into world-changing innovation.

After encountering more plastic than fish while diving in Greece, Slat didn't just lament the problem – he set out to solve it. His approach embodies the risk-taking and resilience we've identified as key traits of innovative leaders. Despite skepticism from many experts, Slat persisted in developing his ocean-cleaning technology.

What's particularly noteworthy about Slat's leadership is his ability to inspire and mobilize others around a grand vision. As he puts it, "Big problems require big solutions" (The Ocean Cleanup, 2021). This ability to communicate a compelling vision and rally resources around it is a hallmark of effective innovation leadership in the digital age.

Slat's journey hasn't been without setbacks – early prototypes failed, and critics were quick to point out flaws. But his resilience and adaptability shone through. He and his team iterated on their designs, learned from their failures, and kept pushing forward. Today, The Ocean Cleanup is making tangible progress in addressing ocean plastic pollution, demonstrating the power of purpose-driven innovation leadership.

Shifting gears, let's examine the case of Tara Bosch, founder of SmartSweets. Bosch started her company at 21, driven by a personal mission to find healthier candy options. Her story illustrates how innovative leaders in the digital age can disrupt established industries by combining empathy with technological innovation.

Bosch's leadership style exemplifies the blend of emotional intelligence and business acumen that characterizes many successful Millennial and Gen-Z leaders. She understood the emotional relationship many people have with candy and used that insight to drive product innovation. As she notes, "I realized there was an opportunity to create a product that addressed the need for reducing sugar intake while still allowing people to enjoy candy" (Glasner, 2020).

What's particularly impressive about Bosch's leadership is her ability to navigate the complexities of the food industry as a young entrepreneur. She faced skepticism from manufacturers and retailers but persisted in her vision. Her adaptability and resilience were put to the test when an early batch of product had to be recalled, but she used this setback as an opportunity to improve quality control and strengthen customer relationships.

Bosch's success – SmartSweets was acquired for $360 million in 2020 – demonstrates how innovative leaders can create significant value by addressing unmet needs in established markets. Her story is a powerful example of how empathy-driven innovation, combined with resilience and adaptability, can lead to breakthrough success.

Finally, let's consider the case of Vitalik Buterin, the co-founder of Ethereum. Buterin's story embodies many of the characteristics we've discussed, particularly the ability to navigate ambiguity and think in systems.

Buterin conceived the idea for Ethereum at just 19, demonstrating the kind of visionary thinking that defines many innovative leaders in the digital age. What sets Buterin apart is his ability to not just envision a radically different future, but to build the technical and community infrastructure to make it a reality.

His leadership style is marked by a deep commitment to decentralization and community governance. As he puts it, "I'm concerned a lot about centralization risks" (Cryptocompare, 2022). This focus on distributed decision-making aligns closely with the collaborative, network-centric approach that characterizes much of Millennial and Gen-Z leadership.

Buterin's journey with Ethereum hasn't been without challenges. The rapid growth of the platform has led to scaling issues and energy consumption concerns. But Buterin's adaptability and commitment to continuous learning have been evident in how he and the Ethereum community have tackled these challenges head-on.

What's particularly noteworthy about Buterin's leadership is his ability to balance technical innovation with social impact. He's been a vocal advocate for using blockchain technology to address global challenges, from financial inclusion to digital identity. This alignment of technological innovation with broader societal goals is a hallmark of many Millennial and Gen-Z innovation leaders.

These case studies – from Whitney Wolfe Herd's empathy-driven disruption of online dating to Boyan Slat's audacious ocean cleanup mission, from Tara Bosch's reinvention of candy to Vitalik Buterin's blockchain revolution – illustrate the multifaceted nature of innovation leadership in the digital age.

These young leaders embody the characteristics we've discussed: comfort with ambiguity, resilience in the face of setbacks, deep empathy for users and stakeholders, adaptability in rapidly changing environments, and a strong sense of purpose that goes beyond profit.

Their stories remind us that innovation leadership in the digital age isn't about having all the answers. It's about asking the right questions, inspiring others to join in the quest for solutions, and creating environments where breakthrough ideas can flourish. As we look to the future, these Millennial and Gen-Z leaders are lighting the way, showing us what's possible when we combine technological savvy with human insight, risk-taking with thoughtful analysis, and visionary thinking with pragmatic execution.

These young innovators are not just leading companies; they're reshaping entire industries and addressing global challenges. They're proving that age is not a barrier to transformative leadership, and that the characteristics we've identified – from adaptability to empathy, from resilience to purpose-driven motivation – are indeed the hallmarks of successful innovation leadership in the digital age.

Moreover, these case studies highlight a key trend among Millennial and Gen-Z innovation leaders: the seamless integration of business goals with social impact. Whether it's Wolfe Herd's mission to empower women in the dating space, Slat's determination to clean up our oceans, Bosch's drive to create healthier food options, or Buterin's vision of decentralized, accessible financial systems, these leaders are demonstrating that profit and purpose can go hand in hand.

This alignment of business and societal goals is not just a nice-to-have for these leaders; it's fundamental to their approach to innovation. As a study by Deloitte (2021) found, 44% of Millennials and 49% of Gen-Zs say they have made choices over the type of work they are prepared to do or organizations they'd work for based on their personal ethics. This value-driven approach to leadership is reshaping how we think about innovation and its role in society.

Another common thread among these leaders is their ability to leverage digital platforms and communities to drive innovation. Wolfe Herd's Bumble, Slat's crowdfunding campaigns, Bosch's direct-to-consumer strategy, and Buterin's open-source development model all demonstrate a deep understanding of how to harness the power of digital networks. This network-centric approach allows them to tap into collective intelligence, iterate rapidly based on user feedback, and scale their innovations quickly.

The success of these young leaders also underscores the importance of diversity in driving innovation. Their fresh perspectives and willingness to challenge established norms have allowed them to see opportunities where others saw only obstacles. As research by Boston Consulting Group (Lorenzo et al., 2018) has shown, companies with more diverse management teams have 19% higher innovation revenues. These case studies bring that statistic to life, showing how diverse leadership can lead to breakthrough innovations.

However, it's important to note that the path of these young innovation leaders hasn't been without challenges. They've all faced skepticism, setbacks, and moments of doubt. What sets them apart is their resilience – their ability to view failures as learning opportunities and to persist in the face of adversity. This resilience, combined with their adaptability, has allowed them to navigate the uncertainties of the digital age and emerge as leaders in their fields.

As we look to the future, these Millennial and Gen-Z innovation leaders are setting a new standard for what leadership can look like in the digital age. They're demonstrating that effective innovation leadership is about more than just technical knowledge or business acumen. It's about having the vision to see possibilities where others see problems, the empathy to understand and address real human needs, the courage to take calculated risks, and the resilience to keep pushing forward in the face of setbacks.

Their stories serve as both inspiration and instruction for aspiring innovation leaders. They remind us that age is no barrier to transformative leadership, that purpose and profit can be powerful allies, and that the most impactful innovations often come from a deep understanding of human needs combined with the clever application of technology.

As we conclude this exploration of Millennial and Gen-Z innovation leaders, it's clear that the future of leadership is in good hands. These young innovators are not just adapting to the digital age – they're actively shaping it, creating new paradigms for how businesses can innovate, grow, and make a positive impact on the world.

Their journeys underscore the evolving nature of innovation leadership we discussed earlier in this chapter. They embody the characteristics we identified as crucial for innovative leaders in the digital age – from comfort with ambiguity to empathetic understanding, from adaptability to purpose-driven motivation. In doing so, they're not just leading their own organizations; they're redefining what leadership looks like for a new generation of innovators.

As we move forward, the challenge for organizations will be to create environments where this kind of leadership can flourish. This means embracing diversity, encouraging calculated risk-taking, valuing both technological innovation and human insight, and recognizing that the most powerful innovations often arise when we align business goals with broader societal needs.

The stories of Whitney Wolfe Herd, Boyan Slat, Tara Bosch, and Vitalik Buterin are just a few examples of the incredible innovation leadership emerging from the Millennial and Gen-Z generations. As more young leaders step into prominent roles, we can expect to see continued disruption, transformation, and positive change across industries and societies.

These case studies serve as a powerful reminder that innovation leadership in the digital age is not about having all the answers. It's about asking the right questions, inspiring others to join in the quest for solutions, and creating environments where breakthrough ideas can flourish. As we look to the future, these Millennial and Gen-Z leaders are lighting the way, showing us what's possible when we combine technological savvy with human insight, risk-taking with thoughtful analysis, and visionary thinking with pragmatic execution.

The future of innovation leadership is here, and it's being shaped by a new generation of leaders who are unafraid to challenge the status quo, leverage technology for good, and pursue innovations that can change the world. As we face the complex challenges of the 21st century, these are precisely the kind of leaders we need to guide us into a more innovative, sustainable, and equitable future.

KEY INSIGHTS

- • Innovative leaders create environments that foster creativity and risk-taking
- • They balance vision with pragmatism and embrace ambiguity
- • Empathy and emotional intelligence are crucial for innovation leadership

INNOVATION CHALLENGE

For the next month, practice one aspect of innovative leadership discussed in this chapter (e.g., embracing failure, encouraging diverse perspectives). Keep a journal of how this practice impacts your team or projects.

REFLECTION QUESTIONS

1. What's your current leadership style? How might you adapt it to better foster innovation in your team or organization?

2. How comfortable are you with ambiguity and risk-taking in your leadership approach? How might increasing your tolerance in these areas impact innovation in your team?

3. In what ways could you enhance psychological safety in your team to encourage more innovative thinking?

CHAPTER 9

THE ROLE OF EMPATHY IN INNOVATION

In a world buzzing with technological marvels, you might think the key to groundbreaking innovation lies solely in cutting-edge algorithms or the latest gadgetry. But here's a plot twist for you: one of the most powerful tools in an innovator's arsenal is something uniquely human – empathy. Yes, you heard that right. That ability to understand and share the feelings of another isn't just for heart-to-heart chats; it's a superpower that's revolutionizing how we approach innovation.

For you, the Generation Innovate changemakers, empathy isn't just a soft skill to be tucked away in your personal development folder. It's the secret sauce that transforms good ideas into innovations that truly resonate with users. It's the bridge between technological capability and human needs, the X-factor that can set your innovations apart in a crowded marketplace.

In this chapter, we're going to dive deep into the world of empathy and its crucial role in the innovation process. We'll explore what empathy really means in the context of innovation, examine its profound impact on creativity, uncover practical strategies for cultivating and applying empathy in your work, and look at how empathy and compassion work together to drive meaningful innovation. Whether you're developing the next big app, designing a revolutionary product, or seeking to solve complex social issues, understanding and harnessing the power of empathy can be your key to creating innovations that truly make a difference.

So, buckle up, future world-changers. We're about to embark on a journey that will supercharge your innovation process with the power of human connection. Are you ready to discover how this uniquely human skill can drive the next wave of world-changing innovations? Let's dive in!

9.1 EMPATHY UNVEILED: DEFINITION, SIGNIFICANCE, AND THE COMPASSIONATE DIMENSION

Imagine for a moment that you could step into someone else's mind, see through their eyes, feel their emotions, and understand their thoughts. Sounds like a superpower, right? Well, in a way, it is. This ability is empathy, and it's not just the stuff of science fiction – it's a very real and incredibly powerful human capacity that's revolutionizing the way we approach innovation.

But what exactly is empathy? It's a term we throw around a lot, often conflating it with sympathy or compassion. But empathy is its own unique beast, and to truly harness its power, we need to understand it in all its complexity. At its core, empathy is the ability to understand and share the feelings of another. It's like having an emotional Wi-Fi that connects you to the experiences of others. But it's more than just feeling bad when someone else is sad. As Roman Krznaric, a renowned empathy researcher, puts it, empathy is "the art of stepping imaginatively into the shoes of another person, understanding their feelings and perspectives, and using that understanding to guide your actions" (Krznaric, 2014).

This definition hints at the multifaceted nature of empathy. It's not just about feeling; it's about understanding and action. This aligns with what psychologists often describe as the three components of empathy: cognitive empathy (understanding how others feel), emotional empathy (sharing those feelings), and compassionate empathy (being moved to help if needed). These components work together to create the full empathy experience, like a three-layer cake of human connection – each layer adding depth and richness to our interactions.

Now, here's where it gets really interesting. Empathy isn't just a fixed trait that some people have and others don't. It's a skill that can be developed and honed. Helen Riess, Associate Professor of Psychiatry at Harvard Medical School, has shown through her research that empathy has both innate and learned components (Riess, 2017). We're all born with the capacity for empathy, but like a muscle, it can be strengthened with practice.

But empathy doesn't exist in isolation. It has a close companion that takes it from understanding to action: compassion. While empathy is about understanding and sharing feelings, compassion is the motivation to help or alleviate suffering that arises from that empathetic understanding. In the context of innovation, compassion drives us not just to understand user needs, but to actively work towards improving their situations.

Recent research by Vieten et al. (2024) provides valuable insights into the relationship between empathy and compassion. Their work suggests that while empathy and compassion are distinct constructs, they are closely interrelated and both play crucial roles in prosocial behavior and innovation. For Generation Innovate, this means that cultivating both empathy and compassion can lead to innovations that not only understand user needs but actively strive to improve users' lives.

The significance of empathy in innovation cannot be overstated. It's the key to creating user-centered designs that truly resonate with your target audience. By deeply understanding the experiences, needs, and pain points of your users, you can create solutions that address real problems, not just perceived ones. This leads to innovations that don't just look good on paper, but actually make a meaningful difference in people's lives.

Take the case of Doug Dietz, a designer at GE Healthcare. When Dietz observed children being terrified of the MRI machines he had designed, he was moved to action. By employing empathy and putting himself in the shoes of these young patients, he reimagined the MRI experience. The result? MRI suites transformed into adventures, with machines disguised as pirate ships or space rockets. This empathy-driven innovation not only reduced the need for child sedation but also improved the entire experience for children and their families (Brown, 2009).

But empathy in innovation isn't just about understanding current needs. It's about anticipating future ones. It's about seeing not just what people say they want, but understanding what they might need before they even know it themselves. This predictive power of empathy is what sets truly revolutionary innovations apart.

As we delve deeper into the connection between empathy and creativity in the next section, remember this: empathy isn't just a soft skill or a nice-to-have. It's the cornerstone of meaningful innovation, the key to unlocking human-centered solutions, and perhaps our greatest tool for creating a more understanding and connected world. In a landscape where technology is advancing at breakneck speed, our ability to understand and connect with other humans is what will set truly groundbreaking innovations apart.

So, as you move forward in your innovation journey, keep empathy and compassion at the forefront. Let them be your guide, your inspiration, and your superpower. Because in this age of artificial intelligence and advanced technology, it's our human capacity for empathy and compassion that will enable us to create innovations that don't just change the market, but change lives.

9.2 EMPATHY'S IMPACT ON CREATIVITY AND INNOVATION

Now that we've dived deep into the world of empathy, let's connect the dots to creativity and innovation. Because here's the thing: empathy isn't just about being nice or understanding others better (though those are fantastic side effects). It's a powerful catalyst for creativity and a crucial ingredient in the secret sauce of innovation.

At its core, creativity is about making novel connections, seeing patterns where others see chaos, and imagining new possibilities. Sound familiar? That's right - it's not too far off from what we do when we empathize. When we step into someone else's shoes, we're essentially engaging in a creative act, imagining a reality different from our own. This connection isn't just philosophical musing. There's hard science backing it up.

A study by Carlozzi et al. (1995) found a significant positive correlation between empathy and creativity. They discovered that individuals who scored higher on measures of empathy also tended to perform better on tests of creative thinking. It's like empathy and creativity are two peas in a very innovative pod.

But why is this the case? Let's break it down. First, empathy fuels divergent thinking, a cornerstone of creativity. Research by Grant and Berry (2011) found that perspective-taking enhances creative performance by encouraging individuals to generate ideas that are both novel and useful. It's like having access to multiple brainstorming sessions happening simultaneously in your head. For Generation Innovate, this is crucial. In a world where problems are increasingly complex and interconnected, the ability to see issues from multiple perspectives is invaluable. It's the difference between creating a product that works for a narrow demographic and one that has universal appeal.

Empathy also uncovers unmet needs. By truly understanding others' experiences, we can identify pain points that might not be immediately obvious. It's like being a detective of human experiences, finding clues that others miss. Tim Brown, CEO of IDEO, puts it beautifully: "Empathy is at the heart of design. Without the understanding of what others see, feel, and experience, design is a pointless task" (Brown, 2009). This empathetic approach has led to countless innovations, from better hospital experiences to more intuitive tech interfaces.

Consider the evolution of the smartphone. The leap from clunky button-based devices to sleek touchscreens wasn't just a technological advancement. It was rooted in a deep empathetic understanding of how people interact with technology in their daily lives. Innovators had to step into the shoes of users, understanding their frustrations with existing phones and imagining how a device could become more intuitive, more personal, and more integrated into daily life. This empathetic approach led to devices that didn't just have better specs, but fundamentally changed how we communicate, work, and live.

Moreover, empathy drives motivation in the creative process. When we empathize, we connect emotionally with the problems we're trying to solve. This emotional connection can be a powerful motivator, driving us to push through obstacles and persevere in our creative endeavors. A study by Thrash and Elliot (2003) found that inspiration - a key driver of creativity - is more likely to occur when individuals are open to new experiences and perspectives. And what better way to open yourself to new perspectives than through empathy?

In our interconnected world, creativity is often a team sport. And empathy? Well, it's the MVP of team creativity. Research by Hoever et al. (2012) found that perspective-taking (a key component of empathy) significantly enhanced creative performance in diverse teams. Why? Because empathy allows team members to build on each other's ideas more effectively. It's like playing a game of creative hot potato, where each person can catch and enhance the idea because they truly understand where it's coming from.

Empathy also encourages risk-taking in innovation. When we feel understood and supported - outcomes of an empathetic environment - we're more likely to take creative risks. Amy Edmondson's (1999) work on psychological safety shows that when team members feel safe to take risks without fear of negative consequences, innovation flourishes. Empathy is a key builder of this psychological safety. It's like creating an emotional safety net that allows people to leap into creative unknowns.

But here's where it gets really exciting. Empathy doesn't just enhance creativity; it can fundamentally change how we approach problem-solving in innovation. Design thinking, a methodology that puts empathy at the forefront of innovation, emphasizes the importance of deeply understanding user experiences before even defining the problem to be solved. This empathetic approach to problem definition often leads to reframing issues in ways that open up entirely new solution spaces.

Take the case of Doug Dietz and the MRI machine we mentioned earlier. The initial problem might have been framed as "How do we make the MRI machine less noisy?" or "How do we speed up the scanning process?" But by empathizing deeply with the young patients and their families, Dietz reframed the problem as "How do we make the MRI experience less frightening for children?" This empathy-driven reframing led to a solution that was far more innovative and impactful than any technical tweak to the machine itself could have been.

Empathy also enhances our ability to communicate our innovations effectively. When we understand our audience deeply, we can present our ideas in ways that resonate with their needs, values, and experiences. This is crucial not just for pitching ideas, but for getting buy-in from teammates, leaders, and ultimately, users.

Now, I know what some of you might be thinking. "But wait," you say, "doesn't too much empathy risk stifling creativity? What if we get so caught up in what users say they want that we miss out on revolutionary ideas?" It's a fair question, but here's the thing - true empathy isn't about slavishly following what users say they want. It's about understanding them deeply enough to see beyond their immediate requests to their underlying needs and desires. It's the difference between Henry Ford's apocryphal quote, "If I had asked people what they wanted, they would have said faster horses," and actually understanding people's need for faster, more convenient transportation.

The key is to use empathy not as a constraint, but as a springboard for creativity. It's about using the understanding you gain to fuel "what if" questions and challenge assumptions. Empathy gives you a deep understanding of the current reality that you need to imagine a radically different future.

As we move forward, remember this: empathy isn't just a soft skill or a nice-to-have. It's a creativity supercharger, a perspective-widener, and a neural pathway-blazer. It's the secret weapon that can take your creative thinking from good to groundbreaking. For Generation Innovate, empathy is more than just a tool - it's a mindset that aligns perfectly with your values and aspirations. It allows you to create innovations that are not just technologically advanced, but human-centered. It enables you to tackle complex problems with nuance and depth. And perhaps most importantly, it empowers you to create a future that's not just innovative, but inclusive and meaningful.

In our next section, we'll explore practical strategies for cultivating and applying empathy in your innovation process. Because knowing about empathy's power is one thing - being able to wield that power effectively is where the real magic happens. So stay tuned, future innovators. The best is yet to come.

9.3 Cultivating Empathy: Practical Strategies for Development and Application

Alright, we've explored what empathy is and how it supercharges creativity and innovation. But here's the million-dollar question: How do we actually cultivate this empathy superpower? Because let's face it, empathy isn't just something you can order on Amazon Prime (though wouldn't that be nice?). The good news is that empathy is like a muscle -- the more you use it, the stronger it gets. And just like physical exercise, there are specific "workouts" you can do to build your empathy muscles.

Let's start with active listening. This is Empathy 101, folks. Active listening means fully concentrating on what's being said rather than just passively hearing the message. It's like the difference between watching a movie while scrolling through your phone versus being completely immersed in the story. Next time you're in a conversation, try the "repeat back" method. After the person speaks, paraphrase what they've said to ensure you've understood correctly. It's not about parroting their words, but about capturing the essence of their message. Research backs this up: A study by Weger Jr et al. (2014) found that active listening techniques significantly improved participants' perceptions of feeling understood. It's like giving someone the gift of being truly heard -- and in return, you get deeper insights into their world.

Now, let's talk about empathy mapping. It's a technique used in design thinking to synthesize observations and draw out unexpected insights about users. Imagine creating a mind map, but for someone else's thoughts and feelings. Osterwalder and Pigneur (2010) popularized this tool in their book "Business Model Generation," showing how it can lead to deeper customer insights and more innovative business models. Here's how it works: You create a chart divided into four quadrants representing what the user says, thinks, does, and feels. As you interact with users or analyze data about them, you fill in these quadrants. This visual representation can reveal patterns and insights that might not be obvious from raw data or notes alone.

To truly understand your users, you need to walk a mile in their shoes. Or, you know, maybe just spend a day in their life. This method, often called "ethnographic research" in academic circles, has been shown to uncover deep insights that more traditional research methods miss. A classic example is IDEO's shopping cart redesign, where designers actually followed shoppers around supermarkets to understand their pain points (Kelley & Littman, 2001). They discovered issues that shoppers themselves might not have articulated, like the challenge of pushing a cart while keeping an eye on a child. This led to innovative features like a dedicated child seat facing the parent.

Perspective-taking is another crucial skill in your empathy toolkit. It's about imagining yourself in someone else's situation. Choose a person or group you're trying to innovate for. Spend some time imagining their daily life in detail. What challenges do they face? What brings them joy? What frustrates them? Write it down as if you were writing a character sketch for a novel. Galinsky et al. (2008) found that perspective-taking can reduce stereotyping and enhance social bonds. In the context of innovation, it can help you see beyond surface-level user feedback to deeper, unspoken needs.

Now, let's talk about the fuel that keeps the empathy engine running: curiosity. It's about maintaining a sense of wonder about the world and the people in it. Make it a habit to ask "Why?" more often. When you observe a behavior or hear an opinion that surprises you, resist the urge to judge. Instead, get curious. Ask questions to understand the reasoning behind it. Research by Kashdan et al. (2013) suggests that curiosity is linked to enhanced empathy and reduced aggression towards outgroups. It's like being a friendly detective, always on the lookout for clues about human behavior.

Storytelling is another powerful tool for building empathy. Stories allow us to experience events and emotions from another person's perspective. Encourage your users to share their stories. Instead of just asking for facts, ask for anecdotes and experiences. Then, practice retelling these stories to your team. The act of retelling helps internalize the user's perspective. Researchers at Princeton found that when we hear a story, our brains synchronize with the storyteller's (Stephens et al., 2010). It's like a neural mind-meld, allowing us to truly step into someone else's experience.

Here's a technique that might surprise you: mindfulness. You might think of it as a stress-reduction technique, but it can also increase our awareness of others' emotions and our own reactions. It's like turning up the sensitivity on your emotional antenna. Start with simple mindfulness exercises. For example, take a few minutes each day to sit quietly and focus on your breathing. As thoughts come up, acknowledge them without judgment and return to your breath. A study by Tan et al. (2014) found that mindfulness training enhanced participants' empathic concern and perspective-taking abilities.

Now, let's talk about diversity. Exposing yourself to diverse experiences and viewpoints can broaden your capacity for empathy. It's like adding new instruments to your empathy orchestra. Seek out experiences and viewpoints different from your own. Read books by authors from different cultures. Attend events outside your usual social circle. Travel to new places if you can. Research shows that multicultural experiences can enhance creativity and empathy (Leung et al., 2008). It's like giving your brain a cultural workout, strengthening those empathy muscles through exposure to diverse viewpoints.

Here's a fun one: role-playing exercises. They can help you practice seeing situations from different perspectives. It's like empathy improv. In your team, assign different roles based on your user personas. Act out scenarios relevant to your product or service. The key is to really try to embody the assigned perspective, not just act out stereotypes. Studies have shown that role-playing can increase empathy in various contexts, from healthcare (Bosse et al., 2012) to conflict resolution (Honeyman et al., 2009).

Last but not least, let's talk about vulnerability. Brené Brown's research has shown that vulnerability is key to connection and creativity (Brown, 2012). It's about being brave enough to let your guard down. Start by sharing your own experiences and emotions in your innovation process. If you're struggling to understand a user need, admit it. If a prototype fails, discuss what you learned from it. It's like creating a safe space for authentic human connection, which is the fertile ground where empathy grows.

Remember, cultivating empathy isn't a one-and-done deal. It's an ongoing practice, a way of approaching the world that can continually deepen and evolve. As you work on these exercises, you'll likely find that your capacity for empathy grows, leading to richer insights and more innovative solutions.

But here's the really exciting part -- as you cultivate empathy, you're not just becoming a better innovator. You're becoming a more connected human being. You're developing a superpower that can enhance every aspect of your life, from your personal relationships to your professional success.

For Generation Innovate, this approach to empathy aligns perfectly with your values and aspirations. It allows you to create innovations that are not just technologically advanced, but deeply human-centered. It enables you to tackle complex problems with nuance and depth, considering not just the technical aspects but the human impact of your solutions.

So go forth, future innovators. Flex those empathy muscles. Use these techniques to dive deep into the human experience. Because in the end, the most revolutionary innovations, the ones that truly change the world, are the ones that deeply understand and address human needs. And that, my friends, is the true power of empathy in innovation.

9.4 Challenges and Future Directions: Empathy in the Digital Age

As we've journeyed through the landscape of empathy in innovation, you might be thinking, "This all sounds great, but surely there are some challenges?" And you'd be right. Like any powerful tool, empathy comes with its own set of hurdles and potential pitfalls. But fear not, future innovators! Understanding these challenges is the first step to overcoming them.

Let's start with a biggie: empathy fatigue. Just as compassion fatigue is a real issue for healthcare workers and social service professionals, innovators who constantly immerse themselves in others' experiences can become emotionally drained. A study by Waytz and Epley (2012) found that people have a finite capacity for empathy, and trying to empathize too much can lead to burnout. It's like trying to run a marathon every day – eventually, you're going to hit a wall.

So, how do we combat this? It's all about balance. Practice self-care and set boundaries. Remember, you can't pour from an empty cup. Make sure you're taking time to recharge your own emotional batteries. Mindfulness practices, which we discussed earlier, can be particularly helpful here. They can help you maintain emotional balance while still staying open to others' experiences.

Another challenge is the risk of over-identifying with users. When we deeply empathize with someone, we might start to lose our objectivity. We might become so focused on one user's perspective that we neglect other important viewpoints or business considerations. It's like getting so caught up in one tree that you lose sight of the forest.

To address this, try to maintain a "zoomed out" perspective alongside your empathetic understanding. Use techniques like persona development to represent a range of user types, not just the ones you connect with most strongly. And remember, empathy is about understanding others' perspectives, not necessarily agreeing with or adopting them wholesale.

Now, let's talk about a challenge that's particularly relevant to Generation Innovate: empathy in the digital age. As more of our interactions move online, how do we maintain and cultivate empathy in virtual spaces? A study by Konrath et al. (2011) found a decline in empathy among college students over time, correlating with the rise of digital communication. It's like we're losing our empathy muscles as we exercise them less in face-to-face interactions.

But here's where it gets interesting. Technology doesn't have to be the enemy of empathy. In fact, it can be a powerful tool for cultivating it. Virtual reality, for instance, is being used to create immersive experiences that allow people to "walk in someone else's shoes" in a very literal sense. Researchers at Stanford's Virtual Human Interaction Lab have found that VR experiences can increase empathy and prosocial behavior (Bailenson, 2018).

Looking to the future, AI and machine learning present both challenges and opportunities for empathy in innovation. On one hand, there's a risk that over-reliance on data-driven decision-making could lead us to neglect the human, empathetic side of innovation. On the other hand, AI could potentially help us process and understand human emotions and experiences on a scale never before possible.

Imagine an AI system that could analyze millions of customer service interactions, not just for keywords or sentiment, but for deeper emotional patterns and unmet needs. Or consider how natural language processing could help us understand and empathize with users who speak different languages or come from different cultural backgrounds.

The key will be to use these technologies as tools to enhance our human capacity for empathy, not replace it. As Sherry Turkle puts it in her book "Reclaiming Conversation," "The point is not to reject or disparage technology. It's to develop a more sophisticated relationship with it" (Turkle, 2015).

As we look to the future, the role of empathy in innovation is only going to become more crucial. In a world grappling with complex, interconnected challenges – from climate change to social inequality – we need innovators who can truly understand and address human needs on a global scale.

The innovations of tomorrow will need to be not just technologically advanced, but emotionally intelligent. They'll need to speak to our shared humanity, bridge divides, and create solutions that resonate across diverse cultures and experiences. And that, future innovators, is where your empathy superpower comes in.

As we wrap up this chapter, let's take a moment to reflect on the journey we've been on. We've explored the depths of empathy, from its basic definition to its profound impact on creativity and innovation. We've discovered practical strategies for cultivating empathy and examined the challenges and future directions of empathy in the digital age.

Remember, empathy isn't just a soft skill or a nice-to-have. It's a fundamental capability that can drive truly transformative innovation. It's the key to creating solutions that don't just work, but resonate. It's the difference between innovation that changes the market and innovation that changes lives.

For you, Generation Innovate, empathy is your secret weapon. In a world increasingly driven by technology, your ability to deeply understand and connect with human needs and experiences will set you apart. It will allow you to create innovations that are not just clever, but meaningful. Not just profitable, but impactful.

So go forth and innovate with empathy. Use it to uncover unmet needs, to reframe problems in novel ways, to create solutions that truly resonate with users. Use it to build diverse, collaborative teams and to communicate your ideas in ways that inspire and motivate.

Remember, the most revolutionary innovations of tomorrow won't just be technologically advanced – they'll be deeply human. And with your empathy superpower, you're perfectly equipped to lead that revolution.

The world is waiting for your empathy-driven innovations. Are you ready to deliver?

KEY INSIGHTS

- Empathy is a crucial driver of user-centered innovation
- Empathy and compassion work together to create meaningful innovations
- Empathy can be actively developed and enhanced through specific practices
- Empathetic design leads to more impactful and resonant innovations
- Empathy fuels creativity and enhances team collaboration in the innovation process

INNOVATION CHALLENGE

Conduct an empathy mapping exercise for a user of your product or service. Use this insight to generate three new ideas for improving their experience. Consider how these ideas not only address user needs but also demonstrate compassion by actively improving their situation.

REFLECTION QUESTIONS

1. How might deeper empathy change your approach to a current project or challenge you're facing? What new perspectives might it offer?

2. In what ways do you currently incorporate empathy into your innovation process? How could you enhance this, particularly in digital or remote contexts?

3. Think of a recent innovation failure. How might a more empathetic approach have led to a different outcome?

4. How can you balance empathy with objectivity in your innovation process to avoid over-identification with specific users?

5. Consider the future of empathy in innovation. How might emerging technologies like AI and VR change the way we practice empathy in the innovation process?

CHAPTER 10

THE POWER OF SOCIAL NETWORKS

In the digital age, innovation isn't just about individual genius—it's about connections. Imagine ideas as sparks of light, traveling along invisible pathways, connecting people, colliding and combining to create brilliant flashes of innovation. This is the power of social networks in action.

For Generation Innovate—our Millennials and Gen Z changemakers—social networks are more than just platforms for sharing selfies or memes. They're the neural pathways of collective creativity, the invisible infrastructure that fuels breakthrough ideas and collaborations.

In this chapter, we'll dive into the hidden powerhouse of innovation: social networks. We'll explore how these webs of relationships shape the flow of information, ideas, and opportunities. We'll examine how digital natives are leveraging online platforms to collaborate in unprecedented ways, and we'll uncover strategies for building and nurturing your own innovation ecosystem.

From the strength of weak ties to the power of diverse connections, we'll reveal how understanding and leveraging social networks can supercharge your innovative potential. Whether you're a startup founder, a corporate innovator, or a social entrepreneur, mastering the art of network-driven innovation is crucial in today's interconnected world.

Are you ready to tap into the collective intelligence of your network and unlock new realms of creative possibility? Let's explore how the power of connections can drive the next wave of game-changing innovations.

10.1 The Structure and Dynamics of Social Networks in the Digital Age

Picture a bustling city, with its intricate web of streets, highways, and subway lines connecting people and places. Now, imagine that city existing not in physical space, but in the digital realm. This is the landscape of social networks in the digital age—a complex, dynamic ecosystem where ideas flow, collaborations form, and innovations emerge.

At its core, a social network is simply a set of relationships between individuals or entities. But in the digital age, these networks have taken on new dimensions, transcending geographical boundaries and operating at unprecedented scales and speeds. As sociologist Manuel Castells puts it, we now live in a "network society" where social structures are increasingly organized around digital networks (Castells, 2010).

The structure of these digital social networks is fascinating. They often exhibit what network scientists call "small-world" properties—a phenomenon where most nodes in the network are not directly connected, but can be reached from every other node in a small number of steps. This concept, popularized by sociologist Stanley Milgram's "six degrees of separation" experiment, has profound implications for how information and ideas spread through networks (Watts, 2003).

In the context of innovation, these small-world properties mean that novel ideas can potentially travel quickly through a network, reaching diverse individuals who might build upon or apply them in unexpected ways. For Generation Innovate, who have grown up navigating these digital networks, this rapid diffusion of ideas is second nature. They intuitively understand how to leverage these network properties to spread their innovations and gather diverse inputs.

But the structure of social networks isn't uniform. Some individuals occupy particularly important positions within networks. Malcolm Gladwell, in his book "The Tipping Point," identified key roles like "connectors" (people with unusually large networks), "mavens" (information specialists), and "salesmen" (persuaders) who play crucial roles in spreading ideas (Gladwell, 2000). In the digital age, these roles have evolved, with social media influencers and thought leaders often occupying these pivotal network positions.

For innovators, understanding these network dynamics is crucial. It's not just about having a large network—it's about strategically positioning yourself within networks to access diverse information and opportunities. As network scientist Albert-László Barabási notes, "Success is a collective phenomenon, driven by our position in the networks we inhabit and the behaviors of those around us" (Barabási, 2018).

One of the most powerful concepts in understanding social networks is the "strength of weak ties," introduced by sociologist Mark Granovetter. He found that when it comes to getting new information or opportunities, our weak ties—acquaintances and distant colleagues—are often more valuable than our strong ties (close friends and family). Why? Because our close connections tend to have access to the same information we do, while weak ties can serve as bridges to entirely different social circles (Granovetter, 1973).

For Generation Innovate, this concept has taken on new significance in the digital age. Platforms like LinkedIn or Twitter allow individuals to maintain vast networks of weak ties with unprecedented ease. A study by the Pew Research Center found that the median number of Facebook friends for users aged 18-29 was 300 (Smith, 2021). Each of these connections represents a potential source of new ideas or opportunities.

But it's not just about the number of connections—it's about the diversity of those connections. Research has shown that individuals with more diverse networks are more likely to generate innovative ideas. Ronald Burt's work on "structural holes" demonstrates that individuals who bridge different groups within a network are at an advantage when it comes to having good ideas (Burt, 2004).

This aligns well with the global outlook of many Millennials and Gen Z innovators. Their comfort with digital platforms allows them to easily form connections across geographical and cultural boundaries, creating diverse networks that can fuel innovation.

However, the digital age has also brought new challenges to network dynamics. The ease of forming online connections has led to concerns about the depth and authenticity of these relationships. Sherry Turkle, in her book "Alone Together," argues that our constant digital connections can sometimes come at the expense of deeper, more meaningful relationships (Turkle, 2017).

Moreover, the algorithmic nature of many social media platforms can create echo chambers, where individuals are primarily exposed to ideas and information that align with their existing views. This can potentially limit the diversity of ideas flowing through networks, a crucial ingredient for innovation.

For Generation Innovate, navigating these challenges requires a nuanced understanding of network dynamics. It's about striking a balance between breadth and depth in relationships, between maintaining a vast network of weak ties and cultivating deeper, more collaborative relationships.

As we move forward, understanding and leveraging social network dynamics will be crucial for driving innovation. In our increasingly connected world, the most successful innovators will be those who can effectively navigate these complex social ecosystems, tapping into collective intelligence and fostering collaborations that span boundaries and disciplines.

The power of social networks in the digital age lies not just in their size or reach, but in their potential to connect diverse minds, spark unexpected collaborations, and catalyze breakthrough innovations.

For Generation Innovate, mastering these network dynamics isn't just a skill—it's a superpower that can unlock new realms of creative possibility.

10.2 Leveraging Social Networks for Innovation

In the bustling marketplace of ideas that is the digital age, your network isn't just a list of contacts—it's your innovation ecosystem. For Generation Innovate, social networks are the rich soil from which groundbreaking ideas sprout and flourish. But how exactly do these digital natives harness the power of their networks to drive innovation? Let's dive into the fascinating world of network-driven innovation.

At its core, leveraging social networks for innovation is about tapping into what sociologists call "social capital"—the resources embedded in our relationships and social structures. But in the context of innovation, we're talking about a specific flavor: "innovative social capital." This concept, introduced by management scholars Martin Gargiulo and Mario Benassi, refers to the network resources that can be mobilized specifically for innovation purposes (Gargiulo & Benassi, 2000).

For Millennials and Gen Z, building and leveraging this innovative social capital is second nature. They intuitively understand what network scientists have long argued: that innovation often emerges from the "structural holes" between different groups in a network (Burt, 2004). These structural holes are gaps between different clusters in a network, and individuals who can bridge these gaps often have access to diverse information and ideas—the building blocks of innovation.

Take the case of Boyan Slat, the young Dutch inventor behind The Ocean Cleanup. Slat's ambitious project to rid the oceans of plastic waste didn't just rely on his technical ingenuity—it was powered by his ability to mobilize a global network of supporters, experts, and funders. Through savvy use of social media and crowdfunding platforms, Slat turned his idea into a movement, raising millions of dollars and attracting top talent from around the world (The Ocean Cleanup, 2023).

This story exemplifies how Generation Innovate leverages networks not just for information sharing, but for resource mobilization, problem-solving, and collaborative creation. They understand that in the digital age, innovation is rarely a solo endeavor—it's a team sport played on a global scale.

But it's not just about having a large network—it's about strategically positioning yourself within that network. As Herminia Ibarra's research has shown, the most successful innovators are often "brokers" who bridge different clusters within their networks, bringing together diverse ideas and resources (Ibarra, 2020). These brokers are the connectors, the ones who can translate ideas from one domain to another, sparking unexpected innovations in the process.

For digital natives, this brokerage often happens naturally through their participation in various online communities. A young developer might be part of a coding forum, a startup incubator Slack channel, and a social impact group on Facebook.

By connecting these different worlds, they create opportunities for novel ideas to emerge. It's like being at a continuous, global cocktail party where ideas from different fields are constantly mingling and recombining.

Moreover, Generation Innovate is redefining how we think about mentorship and knowledge sharing within networks. Gone are the days of the one-way, hierarchical mentorship model. Instead, we're seeing the rise of "peer-to-peer learning networks" where knowledge flows multidirectionally. Platforms like Polywork, founded by Millennial entrepreneur Peter Johnston, exemplify this trend. Polywork allows professionals to showcase their multifaceted skills and experiences, facilitating connections based on shared interests and complementary expertise rather than traditional career trajectories (Polywork, 2023).

This peer-to-peer approach aligns perfectly with the collaborative ethos of Millennials and Gen Z. A study by Deloitte found that 75% of Gen Z respondents believe they can learn new skills more quickly from YouTube and other online resources than through traditional educational methods (Deloitte, 2021). This DIY learning mindset, combined with robust peer networks, creates a powerful engine for continuous innovation.

But leveraging networks for innovation isn't without its challenges. The ease of forming digital connections can sometimes lead to "network overwhelm"—a state where the sheer volume of connections and information becomes paralyzing rather than empowering. It's like trying to drink from a firehose of ideas and opportunities.

To combat this, successful innovators in Generation Innovate are becoming adept at what scholar Herminia Ibarra calls "network pruning"—strategically cultivating some connections while letting others go dormant (Ibarra, 2015). It's about quality over quantity, about nurturing the connections that truly fuel creativity and innovation.

Another challenge is the potential for echo chambers in digital networks. The algorithms that power many social media platforms can create filter bubbles, where we're primarily exposed to ideas and information that align with our existing views. This can potentially limit the diversity of ideas flowing through our networks—a crucial ingredient for innovation.

To address this, many young innovators are intentionally seeking out diverse perspectives in their networks. They're joining cross-disciplinary forums, attending unconferences, and engaging in online debates with people who hold different views. It's a recognition that true innovation often comes from the collision of different worldviews and experiences.

As we look to the future, the ability to effectively leverage social networks for innovation will only become more crucial. Emerging technologies like AI and blockchain promise to create new forms of networked collaboration. For instance, Decentralized Autonomous Organizations (DAOs) are experimenting with new models of collective decision-making and resource allocation that could revolutionize how we collaborate for innovation.

Virtual and augmented reality technologies also hold promise for network-driven innovation. Imagine brainstorming sessions where participants from around the world can gather in a virtual space, manipulating 3D models of their ideas in real time. These technologies could help bridge the gap between the global reach of digital networks and the immediacy of face-to-face collaboration.

For Generation Innovate, these emerging tools and platforms are not just novelties—they're the building blocks of a new innovation paradigm. They understand that in our increasingly complex and interconnected world, the most successful innovators will be those who can tap into collective intelligence, foster diverse collaborations, and navigate the rich, sometimes chaotic, landscape of digital social networks.

By harnessing the power of their networks, Millennials and Gen Z aren't just creating new products or services—they're reshaping how innovation happens in the digital age. They're breaking down silos, crossing boundaries, and creating a more collaborative, inclusive innovation ecosystem.

As we move forward, the key will be to strike a balance between the breadth of digital networks and the depth of meaningful connections. It's about creating innovation ecosystems that are both globally connected and locally rooted, that can generate a constant stream of new ideas while also providing the support and resources to turn those ideas into reality.

In this new paradigm of network-driven innovation, success isn't just about what you know or even who you know—it's about how effectively you can mobilize your network to create value. For Generation Innovate, this isn't just a skill—it's a fundamental part of their innovative DNA, a superpower that's driving the next wave of world-changing innovations.

10.3 Digital Networks and Global Collaboration

Imagine a world where a teenager in Mumbai can collaborate with a startup founder in Silicon Valley, a data scientist in Lagos, and an environmental activist in Stockholm—all in real time, working together to solve a global challenge. This isn't science fiction; it's the reality of digital networks and global collaboration in the 21st century.

For Generation Innovate, these borderless collaborations are more than just a possibility—they're an everyday occurrence. Digital platforms have shattered geographical barriers, creating a global innovation ecosystem where ideas can flow freely across continents and cultures.

At the heart of this phenomenon is what Thomas Friedman calls the "flat world"—a global, web-enabled playing field that allows for multiple forms of collaboration (Friedman, 2005). But it's not just about technology. It's about a mindset shift, a willingness to engage with diverse perspectives and co-create solutions on a global scale.

Take the case of Foldit, an online puzzle game about protein folding that has led to real scientific breakthroughs. In 2011, players of Foldit solved the structure of an AIDS-causing virus that had puzzled scientists for years—in just three weeks (Khatib et al., 2011). This isn't just crowdsourcing; it's a new model of global, collaborative problem-solving that leverages collective intelligence in unprecedented ways.

For Millennials and Gen Z, this kind of global collaboration feels natural. They've grown up in a world where connecting with peers across the globe is as easy as sending a text message. A study by Deloitte found that 75% of Gen Z respondents have friends or followers on social media from other countries (Deloitte, 2021). This global outlook translates into a collaborative approach to innovation that transcends national boundaries.

Digital platforms are the enablers of this global collaboration. Tools like Slack, Microsoft Teams, and Zoom have made real-time, cross-border teamwork not just possible, but highly effective. The COVID-19 pandemic accelerated this trend, with remote work becoming the norm for many knowledge workers. A study by McKinsey found that 20 to 25 percent of the workforce in advanced economies could work from home between three to five days a week without a loss in productivity (McKinsey Global Institute, 2021).

But effective global collaboration isn't just about having the right tools—it's about fostering a culture of openness and inclusivity. As Erin Meyer argues in her book "The Culture Map," successful global teams need to navigate complex cultural differences in communication styles, decision-making processes, and attitudes toward hierarchy (Meyer, 2014).

For Generation Innovate, this cultural fluency often comes naturally. Growing up in a globalized world has made them adept at navigating cultural nuances and finding common ground across differences. This skill is invaluable in fostering truly global innovations that can resonate across diverse markets and contexts.

One fascinating aspect of digital networks and global collaboration is the emergence of what Yochai Benkler calls "commons-based peer production" (Benkler, 2006). This is a model of socio-economic production in which large numbers of people work cooperatively to create shared resources. The open-source software movement is a prime example of this, with developers around the world collaborating to create powerful tools that are freely available to all.

For many Millennial and Gen Z innovators, participating in these global, collaborative projects is a way to make a meaningful impact while also developing their skills and networks. Platforms like GitHub have become not just repositories of code, but vibrant communities where developers can showcase their work, contribute to projects, and learn from peers around the world.

However, global collaboration in the digital age isn't without its challenges. Issues of digital divide and unequal access to technology can limit who gets to participate in these global innovation networks. A report by the International Telecommunication Union found that in 2019, only 19% of individuals in least-developed countries were using the Internet, compared to 87% in developed countries (ITU, 2020).

Moreover, the ease of global communication can sometimes lead to a false sense of understanding. As Edward T. Hall warned in his seminal work on intercultural communication, the most dangerous kind of miscommunication often comes from assuming we understand each other when we don't (Hall, 1976).

For Generation Innovate, addressing these challenges is part of the innovation process itself. Many are working on projects to expand internet access in underserved areas or developing tools to facilitate better cross-cultural understanding. They recognize that true global collaboration means ensuring everyone has a seat at the table.

Looking to the future, we can expect digital networks and global collaboration to become even more integral to the innovation process. Emerging technologies like virtual and augmented reality promise to create even more immersive collaborative experiences, potentially revolutionizing how global teams work together.

Blockchain technology also holds promise for global collaboration, offering new ways to establish trust and facilitate transactions in decentralized networks. Initiatives like Ocean Protocol, which aims to create a decentralized data exchange to unlock data for AI, show how blockchain can enable new forms of global, collaborative innovation (Ocean Protocol, 2023).

As we navigate this new landscape of global, digital collaboration, the key will be to harness the power of diverse perspectives while also cultivating deep, meaningful connections. It's about creating a truly global innovation ecosystem where ideas can flow freely, challenges can be tackled collectively, and breakthroughs can emerge from unexpected corners of the world.

For Generation Innovate, this isn't just an aspiration—it's the world they're already building. By leveraging digital networks for global collaboration, they're not just innovating products or services; they're reimagining how innovation itself happens. And in doing so, they're creating a more connected, collaborative, and innovative world for us all.

10.4 BUILDING AND MAINTAINING INNOVATIVE NETWORKS

In the digital age, your network is your net worth—especially when it comes to innovation. For Generation Innovate, building and maintaining a vibrant, innovation-driving network is more art than science. It's about cultivating an ecosystem that continuously sparks creativity, challenges assumptions, and opens doors to new opportunities. Let's explore how these digital natives are mastering the art of network building in the pursuit of innovation.

The foundation of an innovative network is diversity. As Scott Page, author of "The Diversity Bonus," argues, cognitive diversity—differences in how people see, categorize, understand, and go about solving problems—is a crucial driver of innovation and complex problem-solving (Page, 2017). For Millennials and Gen Z, this often means actively seeking out connections that span different industries, cultures, and disciplines.

Take the case of Gitanjali Rao, named Time Magazine's first-ever Kid of the Year in 2020. At just 15 years old, Rao had already developed multiple innovations, from a device to detect lead in drinking water to an app that uses AI to detect cyberbullying. Her secret? A diverse network that includes scientists, educators, and fellow young innovators from around the world (Time, 2020). Rao's story exemplifies how Generation Innovate is leveraging diverse networks to tackle complex, multidisciplinary challenges.

But diversity alone isn't enough. The key is to create meaningful connections across these diverse nodes. This is where the concept of "boundary spanning" comes into play. As described by organizational theorist Etienne Wenger-Trayner, boundary spanners are individuals who can translate, coordinate, and align perspectives across different communities of practice (Wenger-Trayner & Wenger-Trayner, 2015).

For Generation Innovate, being a boundary spanner often means actively participating in multiple communities—both online and offline. They might be part of a professional association in their field, a startup incubator program, and a social impact group on Facebook. By moving between these different worlds, they create opportunities for cross-pollination of ideas. It's like being a pollinator in the ecosystem of innovation, carrying ideas from one flower to another and enabling new hybridizations to bloom.

Digital platforms play a crucial role in this network-building process. Tools like Twitter, LinkedIn, and even niche platforms like GitHub for developers or Behance for designers allow innovators to connect with like-minded individuals around the globe. But it's not just about accumulating followers or connections—it's about engaging in meaningful exchanges.

Consider the approach of Vitalik Buterin, the wunderkind behind Ethereum. Buterin didn't just create a new blockchain platform; he built a global community of developers, researchers, and enthusiasts around it. Through active engagement on forums, social media, and conferences, Buterin has cultivated a network that continuously drives innovation in the blockchain space (Ethereum Foundation, 2023). His approach demonstrates how Generation Innovate is using digital platforms not just as networking tools, but as community-building engines that fuel ongoing innovation.

But building an innovative network is only half the battle—maintaining it is equally crucial. This is where many traditional networking approaches fall short. It's not about collecting business cards or making superficial LinkedIn connections. It's about nurturing relationships and consistently providing value to your network.

Adam Grant, in his book "Give and Take," argues that the most successful networkers are often "givers"—those who consistently seek to help others without expecting immediate returns (Grant, 2013). This approach resonates strongly with Generation Innovate, who often prioritize purpose and impact over traditional notions of professional advancement. It's about creating a network based on mutual value creation rather than mere transactional exchanges.

One innovative approach to network maintenance that's gaining traction among Millennials and Gen Z is the concept of "network weaving." Coined by social network analysts, network weaving involves intentionally introducing people in your network to each other, fostering new connections, and strengthening the overall fabric of the network (Holley, 2013). It's like being a master DJ, not just playing great tracks but skillfully mixing them to create something entirely new.

However, maintaining an innovative network in the digital age comes with its own set of challenges. The constant connectivity enabled by digital platforms can lead to what psychologist Sherry Turkle calls "alone together"—a state where we're constantly connected but rarely deeply engaged (Turkle, 2017). This can result in a network that's wide but shallow, lacking the depth of connection necessary for true collaborative innovation.

To combat this, many young innovators are finding ways to blend online and offline networking. They're organizing meetups, hackathons, and unconferences that bring their digital connections into the physical world. These events create opportunities for the kind of serendipitous encounters and deep discussions that often spark innovative ideas. It's about creating spaces where the virtual and physical worlds can collide, generating new possibilities in the process.

Another challenge in maintaining innovative networks is the issue of information overload. With the constant stream of updates, messages, and notifications from our networks, it can be difficult to separate signal from noise. This is where the concept of "attention management" comes into play. As productivity expert Maura Thomas argues, in the digital age, our most valuable resource isn't time—it's attention (Thomas, 2015).

Generation Innovate is developing sophisticated strategies for managing their attention within their networks. This might involve using tools like Forest or Freedom to block distracting websites during focused work periods, or setting up carefully curated lists and filters on social media to ensure they're seeing the most relevant and inspiring content from their network.

Looking ahead, the future of network building for innovation is likely to become even more dynamic and multifaceted. Emerging technologies like virtual and augmented reality promise to create new ways of connecting and collaborating across distances. Imagine brainstorming sessions where your global network can gather in a virtual space, manipulating 3D models of ideas in real-time, or augmented reality business cards that display a person's latest projects and areas of expertise when you meet them.

AI-powered networking tools may help us more effectively identify potential collaborators and opportunities within our extended networks. Imagine an AI assistant that can analyze your network, identify structural holes where you could make valuable new connections, and even suggest talking points based on shared interests or complementary skills.

Blockchain technology also holds promise for network building, offering new ways to establish trust and facilitate transactions in decentralized networks. We might see the emergence of "innovation DAOs" (Decentralized Autonomous Organizations) where members can collectively fund and govern innovation projects, creating new models of networked creativity.

But regardless of the tools and platforms, the fundamental principles of building and maintaining innovative networks remain the same: cultivate diversity, engage authentically, provide value, and stay curious. For Generation Innovate, these principles aren't just networking strategies—they're a way of life that fuels continuous learning, creativity, and innovation.

As we navigate this new landscape of network-driven innovation, the key will be to balance the breadth of our digital connections with the depth of meaningful relationships. It's about creating networks that are both globally connected and locally rooted, that can generate a constant stream of new ideas while also providing the support and resources to turn those ideas into reality.

By mastering the art of building and maintaining innovative networks, Millennials and Gen Z aren't just advancing their own careers or businesses. They're creating vibrant ecosystems of creativity and collaboration that have the potential to solve some of our world's most pressing challenges. In the end, that might be their most important innovation of all—a new model of networked creativity that can harness our collective intelligence to drive positive change on a global scale.

KEY INSIGHTS

- Social networks in the digital age are complex ecosystems that drive innovation
- The structure and dynamics of networks, including "small-world" properties, significantly impact idea flow
- Leveraging both strong and weak ties is crucial for accessing diverse information and resources
- Digital platforms have revolutionized global collaboration, enabling borderless innovation
- Building and maintaining innovative networks requires intentional strategies and continuous effort

INNOVATION CHALLENGE

For the next month, focus on becoming a "network weaver." Identify two distinct groups within your network (e.g., colleagues from different industries or interest groups). Introduce three people from each group to someone in the other group, explaining why you think they should connect. Track these new connections and any collaborative ideas or projects that emerge.

REFLECTION QUESTIONS

1. How does your current network reflect the "small-world" properties discussed in the chapter? Can you identify any structural holes that you could bridge to enhance your innovative potential?

2. Consider your digital and physical networking strategies. How well do they complement each other? How might you better integrate online and offline networking to build stronger, more diverse connections?

3. Reflect on a recent innovation challenge you faced. How could you have leveraged your network more effectively to address it? What types of connections were missing that could have been valuable?

4. How are you currently managing the balance between network breadth and depth? What strategies could you implement to maintain meaningful relationships while expanding your network's diversity?

5. In what ways could emerging technologies (e.g., VR, AI, blockchain) enhance your ability to build and maintain innovative networks? How might you prepare to leverage these technologies in your networking efforts?

CHAPTER 11

FROM IDEAS TO REALITY

Imagine standing at the edge of possibility, a map of innovative ideas in your hands. The path ahead is challenging, filled with unexpected twists, but the promise of what lies beyond is irresistible. This, fellow innovators, is where we find ourselves in the journey of Generation Innovate - at the crucial juncture where ideas transform into reality.

Welcome to the thrilling world of innovation implementation, where visionary concepts take tangible form. As Thomas Edison once quipped, "Vision without execution is hallucination." This chapter is all about that execution - the art and science of turning groundbreaking ideas into concrete realities that can change the world.

But let's be real for a moment. Implementation isn't just a walk in the park. It's more like a complex dance, requiring agility, perseverance, and a dash of creative problem-solving. It's where our innovative spirits are truly put to the test. According to a study by McKinsey, a staggering 70% of complex, large-scale change programs don't reach their stated goals (Bucy et al., 2016). That's a sobering statistic, isn't it?

As we embark on this journey from ideation to implementation, we'll explore a range of powerful tools and methodologies. We'll dive into the world of Business Model Canvas and Lean Canvas, unpack the wisdom of Kotter's 8-Step Change Model, and harness the flexibility of Agile methodologies. We'll also look at strategies for identifying and overcoming the frictions that can hinder implementation.

But here's the thing: implementation isn't just about tools and processes. At its heart, it's a deeply human endeavor. It's about inspiring teams, navigating resistance to change, and fostering an environment where innovation can thrive. As Amy Edmondson's research on psychological safety reminds us, creating a space where people feel safe to take risks and voice their ideas is crucial for successful implementation (Edmondson, 1999).

So, are you ready to transform your ideas into reality? Let's roll up our sleeves and dive in!

11.1 The Implementation Roadmap: Charting Your Course

Picture yourself planning an expedition to climb Mount Everest. You wouldn't just show up at base camp with a backpack and a can-do attitude, would you? Of course not! You'd meticulously plan every stage of the journey, anticipate potential obstacles, and ensure you have the right team and resources in place. Implementing an innovative idea is no different.

Our implementation roadmap begins with a crucial step: clearly defining your vision and goals. This might seem obvious, but you'd be surprised how many promising ideas falter because of a lack of clear direction. Your vision is your North Star, guiding every decision and action along the way. It needs to be compelling enough to inspire your team and concrete enough to provide practical guidance.

Once you have your vision, it's time to break it down into actionable steps. This is where tools like the Business Model Canvas or Lean Canvas come into play. Developed by Alexander Osterwalder and Ash Maurya respectively, these tools help you visualize and structure all the key elements of your idea - from your value proposition and customer segments to your revenue streams and key resources (Osterwalder & Pigneur, 2010; Maurya, 2012).

These canvases aren't just pretty pictures - they're living documents that should evolve as you learn and iterate. As Steve Blank, the godfather of lean startup methodology, often says, "No business plan survives first contact with customers" (Blank, 2013). This iterative approach aligns well with the adaptability we've seen in successful Generation Innovate leaders.

Now, let's talk about timelines. Gantt charts might seem old school in our agile, fast-paced world, but they still have their place in implementation planning. They provide a visual representation of your project timeline, helping you manage dependencies and track progress. But here's a pro tip: don't treat your Gantt chart like it's set in stone. The key is to strike a balance between having a clear plan and remaining flexible enough to adapt to changing circumstances.

Speaking of flexibility, let's dive into the world of Agile methodologies. Born in the software development world but now widely adopted across industries, Agile approaches, particularly Scrum, can be powerful tools for implementing innovative ideas. The core principle of Agile is simple: break your big idea into smaller, manageable chunks, work in short sprints, and continuously gather feedback and iterate.

What's beautiful about Agile is how it embraces uncertainty. Instead of trying to plan everything upfront (which, let's face it, is impossible when you're doing something truly innovative), Agile methodologies allow you to adapt and evolve your implementation as you go. It's like building the plane while you're flying it - scary, yes, but also incredibly empowering.

This iterative approach can also help address what we discussed earlier as "frictions" - the forces that often oppose change and innovation. By breaking the implementation into smaller chunks, you make the change feel more manageable and less overwhelming.

Agile isn't a magic bullet. It requires a shift in mindset and culture. As Jez Humble, co-author of "Accelerate," points out, "Agile is a mindset, described by values and principles. Scrum, XP, etc. are just frameworks for how to implement that mindset" (Humble et al., 2018). So, if you're planning to adopt Agile methodologies, be prepared to invest in training and change management.

No matter how brilliant your idea or how detailed your plan, without proper resources, your implementation efforts are likely to sputter and stall. This isn't just about money (although that's certainly important). It's about people, time, technology, and organizational support.

A study by the Project Management Institute found that 47% of unsuccessful projects failed to meet goals due to poor resource forecasting (PMI, 2017). So, how do you avoid this pitfall? Start by being realistic about what you need. It's tempting to underestimate resources in an attempt to get buy-in, but this often backfires. Instead, do your homework. Benchmark against similar projects, build in contingencies, and be prepared to make a solid business case for the resources you need.

Remember, resource allocation isn't a one-time event. As you progress through implementation, you'll need to continually reassess and adjust. This is where tools like the Theory of Constraints (TOC) can be incredibly useful. Developed by Eliyahu Goldratt, this methodology helps you identify and manage the bottlenecks that are holding back your progress (Goldratt & Cox, 2004). By focusing your efforts on these constraints, you can often achieve significant improvements with minimal additional resources.

TOC offers a powerful framework for identifying and managing bottlenecks in your implementation process. At its core, TOC posits that every system has at least one constraint (or bottleneck) that limits its overall performance. The key steps in applying the powerful approach 1) Identify the constraint, 2) Exploit the constraint (make it as efficient as possible), 3) Subordinate everything else to the constraint (align all other activities to support it), 4) Elevate the constraint (if needed, invest to increase its capacity), and 5) Repeat the process for the next constraint. In the context of implementation, this might mean identifying that your testing phase is the bottleneck, then focusing resources on optimizing testing procedures, adjusting other project phases to smooth the flow into and out of testing, and if necessary, investing in additional testing resources. By systematically addressing constraints, TOC can help you maximize the efficiency of your implementation process and achieve more with your existing resources.

As we wrap up our discussion on the implementation roadmap, let's touch on a critical but often overlooked aspect - celebrating milestones. In the rush to reach the finish line, it's easy to forget to acknowledge the progress you've made along the way. But these celebrations aren't just about boosting morale (although that's important too). They're opportunities to reflect on what's working, what isn't, and how you might need to adjust your course.

Celebrating milestones is a powerful way to maintain enthusiasm for the change, countering the emotional friction that can build up during a long implementation process. It's about fueling motivation alongside reducing friction - a key principle we've seen in successful innovation efforts.

So, as you chart your course from idea to reality, remember: your roadmap is a guide, not a straitjacket. Be prepared to take detours, explore unexpected paths, and even backtrack when necessary. After all, as the old saying goes, "The only constant in life is change." And nowhere is this truer than in the world of innovation implementation.

In the next section, we'll explore how to navigate the human element of implementation - because at the end of the day, it's people who turn innovative ideas into world-changing realities. Are you ready to dive into the interpersonal dynamics of bringing your vision to life? Let's go!

11.2 NAVIGATING THE HUMAN ELEMENT: THE HEART OF IMPLEMENTATION

Now that we've mapped out our implementation journey, let's zoom in on what's arguably the most critical factor in turning ideas into reality - people. You see, at its core, implementation isn't just about processes and tools. It's about human beings, with all their complexities, fears, hopes, and potential. As Peter Drucker, the father of modern management theory, famously said, "Culture eats strategy for breakfast" (Elliot, 2011).

Let's start with a fundamental truth: change is hard. Even positive change, like implementing an exciting new idea, can be met with resistance. Why? Because change disrupts our sense of security and competence. It pushes us out of our comfort zones and into the unknown. This isn't just pop psychology - it's backed by hard science. Neuroscience research shows that organizational change is often experienced in the same way as a threat to our survival, triggering our brain's fight-or-flight response (Rock & Cox, 2012).

So, how do we overcome this natural resistance to change? Enter John Kotter's 8-Step Change Model. Developed based on years of research into why change initiatives fail, Kotter's model provides a comprehensive framework for managing the human side of change (Kotter, 1996). It starts with creating a sense of urgency, builds through forming a guiding coalition and creating a vision, and culminates in anchoring new approaches in the culture.

What's powerful about Kotter's model is how it addresses both the emotional and practical aspects of change. It recognizes that for change to stick, you need to win both hearts and minds. You need to create a compelling case for why change is necessary (that's the urgency), build a strong team to lead the charge (the guiding coalition), and paint a vivid picture of what success looks like (the vision).

But here's where many change initiatives falter - they stop at communication. They assume that if they've explained the change well enough, people will naturally get on board. But as any seasoned change leader will tell you, that's rarely the case. This is where steps like "enable action by removing barriers" and "generate short-term wins" come in. These steps are about creating the conditions for success, making it easier for people to embrace the change and see tangible progress along the way.

Now, let's talk about a concept that's absolutely crucial for successful implementation - psychological safety. Coined by Harvard Business School professor Amy Edmondson, psychological safety refers to a shared belief that the team is safe for interpersonal risk-taking (Edmondson, 1999). In other words, it's an environment where people feel comfortable speaking up, asking questions, and yes, even making mistakes.

Why is this so important for implementation? Because innovation requires experimentation, and experimentation inevitably involves failure. If your team is afraid to take risks or voice concerns, you're likely to miss critical insights that could make or break your implementation efforts. Google's Project Aristotle, a comprehensive study of team effectiveness, found that psychological safety was the most important factor in building a successful team (Duhigg, 2016).

Creating psychological safety can help address what we've discussed earlier as the "emotion" friction - the negative feelings associated with change. When people feel safe to express their concerns and ideas, it can reduce anxiety and increase buy-in for the new idea.

So, how do you foster psychological safety? It starts with leadership. Leaders need to model the behaviors they want to see - admitting when they don't have all the answers, encouraging diverse viewpoints, and treating failures as learning opportunities rather than causes for punishment. It's about creating what Carol Dweck calls a "growth mindset" culture, where challenges are seen as opportunities to learn and grow rather than threats to be avoided (Dweck, 2006).

Creating this kind of culture isn't easy. It requires consistent effort and a willingness to challenge deeply ingrained habits and beliefs. One practical tool that can help is the use of "blameless post-mortems" - structured discussions after setbacks or failures that focus on learning and improvement rather than assigning blame. This practice, popularized in the tech industry, can be a powerful way to build trust and encourage open communication (Allspaw, 2012).

Another critical aspect of the human side of implementation is effective communication. And I'm not just talking about top-down, formal communications (although those are important too). I'm talking about creating a culture of open, honest, two-way communication. This is where tools like regular stand-ups, feedback sessions, and open forums can be incredibly valuable.

Effective communication can help address what we've previously discussed as "reactance" - people's aversion to being changed by others. By involving people in the change process, listening to their concerns, and incorporating their feedback, you can reduce this sense of external control and increase ownership of the new idea.

Communication isn't just about the frequency or format. It's about the quality of the conversations. Are you really listening to your team's concerns and ideas? Are you creating space for dissenting opinions? As Margaret Heffernan argues in her book "Willful Blindness," the ability to have constructive disagreements is crucial for innovation and effective implementation (Heffernan, 2011).

Daniel Pink's research on motivation shows that for complex, creative tasks (like, say, implementing an innovative idea), traditional carrot-and-stick approaches often fall short. Instead, people are motivated by autonomy (the desire to direct our own lives), mastery (the urge to get better at something that matters), and purpose (the yearning to do what we do in service of something larger than ourselves) (Pink, 2011).

This aligns well with what we've seen in successful Generation Innovate leaders - they tap into these intrinsic motivators, creating a powerful drive for change that goes beyond simple compliance. By connecting the implementation to a larger purpose, providing opportunities for skill development, and giving team members autonomy in how they approach their tasks, you can create a more engaged and motivated team.

Remember, implementation isn't a one-size-fits-all process. Different team members may respond to different approaches. Some might thrive on detailed plans and clear guidelines, while others might prefer more freedom to figure things out on their own. As a leader, your job is to understand these individual differences and create an environment where everyone can contribute their best work.

Lastly, don't underestimate the power of storytelling in implementation. Humans are wired for narrative - we make sense of the world through stories. By crafting a compelling narrative around your implementation journey, you can help your team connect emotionally with the vision and stay motivated through the inevitable challenges.

As we wrap up this section on the human element of implementation, remember this: at its core, implementation is about change, and change is fundamentally human. By focusing on creating psychological safety, fostering open communication, tapping into intrinsic motivation, and telling a compelling story, you can create an environment where your innovative ideas have the best chance of becoming reality.

In our next section, we'll explore how to overcome obstacles and adapt your implementation strategy in the face of unexpected challenges. After all, as any seasoned innovator knows, no plan survives contact with reality unchanged. Are you ready to dive into the art of adaptive implementation? Let's go!

11.3 Overcoming Obstacles: The Art of Adaptive Implementation

Now that we've explored the roadmap and the human elements of implementation, let's tackle a reality that every innovator faces: obstacles. If you've ever tried to bring a new idea to life, you know that the path from concept to reality is rarely a straight line. It's more like a winding road, filled with unexpected turns, sudden roadblocks, and the occasional cliff edge. But here's the good news: with the right mindset and tools, these obstacles can become opportunities for growth and innovation.

Let's start with a common challenge: scope creep. You know how it goes - you start with a clear, well-defined idea, but as you get into implementation, the scope starts to expand. New features get added, the target market shifts, and before you know it, your neat little project has turned into a sprawling behemoth. This isn't just a minor inconvenience - scope creep can derail even the most promising innovations. A study by PMI found that 52% of projects experienced scope creep, leading to delays, budget overruns, and in some cases, outright failure (PMI, 2018).

So, how do we combat scope creep? This is where the concept of the Minimum Viable Product (MVP) comes in handy. Popularized by Eric Ries in "The Lean Startup," an MVP is the most basic version of your product that still delivers value to your users (Ries, 2011). The idea is to get something out there quickly, gather feedback, and iterate. It's about progress over perfection.

This approach aligns perfectly with what we've seen in successful Generation Innovate leaders. They're not afraid to launch something that's not fully polished, knowing that real-world feedback is infinitely more valuable than theoretical perfection. By focusing on an MVP, you're not just managing your resources more effectively; you're also reducing the effort required for users to adopt your innovation. It's a double win.

Now, let's talk about a challenge that's become increasingly relevant in our fast-paced world: market shifts. You might start implementing your idea based on one set of market conditions, only to find that by the time you're ready to launch, the landscape has completely changed. This is where the concept of adaptive implementation comes into play.

Adaptive implementation isn't about rigidly sticking to a plan - it's about being flexible and responsive to changing conditions. It's about what Rita McGrath calls "discovery-driven planning," where you make your best guesses about what will work, but then systematically test those assumptions as you go along (McGrath, 2010). This approach allows you to pivot when necessary, without losing sight of your overall vision.

One powerful tool for adaptive implementation is the Build-Measure-Learn loop, another concept from the Lean Startup methodology. The idea is simple: you build something (like your

MVP), measure how it performs, learn from that data, and then use those insights to inform your next steps. It's a cycle of continuous improvement that keeps you aligned with market realities.

Pivoting isn't easy. It can feel like admitting failure or giving up on your original vision. This is where having a strong, adaptable team becomes crucial. As Amy Edmondson points out in her work on teaming, the ability to learn, innovate, and adapt to new challenges is a critical skill in today's rapidly changing business environment (Edmondson, 2012). Foster a culture where change is seen not as a setback, but as an opportunity to get closer to a solution that truly meets market needs.

Another common obstacle in implementation is resource constraints. Whether it's a limited budget, time pressures, or a lack of specific skills within your team, resource challenges can put a serious damper on your implementation efforts. But here's where innovative thinking can really shine.

Consider the concept of "bricolage" in innovation - the art of creating something new from whatever resources you have at hand. As described by researchers Baker and Nelson, bricolage can be a powerful approach when faced with resource constraints (Baker & Nelson, 2005). It's about looking at your limitations not as roadblocks, but as invitations to think creatively.

For example, if you're short on budget, could you leverage open-source tools or freelance talent? If time is tight, could you use rapid prototyping techniques to speed up your development process? If you're missing specific skills, could you form strategic partnerships or invest in upskilling your existing team?

This resourceful approach aligns well with what we've seen from Generation Innovate leaders. They're adept at finding creative solutions to resource constraints, often leveraging their digital fluency and network connections to access resources beyond their immediate environment.

Now, let's talk about a challenge that's particularly relevant in our digital age: information overload. In the implementation phase, you're likely to be bombarded with data - user feedback, market trends, competitor moves, and more. The challenge is not just gathering this information, but making sense of it and using it to guide your decisions.

This is where data visualization tools can be incredibly helpful. Tools like Tableau or even simple Excel dashboards can help you turn raw data into actionable insights. But remember, as we've discussed in earlier chapters, data is just one piece of the puzzle. Successful implementation also requires intuition, empathy, and a deep understanding of your users and market.

Another obstacle you might face is team burnout. Implementation can be a long, demanding process, and it's easy for team members to become exhausted or lose sight of the bigger picture. This is where the concept of "sustainable pace" from Agile methodologies can be helpful. It's about finding a rhythm of work that can be maintained over the long term, rather than sprinting to exhaustion.

Consider implementing regular "innovation days" or "hack weeks" where team members can work on passion projects or explore new ideas. This can help rekindle creativity and enthusiasm, even in the midst of a challenging implementation process.

Finally, let's address the elephant in the room: failure. Despite our best efforts, not every implementation will be successful. But here's the thing - failure, when approached correctly, can be an incredible learning opportunity. As we've seen with many Generation Innovate leaders, the ability to "fail fast" and learn from those failures is often what sets successful innovators apart.

Consider implementing a "failure resume" practice, where team members document their failures and what they learned from them. This not only helps extract valuable lessons from setbacks but also helps create a culture where failure is seen as a natural part of the innovation process, not something to be feared or hidden.

As we wrap up this section on overcoming obstacles, remember this: obstacles in implementation aren't just inevitable - they're opportunities. They're chances to learn, to innovate, and to make your idea even stronger. As you navigate these challenges, stay flexible, stay curious, and above all, stay committed to your vision.

The art of adaptive implementation is about embracing uncertainty, learning continuously, and being willing to evolve your approach as you go. It's about seeing every setback as a chance to gain new insights and every constraint as an invitation to think more creatively. With this mindset, you'll be well-equipped to turn your innovative ideas into reality, no matter what obstacles you encounter along the way.

In our final section, we'll look at some real-world examples of successful implementation, drawing lessons from both triumphs and setbacks. Are you ready to see how all these principles come together in practice? Let's dive in!

11.4 IMPLEMENTATION IN ACTION: LEARNING FROM REAL-WORLD EXAMPLES

Theory is valuable, but as Generation Innovate knows, the real test comes when the rubber meets the road. Let's dive deep into some real-world examples of implementation, both successful and challenging, to see how the principles we've discussed play out in practice. These case studies will provide concrete lessons and inspiration for your own implementation journeys.

Case Study 1: Spotify's "Squad" Model

Spotify, the music streaming giant, provides an excellent example of adaptive implementation at an organizational level. As they grew rapidly from a small startup to a global company, they needed a way to maintain their agility and innovation. Their solution? The "Squad" model.

Squads are small, cross-functional teams of 6-12 people, each responsible for a specific feature or part of the Spotify experience. These squads operate with a high degree of autonomy, making their own decisions about what to build and how to build it.

Squads are then grouped into "Tribes" of up to 150 people, focusing on related areas of the product.

Key aspects of the implementation:

1. Gradual rollout: Spotify didn't implement this model overnight. They started with a few teams and gradually expanded as they learned what worked.
2. Emphasis on autonomy: Squads were given the freedom to choose their own work methods, tools, and even physical workspace setup.
3. Alignment through "missions": While autonomous, each squad is given a long-term mission aligned with company goals, ensuring their work contributes to the bigger picture.
4. Regular synchronization: "Chapter" meetings bring together people with similar skills across squads to share knowledge and maintain consistency.

Results: The Squad model allowed Spotify to scale while maintaining startup-like agility. It enabled rapid experimentation and implementation of new features, contributing to Spotify's ability to stay ahead in a competitive market.

Lessons

1. Autonomy fosters innovation: By trusting teams to make decisions, Spotify accelerated their implementation process.
2. Structure can enable flexibility: The right organizational structure can actually increase adaptability.

3. Alignment is crucial: Autonomy works when there's a clear overarching mission and regular communication.

Case Study 2: Airbnb's Implementation of "Experiences"

When Airbnb decided to expand beyond home rentals into offering local experiences in 2016, they faced a significant implementation challenge. They needed to create a new marketplace, attract a different type of supplier, and shift customer perceptions.

Their approach:

1. Started with an MVP: They launched Experiences in just 12 cities, allowing them to learn and iterate quickly.
2. Leveraged existing network: They tapped into their host community to find initial experience providers, using an existing trusted network to jumpstart the new offering.
3. Quality over quantity: They carefully curated experiences to ensure a high-quality offering from the start, even if it meant slower growth.
4. Host education: Airbnb invested heavily in educating and supporting Experience hosts, recognizing that their success was crucial to the overall success of the initiative.
5. Integrated user experience: They seamlessly integrated Experiences into their existing platform, making it easy for users to discover and book alongside accommodations.
6. Iterative improvement: Based on early feedback, they made numerous adjustments, including introducing

lower price points and shorter experiences to increase accessibility.

Results: By 2019, Experiences had become one of Airbnb's fastest-growing products, with bookings growing by 7x year-over-year. By early 2020, they were offering over 40,000 experiences in more than 1,000 cities.

Lessons:

1. Start small and iterate: The limited initial rollout allowed for rapid learning and adjustment.
2. Leverage existing strengths: Airbnb's use of their host community shows the value of building on existing assets.
3. Focus on quality: Prioritizing quality over rapid expansion helped establish credibility for the new offering.
4. Continuous improvement: Airbnb's willingness to adjust based on feedback was crucial to the success of Experiences.

Case Study 3: Google Glass - When Implementation Falters

Not every implementation goes smoothly, and we can learn just as much from setbacks. Google Glass, the company's foray into wearable tech, provides a cautionary tale of implementation challenges.

Launched with significant hype in 2013, Google Glass was a head-mounted display in the shape of eyeglasses. It allowed users to access the internet, take photos, and record videos hands-free.

Implementation challenges:

1. Unclear value proposition: Google struggled to articulate clear use cases for Glass that resonated with everyday consumers.
2. Privacy concerns: The device's ability to record video inconspicuously led to public backlash and bans in some establishments.
3. Technical limitations: Short battery life and overheating issues hampered the user experience.
4. High price point: The initial cost of $1,500 was prohibitive for many potential users.
5. Social acceptance: The design of Glass was seen as awkward by many, earning users the unflattering nickname "Glassholes."
6. Regulatory issues: Concerns about using Glass while driving led to legal questions in some jurisdictions.

Google's response: In 2015, Google pulled Glass from the consumer market. However, they didn't abandon the project entirely. Instead, they refocused on enterprise applications, where the hands-free nature of Glass provided clear value in industries like manufacturing and healthcare.

Results: While Glass failed to achieve widespread consumer adoption, the enterprise version, Google Glass Enterprise Edition, has found success in niche markets. Companies like Boeing, DHL, and Volkswagen have utilized Glass to improve efficiency in areas like assembly, logistics, and quality control.

Lessons:

1. Clear value proposition is crucial: Without a compelling reason for adoption, even innovative technology can struggle.
2. Consider social and ethical implications: The privacy concerns around Glass show the importance of considering broader impacts.
3. Iterative approach is valuable: Google's pivot to enterprise applications demonstrates the importance of learning from setbacks and being willing to change direction.
4. Price sensitivity matters: The high cost of Glass limited its potential user base, highlighting the need to consider pricing strategy in implementation.

Synthesis of Lessons:

Looking across these case studies, we can extract some key principles for successful implementation:

1. Start small and iterate: Both Spotify and Airbnb began with limited rollouts that allowed for learning and adjustment. This approach allows for rapid learning and course correction.
2. Maintain flexibility: All three cases demonstrate the importance of being able to adapt to feedback and changing circumstances.

3. Focus on user needs: Airbnb's success and Google Glass's struggles both highlight the crucial importance of addressing real user needs and concerns.
4. Consider broader implications: Google Glass's privacy issues remind us to think beyond just the product itself to its wider impact.
5. Leverage existing strengths: Airbnb's use of their host community shows how building on existing assets can accelerate implementation.
6. Align autonomy with overall goals: Spotify's squad model demonstrates how giving teams freedom within a clear overall framework can drive innovation.
7. Be prepared to pivot: Google's shift to enterprise applications for Glass shows how a failed implementation can sometimes lead to new opportunities if you're willing to adapt.

As we can see from these examples, successful implementation often involves a delicate balance of planning and flexibility, vision, and adaptability. It's about having a clear direction but being willing to adjust your course based on real-world feedback and changing circumstances.

For Generation Innovate, these case studies offer both inspiration and caution. They demonstrate the potential for transformative implementation when approached with creativity, adaptability, and a deep understanding of user needs. At the same time, they remind us of the complex challenges that can arise when bringing innovative ideas to life.

As you embark on your own implementation journeys, keep these lessons in mind. Stay curious, stay flexible, and above all, keep pushing to turn those groundbreaking ideas into world-changing realities. The path may not always be straight, but with persistence and adaptability, you can navigate the complex terrain of implementation and bring your innovative visions to life.

KEY INSIGHTS

- Implementation requires a clear roadmap that balances structure with flexibility
- Navigating the human element, including change resistance and psychological safety, is crucial
- Adaptive implementation strategies help overcome obstacles and resource constraints
- Learning from real-world successes and failures can inform better implementation practices

INNOVATION CHALLENGE

Choose a recent innovative idea. Over the next two weeks, apply the Build-Measure-Learn loop from Lean Startup methodology. Create a basic prototype or MVP, test it with at least three potential users, document their feedback, and plan your next iteration based on what you've learned.

REFLECTION QUESTIONS

1. How might you apply the Theory of Constraints to identify and address bottlenecks in your current or future implementation projects?

2. Consider a recent implementation challenge you faced. How could principles of adaptive implementation have helped you navigate this situation more effectively?

3. Reflecting on the case studies discussed, which lessons resonate most with your experience? How might you apply these insights in your next implementation project?

4. How can you foster psychological safety in your team or organization to support more effective implementation of innovative ideas?

PART IV

THE INNOVATION MODEL UNVEILED

CHAPTER 12

THE CAS MODEL OF INNOVATION

As we reach the culmination of our journey through Generation Innovate, we arrive at our CAS Model of Innovation - a synthesis of the insights and strategies we've explored throughout this book. This model isn't a rigid blueprint, but a dynamic, adaptive system reflecting the complexity of innovation itself and the fluid, interconnected world that Millennials and Gen Z navigate with such ease.

Drawing from complex adaptive systems theory, our model focuses on creating the right conditions for innovation to flourish, much like Generation Innovate thrives in environments of constant change and uncertainty. We'll explore how this model embraces their digital fluency, global connectivity, and adaptability, providing a framework that resonates with their natural approach to problem-solving and creation.

Let's embark on this final leg of our journey, where theory meets practice, and the CAS Model of Innovation comes to life in the hands of our young innovators.

12.1 INTRODUCTION TO THE CAS MODEL OF INNOVATION

Throughout this book, we've explored the unique characteristics that define Generation Innovate - their digital nativity, their comfort with rapid change, their desire for purpose-driven work, and their innate ability to connect and collaborate across traditional boundaries. These traits aren't just incidental; they're fundamental to how Millennials and Gen Z approach innovation. Our CAS Model of Innovation is designed to harness these strengths, providing a framework that aligns with their natural tendencies and amplifies their innovative potential.

But first, let's understand what we mean by a Complex Adaptive System (CAS). In essence, a CAS is a system composed of many interacting parts that learn and adapt in response to their interactions with each other and their environment. This concept, pioneered by researchers like John H. Holland, has revolutionized fields from biology to economics, and now, we're applying it to innovation (Holland, 1995).

Why is this relevant to Generation Innovate? Because the world they've grown up in - a world of social media, global connectivity, and rapid technological change - is itself a complex adaptive system. They intuitively understand that outcomes can't always be predicted, that small actions can have large consequences, and that adaptation is key to survival and success.

Our CAS Model of Innovation reflects this reality. Unlike traditional, linear models of innovation that emphasize control and predictability, our model recognizes innovation as an emergent property of a complex system. It focuses on creating the conditions for innovation to arise organically, embracing uncertainty and valuing diverse inputs - all qualities that resonate deeply with Millennial and Gen Z innovators.

The model consists of five key components:

1. Leadership: Not top-down control, but adaptive and enabling leadership that creates space for innovation to emerge.
2. Empathy: Deep understanding of users and stakeholders, reflecting Generation Innovate's desire for purpose and human connection.
3. Creativity and Flow: Creating conditions for optimal creative performance, tapping into the state of deep engagement that many young innovators naturally seek.
4. Social Networks: Leveraging the power of connections, mirroring the networked world that Millennials and Gen Z inhabit.
5. Implementation: Continuous experimentation and adaptation, aligned with the iterative, fail-fast mentality of many young entrepreneurs.

These components don't operate in isolation but interact in complex ways, influencing and being influenced by each other. This reflects the interconnected thinking that characterizes Generation Innovate, who often break down traditional silos and blend disciplines in their approach to problem-solving.

By viewing innovation through the lens of complex adaptive systems, we open up new possibilities. We move away from trying to control or direct innovation and instead focus on nurturing the conditions where it can spontaneously emerge. This approach aligns perfectly with the entrepreneurial spirit of Millennials and Gen Z, who often prefer creating their own opportunities to following predetermined paths.

As we delve deeper into each component of the model, we'll explore how it relates to the strengths and preferences of Generation Innovate. We'll see how this model not only describes their natural approach to innovation but also provides a framework for organizations to tap into their potential more effectively.

The CAS Model of Innovation isn't just a theoretical construct - it's a practical tool for navigating the complex, rapidly changing landscape of modern innovation. It's a model that embraces uncertainty, values diversity, and thrives on adaptation - all qualities that Generation Innovate embodies.

As we explore this model, remember: you're not just learning about a system, you're part of it. Your actions, ideas, and connections all contribute to the ever-evolving landscape of innovation. The question is, how will you use this understanding to shape the future?

12.2 Components of the CAS Model of Innovation

Our CAS Model of Innovation comprises five key components, each reflecting crucial aspects of how Generation Innovate approaches creativity and problem-solving. Let's explore each of these components in detail, understanding how they function within the complex adaptive system of innovation.

Leadership: Adaptive and Enabling

In our model, leadership takes on a different role than in traditional hierarchies. It's not about command and control, but about creating what complexity leadership theorists call "adaptive space" (Uhl-Bien & Arena, 2018). This aligns perfectly with the flatter, more collaborative structures that Millennials and Gen Z often prefer.

Adaptive leadership in this context involves:

- Fostering an environment where ideas can freely emerge and evolve
- Encouraging experimentation and viewing failures as learning opportunities
- Facilitating connections between different parts of the organization
- Sensing and responding to changes in the system rather than trying to predict and control them

For example, Supercell, the Finnish mobile game developer known for hits like Clash of Clans, operates with a highly decentralized structure. Small, autonomous teams (which they call "cells") have the freedom to develop and kill projects without top-down interference. This approach has allowed them to consistently innovate in the fast-paced mobile gaming market (Osterwalder & Pigneur, 2016).

Empathy: Deep Understanding and Engagement

Empathy in our model goes beyond traditional market research. It's about developing a profound, almost intuitive understanding of users, team members, and all stakeholders in the innovation process. This resonates with Generation Innovate's desire for purpose and human connection in their work.

Key aspects of empathy in the CAS Model include:

- Immersive user research to uncover latent needs
- Creating feedback loops that allow for continuous user input
- Fostering a culture of psychological safety within teams
- Considering the broader impact of innovations on society and the environment

Airbnb's approach to empathy-driven innovation provides a great example. Their "Snow White" project involved creating storyboards of the entire user journey, allowing them to identify and address pain points that users themselves might not have articulated (Moran, 2014).

Creativity and Flow: Optimal Creative Performance

Flow, as conceptualized by Mihaly Csikszentmihalyi, is a state of optimal experience where one is fully immersed in a task, experiencing a sense of energized focus and enjoyment (Csikszentmihalyi, 1990). In our CAS Model, creating conditions for flow is crucial for unleashing the creative potential of Generation Innovate.

Elements of flow in the innovation context include:

- Balancing challenge and skill level to keep tasks engaging but not overwhelming
- Providing clear goals and immediate feedback
- Minimizing distractions and creating space for deep work
- Encouraging intrinsic motivation by connecting work to larger purpose

Companies like Valve have structured their entire work environment around the concept of flow. Their famous "flatland" structure allows employees to freely choose which projects to work on, optimizing for engagement and intrinsic motivation (Valve, 2012).

Social Networks: Leveraging Connections

In our CAS Model, innovation doesn't happen in isolation. It emerges from the complex web of connections within and beyond the organization. This component taps into the natural networking abilities of Millennials and Gen Z, who are often described as "Digital natives" (Prensky, 2001).

Key aspects of social networks in innovation include:

- Fostering diverse connections to bring in fresh perspectives
- Utilizing weak ties to access novel information (Granovetter, 1973)

- Creating platforms for idea exchange and collaboration
- Leveraging external networks through open innovation approaches

Glossier, the beauty company founded by Millennial entrepreneur Emily Weiss, exemplifies this approach. They've built a devoted community of customers who actively contribute to product development, effectively turning their social network into a powerful innovation engine (Segran, 2017).

Implementation: Continuous Experimentation

In our CAS Model, implementation isn't a final stage but an ongoing process of experimentation and adaptation. This aligns with the "fail fast, learn fast" mentality often associated with Generation Innovate.

Key elements of this approach include:

- Rapid prototyping and MVP (Minimum Viable Product) development
- A/B testing and data-driven decision making
- Agile methodologies that allow for quick pivots
- Treating each implementation as a learning opportunity that feeds back into the system

Spotify's "squad" model of product development embodies this approach. Small, cross-functional teams work autonomously on specific features, allowing for rapid experimentation and iteration (Mankins & Garton, 2017).

These five components don't operate in isolation but interact in complex ways within our model. In the next section, we'll explore the dynamics of these interactions and how they give rise to emergent innovation.

12.3 DYNAMICS OF THE CAS MODEL

Understanding the components of our CAS Model is just the beginning. The real power of this model lies in how these elements interact and influence each other, creating a dynamic system that's greater than the sum of its parts. This section will explore four key dynamics that characterize our CAS Model of Innovation: emergence, co-evolution, self-organization, and feedback loops.

Emergence: The Birth of Innovation

Emergence is a fundamental concept in complex adaptive systems. It refers to the way that novel and coherent structures, patterns, and properties arise from the interactions of the system's components. In our innovation model, breakthrough ideas and solutions often emerge from the interplay of leadership, empathy, flow, social networks, and implementation.

For Generation Innovate, this concept of emergence aligns with their intuitive understanding that great ideas can come from unexpected places. They're less likely to believe in the "lone genius" model of innovation and more likely to embrace collaborative, interdisciplinary approaches.

Example: Consider the story of Snapchat. The idea for disappearing messages emerged not from a deliberate attempt to create a new social media platform, but from a confluence of factors: the founders' understanding of how young people communicate (empathy), their willingness to experiment with new ideas (implementation), and their connection to a network of college students who became early adopters (social networks) (Gallagher, 2018).

Co-evolution: Mutual Adaptation

In a complex adaptive system, components don't just interact; they co-evolve, mutually influencing each other's development over time. In our innovation model, this means that as one component changes, it creates ripple effects throughout the system.

This dynamic resonates with Millennials and Gen Z's comfort with change and their understanding of the interconnected nature of global systems.

Example: At Pixar, the introduction of their Braintrust meetings (a manifestation of empathy and social networks in our model) led to changes in leadership style, fostering a more open and collaborative culture. This, in turn, influenced their implementation processes, encouraging more iteration and experimentation in storytelling (Catmull, 2014).

Self-organization: Spontaneous Order

Self-organization refers to the spontaneous emergence of order out of seeming chaos. In our CAS Model, this manifests as the ability of innovative solutions and practices to arise without top-down direction.

This aligns with Generation Innovate's preference for flatter hierarchies and their belief in the power of grassroots movements and bottom-up innovation.

Example: GitHub, the software development platform, exemplifies self-organization in innovation. Their system allows developers worldwide to collaborate on projects, with valuable contributions rising to the top through a decentralized process of peer review and iteration (Zagalsky et al., 2015).

Feedback Loops: The Engine of Adaptation

Feedback loops are crucial in complex adaptive systems. They allow the system to learn from its outputs and adjust its behavior accordingly. In our innovation model, feedback loops exist within and between all components, driving continuous adaptation and improvement.

This dynamic fits well with Millennials and Gen Z's affinity for rapid iteration and their expectation of quick feedback in their work.

Example: Tesla's approach to vehicle development embodies this principle. They collect vast amounts of data from their vehicles in use, creating a continuous feedback loop that informs everything from software updates to the design of future models (Korn, 2019).

The Interplay of Dynamics

These dynamics don't operate in isolation but interact in complex ways. For instance, feedback loops can drive co-evolution, which can lead to emergent properties, which in turn might result in new self-organized structures. Understanding these interactions is key to leveraging the full power of the CAS Model.

For Generation Innovate, this systemic view of innovation often comes naturally. They've grown up in a world of complex, interconnected systems - from social media networks to global supply chains. They're well-positioned to navigate and harness these dynamics in their innovative endeavors.

By embracing these dynamics, organizations can create innovation ecosystems that are more resilient, adaptable, and capable of producing breakthrough ideas. In the next section, we'll explore how Generation Innovate is putting these principles into action in real-world scenarios.

12.4 Applying the CAS Model: Generation Innovate in Action

The true test of any model lies in its practical application. In this section, we'll explore how Millennial and Gen Z-led companies are leveraging the principles of our CAS Model of Innovation, often intuitively, to drive success in various industries. We'll also examine the challenges they face and the opportunities that arise when implementing this approach.

Case Study 1: Notion - Emergent Collaboration

Notion, the all-in-one workspace platform, exemplifies how the CAS Model can drive innovation in software development. Founded by millennials Ivan Zhao and Simon Last, Notion's approach incorporates several key elements of our model:

- Leadership: Notion's flat structure and emphasis on autonomy create an adaptive space where ideas can flourish.
- Empathy: The product itself is a result of deep empathy with users' needs for flexible, customizable workspaces.
- Flow: Notion's block-based system allows users to enter a state of flow, seamlessly moving between different types of content.
- Social Networks: The company leverages its user community for idea generation and product refinement.
- Implementation: Rapid iteration based on user feedback is a core part of their development process.

The emergent nature of innovation in Notion is evident in how users have found creative ways to use the platform beyond its original conception, leading to new features and use cases (Notion, 2021).

Case Study 2: Oatly - Co-evolution of Product and Message

Oatly, the oat milk company that has taken the alternative dairy market by storm, demonstrates the principle of co-evolution in our CAS Model. Under the leadership of millennial CEO Toni Petersson, Oatly has:

- Adapted its leadership style to match its irreverent brand voice
- Used empathy to understand changing consumer attitudes towards sustainability

- Created flow in its marketing campaigns, allowing for spontaneous, authentic messaging
- Leveraged social networks, particularly Instagram, to build a community around its brand
- Implemented an agile approach to product development and marketing

The co-evolution is evident in how Oatly's product development and marketing message have evolved together, each informing and strengthening the other (Oatly, 2021).

Case Study 3: Glossier - Self-Organization in Beauty

Glossier, founded by millennial entrepreneur Emily Weiss, has revolutionized the beauty industry by embracing self-organization principles from our CAS Model:

- Leadership: Weiss fosters a culture where ideas can come from anywhere in the organization.
- Empathy: Glossier's entire product line is developed based on deep engagement with its community.
- Flow: The company creates conditions for creative flow by encouraging employees to think like founders.
- Social Networks: Glossier's "rep" program turns customers into micro-influencers, creating a self-organizing marketing network.
- Implementation: Product development is highly iterative, with constant feedback from the community.

The self-organizing nature of Glossier's approach is particularly evident in how their community contributes to product development and marketing, creating a beauty brand that feels authentically co-created with its customers (Segran, 2017).

Challenges and Opportunities

While these case studies demonstrate the power of the CAS Model, implementing this approach is not without challenges:

1. Balancing Structure and Chaos: Many organizations struggle to find the right balance between providing enough structure for coherence and enough freedom for emergence.
2. Scaling Complexity: As organizations grow, maintaining the adaptive, emergent qualities of a CAS becomes more challenging.
3. Measuring Success: Traditional metrics often fall short in capturing the value created by a CAS approach to innovation.
4. Resistance to Change: Older organizations may resist the shift to a more fluid, unpredictable innovation process.

However, these challenges also present opportunities:

1. New Leadership Models: The CAS approach opens the door for new, more distributed forms of leadership that resonate with Generation Innovate.
2. Enhanced Adaptability: Organizations that master the CAS Model are better positioned to thrive in rapidly changing environments.
3. Deeper Engagement: The emphasis on empathy and social networks in the CAS Model can lead to stronger connections with customers and employees.

4. Breakthrough Innovations: By embracing emergence and self-organization, organizations increase their chances of stumbling upon truly disruptive ideas.

As we can see, the CAS Model of Innovation aligns naturally with many of the intuitive approaches of Generation Innovate. By consciously applying these principles, Millennial and Gen Z leaders can amplify their innovative potential and create organizations that are more resilient, adaptive, and creative.

In our final section, we'll look towards the future, exploring how the CAS Model prepares organizations for ongoing change and evolution.

12.5 The Future of Innovation: CAS Model as a Framework for Continuous Adaptation

As we look towards the horizon of innovation, it's clear that the only constant will be change. The CAS Model of Innovation isn't just a framework for today; it's a roadmap for navigating the uncertainties of tomorrow. In this section, we'll explore how this model prepares organizations for ongoing change, consider potential evolutions of the model itself, and issue a call to action for Generation Innovate to leverage their natural affinity for CAS thinking.

Preparing for Perpetual Change

The CAS Model of Innovation inherently embraces change as a fundamental aspect of the innovation process. This makes it particularly well-suited for the rapidly evolving landscape that organizations face today and will continue to face in the future. Here's how:

1. Adaptability as Core Competence: By treating adaptability as a core competence rather than a reactive necessity, organizations can stay ahead of disruptions rather than merely responding to them.
2. Resilience Through Diversity: The emphasis on diverse networks and perspectives in the CAS Model builds organizational resilience, allowing companies to draw on a wide range of resources and ideas when facing new challenges.
3. Continuous Learning: The feedback loops inherent in the CAS Model create a culture of continuous learning and improvement, essential for keeping pace with technological and social changes.
4. Emergent Strategy: Rather than relying solely on top-down strategic planning, the CAS Model allows for strategy to emerge organically in response to changing conditions, an approach that aligns well with the fast-paced, unpredictable nature of many industries today.

Potential Evolutions of the CAS Model

As with any complex adaptive system, our model itself will likely evolve over time. Some potential directions for this evolution include:

1. AI Integration: As artificial intelligence becomes more sophisticated, it could become an active component in the CAS Model, potentially acting as an additional 'agent' in

the system, contributing to idea generation, pattern recognition, and even decision-making.

2. Virtual and Augmented Reality: These technologies could enhance the 'empathy' component of our model, allowing for more immersive user research and more engaging collaborative environments.
3. Blockchain and Decentralized Systems: The principles of decentralization inherent in blockchain technology align well with the self-organizing aspects of the CAS Model. We might see new organizational structures emerge that leverage these technologies to create even more distributed innovation ecosystems.
4. Neurotechnology: Advances in brain-computer interfaces and neurofeedback could enhance the 'flow' component of our model, allowing for more precise cultivation of optimal creative states.
5. Quantum Computing: The ability to process vast amounts of data and model complex systems could take the 'social networks' component of our model to new levels, allowing for more sophisticated network analysis and prediction.

A Call to Action for Generation Innovate

For Millennials and Gen Z, the CAS Model of Innovation isn't just a theoretical construct—it's a reflection of how many of you already think and work. Your generation's comfort with complexity, adaptability, and interconnectedness makes you natural practitioners of this approach. Here's how you can leverage this affinity to drive innovation forward:

1. Embrace Your Natural CAS Thinking: Recognize that your intuitive approach to problem-solving and creation often aligns with CAS principles. Trust these instincts and articulate them using the language of complex adaptive systems to bring others along.
2. Be Agents of Change: Use your understanding of the CAS Model to drive organizational transformation. Help older institutions adapt to this more fluid, emergent approach to innovation.
3. Push the Boundaries: Don't just apply the model—evolve it. Your unique perspectives and experiences can help refine and expand our understanding of how innovation emerges in complex systems.
4. Foster Cross-Generational Collaboration: While you may have a natural affinity for CAS thinking, there's much to be gained from the experience and insights of older generations. Create bridges that allow for the free flow of ideas across generational lines.
5. Think Globally, Act Systemically: The challenges facing our world—from climate change to social inequality—are complex, adaptive problems. Apply CAS thinking not just to business innovation, but to social innovation as well.

In conclusion, the CAS Model of Innovation offers a powerful framework for navigating the complexities of modern innovation. It aligns naturally with the strengths and inclinations of Generation Innovate, providing a structure that amplifies your creative potential while maintaining the flexibility to adapt to an ever-changing world.

As we stand on the brink of unprecedented technological and social change, your ability to think in terms of complex adaptive systems will be more valuable than ever. You have the opportunity not just to participate in the future of innovation, but to actively shape it.

The symphony of innovation is playing, and you, Generation Innovate, are both the composers and the performers. The stage is set, the audience is waiting, and the future is unfolding. What masterpiece will you create?

KEY INSIGHTS

- Innovation emerges from the interplay of leadership, empathy, flow, social networks, and implementation in a complex adaptive system
- Successful innovation involves creating conditions for creativity to flourish and adapt to changing circumstances
- The CAS Model of Innovation prepares organizations and individuals for ongoing change and future challenges

INNOVATION CHALLENGE:

Over the next month, apply the Innovation Model as a complex adaptive system in your workplace or personal project. Focus on creating an "adaptive space" where ideas can emerge and evolve. Document how the different elements of the model (leadership, empathy, flow, social networks, and implementation) interact and influence each other throughout the process.

As you document the interactions, also consider how emerging technologies or future trends might influence these dynamics.

REFLECTION QUESTIONS

1. How does viewing innovation as a complex adaptive system change your approach to leadership and decision-making in your organization or projects?

2. In what ways can you foster greater empathy and create more opportunities for flow states in your innovation processes? How might these changes impact the overall system?

3. Consider your current social networks, both within and outside your organization. How can you leverage these connections more effectively to drive innovation? What new connections might you need to cultivate?

4. How might the CAS Model of Innovation evolve in the future as new technologies emerge? How can you prepare yourself or your organization to adapt to these potential changes?

CHAPTER 13

INNOVATION IN ACTION - STORIES FROM THE FRONT LINES

In this chapter, we'll explore real-world examples of the Complex Adaptive Systems (CAS) Model of Innovation in action. Through four diverse case studies, we'll see how visionary leadership, empathetic understanding, flow-state creativity, social network synergy, and agile implementation come together to drive groundbreaking innovations. These stories will illustrate the power and versatility of our model across different sectors and challenges.

13.1 Environmental Innovation: Boyan Slat and The Ocean Cleanup

Picture this: A 16-year-old boy scuba diving in Greece, expecting to see vibrant marine life, but instead encountering more plastic bags than fish. For most of us, this might be a disappointing vacation memory. For Boyan Slat, it was the spark that ignited a world-changing innovation.

Slat's journey from that eye-opening dive to founding The Ocean Cleanup is a masterclass in how the Complex Adaptive Systems (CAS) Model of Innovation can turn a bold vision into reality. It's a story that reminds us that age is no barrier to innovation, and that some of the most powerful solutions emerge when we dare to think differently about complex problems.

Let's start with visionary leadership. Slat didn't just see a problem; he imagined a solution on a scale that matched the enormity of the challenge. His vision? To develop a passive system that could remove 90% of ocean plastic by 2040. That's not just ambitious; it's audacious. As Slat himself put it, "Big problems require big solutions" (The Ocean Cleanup, 2021).

This vision exemplifies what management guru Peter Senge calls "personal mastery" - the discipline of continually clarifying and deepening our personal vision (Senge, 1990). Slat's ability to articulate and commit to such a bold vision at a young age set the stage for everything that followed.

But vision alone isn't enough. This is where empathetic understanding comes into play. Slat's approach wasn't just about removing plastic; it was rooted in a deep empathy for marine ecosystems and future generations. He spent countless hours studying ocean currents, marine life behavior, and the impact of plastic pollution. This wasn't just academic research; it was an empathetic immersion into the complex system he was trying to change.

This deep dive into the problem space aligns with what design thinking pioneer David Kelley calls "empathic design" - the ability to see and experience issues from the perspective of others, including, in this case, marine life and ecosystems (Kelley & Kelley, 2013). This empathetic understanding guided Slat's innovative approach, ensuring that his solution worked with nature, not against it.

Now, let's talk about flow-state creativity. Slat's eureka moment came during a school project. He found himself in what psychologist Mihaly Csikszentmihalyi describes as a flow state - a period of intense focus and creativity where time seems to stand still (Csikszentmihalyi, 1990). In this state, Slat connected two seemingly unrelated ideas: the way plastic spreads through the ocean and how it could be concentrated for removal.

This creative leap led to the core idea behind The Ocean Cleanup: using the ocean's currents to concentrate plastic waste for easy collection. It's a perfect example of what Steven Johnson calls "the adjacent possible" in innovation - taking existing elements and recombining them in novel ways (Johnson, 2010).

But having a great idea is one thing. Turning it into reality? That's where social network synergy comes into play. Slat's 2012 TEDx talk was a masterclass in leveraging networks. The talk went viral, reaching millions and catching the attention of scientists, environmentalists, and potential funders worldwide.

This virality demonstrates what network scientists call "the strength of weak ties" (Granovetter, 1973). By reaching beyond his immediate network, Slat accessed diverse knowledge, resources, and support that propelled his idea forward. It's a powerful reminder that in our connected world, a single talk can spark a global movement.

The journey from concept to implementation, however, was far from smooth sailing (pun intended). This is where we see agile implementation in action. The Ocean Cleanup's first prototype, launched in 2018, failed spectacularly, breaking apart after a few months at sea. For many, this would have been the end of the road. But in the world of complex adaptive systems, failure is often a stepping stone to success.

Slat and his team exemplified what Eric Ries calls the "build-measure-learn" feedback loop in his Lean Startup methodology (Ries, 2011). They quickly analyzed the failure, gleaned valuable insights, and pivoted their approach. They redesigned the system, making it more durable and efficient. This iterative process, characterized by rapid learning and adaptation, is a hallmark of innovation in complex systems.

Their persistence paid off. By 2023, The Ocean Cleanup had removed over 456,000 kg of plastic from the Great Pacific Garbage Patch (The Ocean Cleanup, 2023). But the impact goes beyond the plastic removed. The project has raised global awareness about ocean pollution, inspired countless cleanup initiatives, and demonstrated the power of innovative thinking in tackling environmental challenges.

What's particularly inspiring about The Ocean Cleanup's story is how it continues to evolve. True to the nature of complex adaptive systems, the organization isn't resting on its laurels. They've expanded their focus to include river cleanup systems, recognizing that preventing plastic from entering the oceans is as crucial as removing what's already there. They're also exploring ways to recycle the collected plastic into products, creating a circular economy model.

This ongoing evolution echoes what organizational theorist Peter Senge calls "systems thinking" - the ability to see and work with the interconnectedness of complex systems (Senge, 1990). By addressing the problem at multiple points in the system - from rivers to oceans to recycling - The Ocean Cleanup is creating a more comprehensive and sustainable solution.

Slat's journey with The Ocean Cleanup is a powerful illustration of the CAS Model of Innovation in action. It shows how visionary leadership can inspire global action, how empathetic understanding can lead to nature-inspired solutions, how flow-state creativity can generate breakthrough ideas, how social networks can amplify impact, and how agile implementation can turn setbacks into opportunities for improvement.

But perhaps most importantly, it reminds us that age is no barrier to world-changing innovation. Slat was just a teenager when he started this journey. His story challenges us all to look at the complex problems around us with fresh eyes and daring imagination. As Slat himself often says, "Everyone can do something to combat ocean plastic pollution" (The Ocean Cleanup, 2021).

So, the next time you're faced with a daunting challenge, remember Boyan Slat and The Ocean Cleanup. Remember that with vision, empathy, creativity, connection, and persistence, even the most complex problems can be tackled. Who knows? The next world-changing innovation could be yours.

13.2 Social and Technological Innovation: Trisha Prabhu's ReThink and Nishant Biswas's Runway

In our hyper-connected digital age, innovation often emerges at the intersection of social needs and technological possibilities. This convergence is beautifully illustrated by the stories of Trisha Prabhu, creator of ReThink, and Nishant Biswas, co-founder of Runway. These young innovators show us how the Complex Adaptive Systems (CAS) Model can drive solutions that not only push technological boundaries but also address pressing social issues.

Let's start with Trisha Prabhu's ReThink, an app designed to combat cyberbullying. Prabhu's journey began when she was just 13, after reading about an 11-year-old girl who took her own life due to relentless online bullying. This moment of empathy – feeling deeply the pain of a stranger – became the catalyst for an innovation that would impact millions of lives.

Prabhu's approach exemplifies what psychologist Daniel Goleman calls "emotional intelligence" – the ability to recognize and understand emotions in ourselves and others (Goleman, 1995). Her empathy didn't just fuel her motivation; it shaped her entire approach to solving the problem.

Drawing on insights from psychology, particularly the fact that the teenage brain is not fully developed in areas responsible for decision-making and impulse control, Prabhu had an idea. What if there was a way to give teens a chance to reconsider before posting potentially hurtful messages online?

This idea led to the creation of ReThink, an app that detects potentially offensive messages and prompts users to reconsider before posting. The development of ReThink showcases what psychologist Mihaly Csikszentmihalyi describes as "flow" – a state of deep focus and creativity where time seems to stand still (Csikszentmihalyi, 1990). Prabhu, who taught herself coding, often lost track of time as she worked on developing the app, fully immersed in the process of bringing her vision to life.

But having a great idea and even a working prototype isn't enough in the competitive world of apps. This is where Prabhu's skill in leveraging social network synergy shone through. She participated in science fairs, pitched at entrepreneurship competitions, and even appeared on Shark Tank, expanding her network and gathering valuable insights (ABC, 2016).

This approach to building connections and gaining exposure demonstrates what sociologist Mark Granovetter calls "the strength of weak ties" – the idea that our acquaintances, rather than close friends, are often our greatest source of new ideas and information (Granovetter, 1973). Each presentation, each competition, was not just about winning awards, but about refining the idea, gaining supporters, and opening new opportunities.

The results of Prabhu's efforts have been remarkable. Research has shown that ReThink is effective in preventing cyberbullying in 93% of cases. The app has been recognized by Google, MIT, and even the White House, with Prabhu being invited to present her work to President Obama (ReThink, 2023).

Now, let's shift our focus to Nishant Biswas and Runway, an AI-powered fashion app that's revolutionizing how people discover and shop for clothes. Biswas's journey illustrates how empathy can drive innovation even in seemingly superficial industries like fashion.

Before writing a single line of code, Biswas and his team spent months interviewing potential users. They immersed themselves in the frustrations people face with online shopping, from inconsistent sizing to the overwhelming number of choices. This deep dive into user experiences exemplifies what design thinking pioneer David Kelley calls "empathic design" – the process of understanding users' unarticulated needs (Kelley & Kelley, 2013).

One key insight that emerged from this research was the disconnect between how people think about their style and how online fashion platforms typically categorize clothing. This realization led to the development of Runway's unique AI-powered recommendation system. Instead of traditional category-based browsing, Runway uses advanced machine learning algorithms to understand a user's personal style and recommend items accordingly.

The creation of Runway's AI algorithm is a testament to what computer scientist John McCarthy described as the goal of AI: "to develop machines that behave as though they were intelligent" (McCarthy, 2007). By mimicking the nuanced way humans think about fashion, Runway's AI creates a more intuitive and personalized shopping experience.

Biswas and his team didn't work in isolation. They leveraged what management theorist Henry Chesbrough calls "open innovation" – the use of external as well as internal ideas to advance technology (Chesbrough, 2003). They tapped into connections in both the tech and fashion industries to gather insights, secure partnerships with clothing brands, and attract investors.

Runway's development process also exemplifies what Eric Ries calls the "build-measure-learn" feedback loop in his Lean Startup methodology (Ries, 2011). The team released early versions of the app to a select group of beta testers and iterated based on their feedback. This approach allowed them to quickly identify and address issues, continuously improving the user experience.

By 2023, Runway had grown to over 500,000 users and secured partnerships with major fashion brands (TechCrunch, 2023). But perhaps more importantly, it has changed the way many people interact with fashion, making style discovery more intuitive and personalized.

The stories of ReThink and Runway demonstrate how the CAS Model of Innovation can be applied to create solutions that are not only technologically advanced but also deeply attuned to human needs and behaviors. They show us that empathy isn't just a feel-good concept, but a powerful driver of technological innovation.

Moreover, these stories highlight the importance of youth in driving innovation. As management guru Peter Drucker once said, "The best way to predict the future is to create it" (Drucker, 1993). Prabhu and Biswas, like many young innovators, aren't constrained by traditional thinking. They see problems with fresh eyes and dare to imagine radical solutions.

As we look to the future, the convergence of social understanding and technological advancement will undoubtedly continue to be a fertile ground for innovation. The success of ReThink and Runway challenges us all to think about how we can use technology not just to create new products, but to address real human needs and improve lives.

In our next section, we'll explore how this empathy-driven approach to innovation can transform even the most unlikely industries, as we delve into the sweet world of candy with a healthy twist.

13.3 Health and Sustainability Innovation: Tara Bosch and SmartSweets

From the digital realm of cyberbullying prevention and AI-powered fashion, let's shift our focus to an unlikely arena for innovation: the candy aisle. Here, we find Tara Bosch, a young entrepreneur who decided to tackle another kind of pollution – the excess sugar in our diets. Bosch's journey with SmartSweets is a delicious example of how the Complex Adaptive Systems (CAS) Model can drive innovation in established industries, blending health concerns with sustainability and challenging our notions of indulgence.

Bosch's story begins with a personal struggle. As a self-proclaimed "candy addict," she had firsthand experience with the negative health impacts of excessive sugar consumption. This personal connection exemplifies what psychologist Carl Rogers called "unconditional positive regard" – a deep empathy and acceptance for oneself and others (Rogers, 1957). Bosch didn't just identify a market opportunity; she felt the problem deeply and personally.

At the age of 21, Bosch made a decision that would change her life and potentially impact the health of millions. She dropped out of college to pursue her vision: creating candy that people could enjoy without the negative health impacts of excessive sugar. This bold move demonstrates what management theorist Peter Drucker described as "entrepreneurial judo" – using unexpected moves to create new markets (Drucker, 1985).

Bosch's approach to developing SmartSweets is a masterclass in what psychologist Mihaly Csikszentmihalyi calls "flow-state creativity" (Csikszentmihalyi, 1996). She spent countless nights in her kitchen, experimenting with different recipes and ingredients. This intense focus, characteristic of flow states, allowed her to make rapid progress in developing her product. She describes losing track of time, often working through the night as she pursued the perfect formulation.

But creating a tasty, low-sugar candy was just the beginning. Bosch faced skepticism from manufacturers who said it couldn't be done and retailers who doubted that sugar-free candy could sell. This is where we see the importance of what organizational theorist Karl Weick calls "sensemaking" – the process of creating meaning in uncertain or ambiguous contexts (Weick, 1995). Bosch had to navigate this uncertainty, constantly interpreting feedback and adjusting her approach.

Here's where social network synergy came into play. Bosch leveraged every connection she could, cold-emailing buyers, reaching out to industry veterans for mentorship, and using social media to build buzz around her product. She even stood outside grocery stores, offering samples to customers and buyers alike. This grassroots approach to building a network demonstrates what sociologist Mark Granovetter calls "the strength of weak ties" – the idea that our acquaintances, rather than close friends, are often our greatest source of new opportunities (Granovetter, 1973).

Bosch's efforts paid off. SmartSweets secured shelf space in major retailers and caught the eye of investors. By 2019, just three years after its founding, SmartSweets was projecting $50 million in sales. This rapid growth illustrates what business theorist Clayton Christensen calls "disruptive innovation" – innovations that create new markets and value networks, ultimately disrupting existing ones (Christensen, 1997).

However, success brought its own challenges. In 2019, an early batch of product had to be recalled due to a packaging issue that could potentially cause mold. This crisis threatened to derail all of Bosch's hard work. But here's where we see agile implementation in action. Instead of trying to downplay the issue,

Bosch took it head-on. She communicated transparently with customers, explaining the problem and the steps being taken to resolve it.

This approach aligns with what crisis communication expert Timothy Coombs calls the "rebuilding posture" – taking full responsibility for the crisis and offering compensation to victims (Coombs, 2007). By handling the recall with transparency and efficiency, SmartSweets reinforced its brand image as a company that truly cares about its customers' health and well-being.

The result of all this hard work, creativity, and adaptability? By 2020, SmartSweets had become one of the fastest-growing confectionery companies in North America. In November of that year, the company was acquired by TPG Growth for a reported $360 million (Glasner, 2020). This exit, impressive for any startup, is particularly remarkable given that Bosch was just 25 years old at the time.

But the story of SmartSweets doesn't end with its acquisition. True to the nature of complex adaptive systems, the company continues to evolve. They've expanded their product line, introduced new flavors, and continued to innovate in the healthy snacking space. This ongoing evolution demonstrates what organizational theorist Peter Senge calls "systems thinking" – the ability to see and work with the interconnectedness of complex systems (Senge, 1990).

SmartSweets' success also highlights an important aspect of innovation in the modern era – the power of purpose-driven businesses. By aligning profit with a mission to improve health,

SmartSweets tapped into what management professor Rosabeth Moss Kanter calls "institutional logic" – the idea that companies can create value for society while also creating value for shareholders (Kanter, 2011).

As we reflect on Bosch's journey with SmartSweets, we see a powerful illustration of how the CAS Model of Innovation can transform even the most traditional industries. From the empathy that drove the initial concept, to the flow-state creativity that fueled product development, to the network synergy that enabled rapid growth, to the agile implementation that turned crises into opportunities – each element of the model played a crucial role in SmartSweets' success.

Moreover, SmartSweets' story challenges us to think differently about sustainability in business. It's not just about reducing environmental impact (though that's important too), but about creating products and business models that sustain human health and well-being. As we face growing global health challenges, innovations like SmartSweets point the way towards a future where indulgence and health can coexist.

In our final section, we'll see how these principles of empathy-driven, adaptive innovation can be applied not just to products, but to movements that aim to change the world. Get ready to meet a young activist who's shaking up the global conversation on climate change.

13.4 ACTIVISM AS INNOVATION: GRETA THUNBERG AND CLIMATE ACTION

From the sweet world of candy, we now turn to a bitter reality: the global climate crisis. Here, we meet Greta Thunberg, a young Swedish activist who has revolutionized climate activism and reshaped the global conversation on environmental action. Thunberg's story illustrates how the Complex Adaptive Systems (CAS) Model of Innovation can be applied beyond products and services to catalyze social movements and drive systemic change.

Thunberg's journey began with a profound sense of empathy – not just for current generations affected by climate change, but for all future inhabitants of our planet. This empathetic understanding, a core component of our CAS Model, became the driving force behind her actions. At the age of 15, Thunberg's concern about climate change was so intense that it affected her health, leading to depression and selective mutism. This deep emotional connection to the issue exemplifies what psychologist Daniel Goleman calls "ecological intelligence" – the ability to adapt to our ecological niche (Goleman, 2009).

Thunberg's approach to climate activism showcases several elements of our CAS Model of Innovation. Her clear, uncompromising message about the urgency of climate action is a prime example of what leadership expert Simon Sinek calls "starting with why" (Sinek, 2009). In August 2018, she decided to skip school and protest outside the Swedish Parliament, holding a sign that read "School Strike for Climate." This solitary act, born from a place of deep concern and frustration, demonstrates the kind of audacious thinking that often precedes world-changing innovations.

Flow-state creativity manifests in Thunberg's powerful speeches and innovative protest methods. Her focused passion is evident in her communications, which often come from intense periods of research and writing. In her speech at the UN Climate Action Summit in 2019, Thunberg's emotional delivery and pointed questions to world leaders showcased what rhetoric scholar Keith Keith-Spiegel calls "ethical appeal" – the use of character and credibility in persuasion (Keith-Spiegel, 1994).

But perhaps the most striking aspect of Thunberg's impact is her mastery of social network synergy. Through skillful use of social media and public appearances, Thunberg turned her solo protest into a global movement. The school strikes for climate that she inspired, known as Fridays for Future, have involved millions of participants worldwide. This demonstrates what network scientists Albert-László Barabási and Réka Albert call "preferential attachment" in scale-free networks – the tendency of new connections to form around already well-connected nodes (Barabási & Albert, 1999).

Thunberg's movement has also shown remarkable agile implementation, adapting to challenges and opportunities as they arise. When the COVID-19 pandemic made in-person protests impossible, Thunberg quickly pivoted to organizing digital strikes. This flexibility in the face of obstacles is what organizational theorist Karl Weick calls "improvisation" – the ability to recombine known materials in novel ways to address unexpected situations (Weick, 1998).

The impact of Thunberg's activism has been profound and measurable. A study by Bugden (2023) found that her efforts have significantly increased public engagement with climate change issues, particularly among young people. By innovating in the realm of activism, Thunberg has changed the global conversation around climate change, influencing policy discussions and corporate decision-making.

Thunberg's approach aligns with what social movement theorists Doug McAdam, Sidney Tarrow, and Charles Tilly call "contentious politics" – the use of disruptive techniques to make political claims (McAdam et al., 2001). However, Thunberg has innovated within this framework, combining traditional protest methods with savvy use of media and a powerful personal narrative.

Critics might argue that awareness doesn't equate to action, but Thunberg's influence extends beyond public opinion. Her activism has contributed to concrete policy changes, such as the European Union's commitment to carbon neutrality by 2050 and numerous countries declaring climate emergencies. This demonstrates what political scientist John Kingdon calls "policy windows" – opportunities for action on given initiatives (Kingdon, 1984).

Moreover, Thunberg's movement showcases what sociologist Manuel Castells terms "networked social movements" – decentralized, internet-based movements that can quickly mobilize large numbers of people (Castells, 2015). The global reach and rapid growth of Fridays for Future illustrate the power of this networked approach to activism.

As we reflect on Thunberg's journey, we see a powerful illustration of how the CAS Model of Innovation can be applied to social movements. Her deep empathy for the planet and future generations provided the emotional fuel. Her clear, uncompromising message demonstrated visionary leadership. Her powerful speeches and protest methods showcased flow-state creativity. Her skillful use of social media exemplified network synergy. And her ability to adapt to challenges like the pandemic showed agile implementation.

Thunberg's story challenges us to think broadly about what constitutes innovation. It's not just about new technologies or products; it's about new ways of thinking, communicating, and mobilizing for change. As management guru Peter Drucker once said, "The greatest danger in times of turbulence is not the turbulence; it is to act with yesterday's logic" (Drucker, 1980). Thunberg's approach to climate activism represents a new logic for our turbulent times.

As we face unprecedented global challenges, from climate change to social inequality, Thunberg's example reminds us of the power of youth-driven, empathy-based innovation. It shows us that sometimes, the most powerful innovations don't come from labs or boardrooms, but from individuals who dare to stand up and demand change.

In conclusion, these four case studies – from ocean cleanup to cyberbullying prevention, from healthier candy to climate activism – demonstrate the versatility and power of the CAS Model of Innovation. They show us that whether we're developing new technologies, reimagining industries, or mobilizing global movements, the principles of empathy, leadership, creativity, network synergy, and agile implementation can guide us towards meaningful, impactful innovation.

As we look to the future, these stories challenge us all to think about how we can apply these principles in our own work and lives. How can we leverage empathy to uncover unmet needs? How can we use our networks to amplify our impact? How can we stay agile in the face of rapid change? The answers to these questions could lead to the next world-changing innovation. And who knows? That innovation might just come from you.

KEY INSIGHTS

- Real-world examples provide valuable lessons for applying innovation principles
- Successful innovation often involves adapting strategies to specific contexts
- Learning from both successes and failures is crucial for developing innovation skills

INNOVATION CHALLENGE

Identify an organization or individual from the case studies that resonates with your own context. Over the next month, try to implement one of their strategies or approaches in your own work. Reflect on the results and how you needed to adapt the approach.

Reflection Questions

1. Which case study did you find most relevant to your own work or challenges? Why?

2. What common themes or strategies did you notice across the successful innovation case studies? How might you apply these in your own context?

3. Think about a recent innovation failure in your own experience. How does it compare to the challenges faced in the case studies? What new strategies could you apply based on these examples?

CONCLUSION

THE SYMPHONY OF INNOVATION

As we close our exploration of **Generation Innovate**, we find ourselves at the dawn of a new era of creativity and innovation. Throughout this book, we've uncovered how Millennials and Gen-Z are reshaping industries with a unique blend of digital fluency, empathy, creativity, and a deep connection to global networks. These qualities have formed the foundation of the **Complex Adaptive Systems (CAS) Model of Innovation**, a framework that reflects the dynamic, interconnected nature of innovation in today's world.

We began by recognizing the defining traits of **Generation Innovate**—their comfort with change, their passion for purpose-driven work, and their innate ability to **connect and collaborate** across boundaries. These traits are not just incidental; they are the bedrock of their innovative power, and they have guided our journey through this book.

From the rise of the Creator Economy to the power of **flow states** in unleashing creativity, and from the crucial role of **empathy** to the transformative strength of **social networks**, we've seen how these generations are not merely adapting to the digital age but actively shaping it. Their innovations are not confined to products—they are creating new systems of thought, new ways of working, and new ways of relating to the world.

The **CAS Model of Innovation**, with its focus on **empathy, flow and creativity, social networks**, and **implementation**, provides a fresh way to understand how ideas emerge, evolve, and scale in our complex world. It shows us that innovation is not a linear process, but a dynamic, adaptive system—one that thrives on the **interplay of diverse elements** much like a symphony comes to life through the harmony of individual instruments.

- **Empathy** forms the emotional core, ensuring that innovations resonate deeply with the needs and desires of users.
- **Flow and creativity** create the melody, where the challenge of creation meets the skill to deliver breakthrough ideas.
- **Social networks** provide the harmony, the connective force that amplifies individual creativity into collaborative achievements.
- **Implementation** is the rhythm that brings ideas to life, allowing innovations to move from concept to reality with agility.

But perhaps the most powerful aspect of the **CAS Model** is its adaptability. Just as **Generation Innovate** thrives on change, this model is designed to evolve. As new technologies emerge, as social and economic systems shift, and as global challenges intensify, this model provides a roadmap for navigating uncertainty and driving meaningful innovation.

As we look toward the future, the world's most pressing challenges—climate change, social inequality, public health crises, and the ethical implications of new technologies—demand **innovative thinking on an unprecedented scale**. In **Generation Innovate**, with their blend of **technological savvy**, **global consciousness**, and **purpose-driven motivation**, we have a powerful force for positive change.

The **CAS Model of Innovation** offers a way to channel this potential—not just for individual success, but for the **collective good**. It's a model that meets the complexity of our world with the complexity of thought that Millennials and Gen-Z naturally bring to the table.

As we conclude this book, remember that the **symphony of innovation** is still being composed. Whether you are a member of **Generation Innovate** or someone inspired by their approach, you have a unique part to play. Your ideas, your connections, your creativity—they are all essential to shaping the future.

Innovation isn't about isolated breakthroughs. It's about creating **ecosystems** where creativity can flourish, where diverse perspectives combine in unexpected ways, and where **collective intelligence** drives solutions to the challenges that face us all.

Generation Innovate, you have the tools, the mindset, and the opportunity to lead this charge. Armed with the insights from this book and your own understanding of our interconnected world, you are ready to compose the next movement in the symphony of human progress.

The stage is set. The instruments are tuned. What melody will you create? How will you harmonize **technology with humanity**, **creativity with compassion**, and **innovation with purpose**?

The future of innovation is in your hands. The world is waiting for your unique contribution. **Let the music begin.**

EPILOGUE

TAKING THE FIRST STEPS

As we conclude our exploration of **Generation Innovate and the Complex Adaptive Systems (CAS) Model of Innovation,** you may be asking yourself, "Where do I go from here?" This epilogue is designed to help you translate the insights from this book into actionable steps. Remember, innovation isn't just something to understand—it's a skill to be practiced and honed over time. Here are six key steps to guide you as you begin or enhance your innovation journey:

1. Conduct a Personal Innovation Audit

Start by assessing your strengths and areas for growth using the **CAS Model of Innovation**. Reflect on your capacity for adaptive leadership, empathetic understanding, flow-state creativity, social network synergy, and agile implementation. Identify areas where you excel and where you can improve. This self-awareness will shape your development and help you prioritize your next steps.

2. Cultivate Creativity and Continuous Learning

Develop your creative muscle and stay adaptable by engaging in two daily practices:

- **Keep a Creativity Journal**: Document your ideas, inspirations, and reflections regularly. This habit helps you capture creative thoughts, recognize patterns, and connect seemingly unrelated ideas.
- **Commit to Continuous Learning**: Challenge yourself to learn one new skill or tool each month—whether it's a technical skill, a soft skill, or a new hobby. Stay curious, and remember that adaptability is essential in the ever-changing landscape of innovation.

3. Expand Your Network

Social networks are critical to both discovering novel ideas and accelerating implementation. Actively seek new connections by joining online communities, attending meetups, or participating in industry events. Don't limit yourself to your area of expertise—innovation thrives at the intersection of diverse fields. Build **strong and weak ties**, as the latter often expose you to fresh perspectives that can inspire breakthroughs.

4. Build Empathy and Collaborate Across Generations

Empathy is at the heart of innovation. Practice putting yourself in others' shoes by engaging in active listening, conducting user interviews, or volunteering for a cause. At the same time, seek out intergenerational collaborations. If you're a younger innovator, connect with experienced professionals for mentorship. If you're more seasoned, engage with younger colleagues for reverse mentorship. These cross-generational exchanges foster mutual learning and spark new ideas.

5. Experiment with Rapid Prototyping

Apply the principle of **agile implementation** by prototyping an idea you've been considering. Build a rough version, test it quickly, gather feedback, and iterate. Don't be afraid to fail fast—every iteration brings you closer to a refined solution. This hands-on experience is essential for cultivating an agile mindset and staying adaptable in the face of uncertainty.

6. Practice Adaptive Leadership

Experiment with creating **adaptive spaces**—environments where creativity can flourish organically. In your work or personal projects, focus on enabling innovation by guiding the process rather than controlling outcomes. By embracing the unpredictability of innovation and letting ideas evolve naturally, you foster more resilient and creative solutions.

7. Embrace the Journey

Innovation is a journey, not a destination. These steps are not a one-time checklist but ongoing practices to integrate into your life and work. Be patient with yourself, celebrate small wins, and don't be afraid to fail—each setback is a learning opportunity that brings you closer to your next breakthrough.

As you take these steps, remember to view your innovation journey through the lens of a **complex adaptive system**. Embrace uncertainty, look for emerging patterns, and be ready to adapt your approach as you go. The future of innovation is in your hands, and by consistently applying these practices, you'll not only enhance your own abilities but also contribute to the broader ecosystem of creativity and problem-solving that the world needs.

So, what will your first step be? The journey of a thousand innovations begins with a single idea. **Your next big breakthrough could be just around the corner. Are you ready to take that step?**

GLOSSARY

Adaptability: The ability to adjust to new conditions and environments, often associated with continuous learning and flexibility in the face of rapid changes.

Agile Methodology: A flexible, iterative approach to project management and software development that emphasizes collaboration, customer feedback, and incremental progress.

AI-Enhanced Creativity: The use of artificial intelligence (AI) tools to augment human creativity, assisting in generating ideas or automating repetitive tasks.

Ambidextrous Organizations: Organizations that balance efficiency in current operations with exploration of new ideas and innovations.

Authentic Leadership: A leadership style that emphasizes transparency, genuineness, and alignment between leaders' values and actions.

Behavioral Economics: A field studying how psychological, emotional, and social factors influence economic decision-making.

Big Data: Large sets of structured and unstructured data analyzed for insights to improve decision-making.

Blockchain: A decentralized digital ledger technology that allows secure, transparent transactions.

Cognitive Diversity: The inclusion of people with different thinking styles, perspectives, and problem-solving approaches.

Collaborative Intelligence (CI): The collective intelligence that emerges from collaboration and teamwork, allowing for innovative problem-solving.

Complex Adaptive System (CAS): A model used to describe dynamic systems where diverse agents interact in unpredictable ways.

Creative Confidence: The belief in one's ability to generate creative solutions.

Crisis Innovation: The development of new solutions in response to a crisis.

Crowdsourcing: Obtaining input, services, or ideas from a large group, often via the Internet.

Cyber-Physical Systems (CPS): Systems integrating computation, networking, and physical processes.

Design Thinking: A problem-solving framework emphasizing empathy, ideation, and iterative prototyping.

Digital Fluency: The ability to navigate and use digital tools effectively.

Digital Well-Being: The practice of maintaining a healthy relationship with technology, balancing screen time, productivity, and mental health.

Emotional Intelligence (EQ): The ability to recognize and manage one's own emotions, as well as the emotions of others.

Empathy: The ability to understand and share the feelings of others.

Empathy Mapping: A tool used to visualize and understand the emotional experiences of users.

Entrepreneurial Mindset: A set of attitudes and behaviors focused on opportunity-seeking, innovation, and calculated risk-taking.

Flow State: A state of optimal focus and immersion in a task, often leading to peak creativity and performance.

Future of Work: The evolving trends, technologies, and societal shifts that are reshaping work environments and careers.

Generative AI: A form of AI that generates new content such as text, images, or music.

Gig Economy: An economy made up of freelance or contract-based work, rather than permanent jobs.

Growth Mindset: The belief that intelligence and abilities can be developed through effort and learning.

Hybrid Work: A flexible work model combining in-office and remote work.

Innovation Ecosystem: A network of organizations, institutions, and individuals collaborating to drive innovation.

Iterative Design: A design methodology that involves continuous prototyping, testing, and refining based on feedback.

Lean Startup: A methodology that focuses on launching a minimal viable product (MVP) quickly, gathering feedback, and iterating based on data.

Neuroplasticity: The brain's ability to reorganize itself by forming new neural connections.

Open Innovation: A model that emphasizes using external ideas, collaborations, and partnerships to drive innovation.

Platform Cooperativism: A movement that advocates for digital platforms that are owned and governed by their users rather than corporations.

Portfolio Careers: Careers in which individuals work multiple jobs or projects simultaneously, often across different industries.

Psychological Safety: A condition where individuals feel safe to express ideas, ask questions, or admit mistakes without fear of negative consequences.

Rapid Prototyping: A fast, iterative process of creating and testing models or prototypes.

Remote Collaboration: Using digital tools and platforms to work with teams or individuals across different geographic locations.

Resilience: The ability to recover from setbacks and persist in the face of adversity.

Reskilling: The process of learning new skills to transition into a different job or industry.

Scrum: An agile project management framework that promotes teamwork, accountability, and iterative progress.

Self-Efficacy: A person's belief in their ability to succeed in specific situations.

Social Capital: The networks of relationships and trust that enable individuals and groups to work together effectively.

Systems Thinking: A holistic approach to problem-solving that considers the interconnectedness of all elements within a system.

T-Shaped Skills: A concept referring to professionals who have deep expertise in one area but also broad knowledge across other disciplines.

Thousand True Fans: A concept suggesting that creators only need 1,000 dedicated followers to be successful.

Transdisciplinary Collaboration: Collaboration that integrates knowledge from multiple disciplines to solve complex problems.

User-Centric Innovation: An innovation approach that places the needs and preferences of the end user at the center of the development process.

VUCA (Volatility, Uncertainty, Complexity, Ambiguity): A framework for understanding the unpredictable, dynamic nature of the modern world.

Web3: The next evolution of the web, characterized by decentralized networks and blockchain technology, enabling users to control their data and digital assets.

REFERENCES

ABC. (2016). Shark Tank, Season 8, Episode 8.

Adobe. (2023). Creative AI Survey.

Alter, A. (2017). Irresistible: The Rise of Addictive Technology and the Business of Keeping Us Hooked. Penguin.

Amabile, T. M. (1982). Social psychology of creativity: A consensual assessment technique. Journal of Personality and Social Psychology, 43(5), 997-1013.

Amabile, T. M. (1983). The social psychology of creativity: A componential conceptualization. Journal of Personality and Social Psychology, 45(2), 357-376.

Amabile, T. M. (1985). Motivation and creativity: Effects of motivational orientation on creative writers. Journal of Personality and Social Psychology, 48(2), 393-399.

Amabile, T. M. (1996). Creativity in context: Update to "The Social Psychology of Creativity." Westview Press.

Amabile, T. M., & Kramer, S. J. (2011). The progress principle: Using small wins to ignite joy, engagement, and creativity at work. Harvard Business Press.

American Psychological Association. (2023). Stress in America 2023.

Amway. (2023). Global Entrepreneurship Report.

Aral, S., Dellarocas, C., & Godes, D. (2013). Introduction to the special issue—social media and business transformation: A framework for research. Information Systems Research, 24(1), 3-13.

Arena, M. (2018). Adaptive space: How GM and other companies are positively disrupting themselves and transforming into agile organizations. McGraw-Hill Education.

Aron, E. N. (1997). The highly sensitive person: How to thrive when the world overwhelms you. Broadway Books.

Arute, F., Arya, K., Babbush, R., et al. (2019). Quantum supremacy using a programmable superconducting processor. Nature, 574(7779), 505-510.

Baer, M. (2010). The strength-of-weak-ties perspective on creativity: A comprehensive examination and extension. Journal of Applied Psychology, 95(3), 592-601.

Bailenson, J. (2018). Experience on Demand: What Virtual Reality Is, How It Works, and What It Can Do. W. W. Norton & Company.

Baker, T., & Nelson, R. E. (2005). Creating something from nothing: Resource construction through entrepreneurial bricolage. Administrative Science Quarterly, 50(3), 329-366.

Bakhshi, H., & Throsby, D. (2011). Culture of Innovation: An economic analysis of innovation in arts and cultural organisations. NESTA.

Bauer, A. A., Loy, L. S., Masur, P. K., & Schneider, F. M. (2017). Mindful instant messaging: Mindfulness and autonomous motivation as predictors of well-being in smartphone communication. Journal of Media Psychology, 29(3), 159-165.

BBC. (2020). Greta Thunberg: Climate change 'as urgent' as coronavirus.

Beals, G. (2016). Thomas Edison: Inventing the Modern Age. Grosset & Dunlap.

Beaty, R. E., Benedek, M., Silvia, P. J., & Schacter, D. L. (2016). Creative cognition and brain network dynamics. Trends in Cognitive Sciences, 20(2), 87-95.

Beaty, R. E., Benedek, M., Wilkins, R. W., Jauk, E., Fink, A., Silvia, P. J., ... & Neubauer, A. C. (2014). Creativity and the default network: A functional connectivity analysis of the creative brain at rest. Neuropsychologia, 64, 92-98.

Beaty, R. E., Kenett, Y. N., Christensen, A. P., Rosenberg, M. D., Benedek, M., Chen, Q., ... & Silvia, P. J. (2018). Robust prediction of individual creative ability from brain functional connectivity. Proceedings of the National Academy of Sciences, 115(5), 1087-1092.

Beaty, R. E., Seli, P., & Schacter, D. L. (2020). Thinking about the past and future in daily life: an experience sampling study of individual differences in mental time travel. Psychological Research, 84(7), 1530-1549.

Belsky, S. (2012). Making Ideas Happen: Overcoming the Obstacles Between Vision and Reality. Portfolio.

Belsky, S. (2018). The Messy Middle: Finding Your Way Through the Hardest and Most Crucial Part of Any Bold Venture. Portfolio.

Benjamin, W. (1935). The work of art in the age of mechanical reproduction. Illuminations, 1969.

Beyens, I., Pouwels, J. L., van Driel, I. I., Keijsers, L., & Valkenburg, P. M. (2020). The effect of social media on well-being differs from adolescent to adolescent. Scientific Reports, 10(1), 1-11.

Bezos, J. (2016). 2016 Letter to Shareholders. Amazon.com, Inc.

Blank, S. (2013). Why the lean start-up changes everything. Harvard Business Review, 91(5), 63-72.

Bock, L. (2015). Work Rules!: Insights from Inside Google That Will Transform How You Live and Lead. Twelve.

Boden, M. A. (2004). The creative mind: Myths and mechanisms. Routledge.

Bosse, H. M., Schultz, J. H., Nickel, M., Lutz, T., Möltner, A., Jünger, J., ... & Nikendei, C. (2012). The effect of using standardized patients or peer role play on ratings of undergraduate communication training: A randomized controlled trial. Patient Education and Counseling, 87(3), 300-306.

Botvinick, M. M., Cohen, J. D., & Carter, C. S. (2004). Conflict monitoring and anterior cingulate cortex: an update. Trends in Cognitive Sciences, 8(12), 539-546.

Boyd, D. (2014). It's Complicated: The Social Lives of Networked Teens. Yale University Press.

Bratman, G. N., Hamilton, J. P., Hahn, K. S., Daily, G. C., & Gross, J. J. (2015). Nature experience reduces rumination and subgenual prefrontal cortex activation. Proceedings of the National Academy of Sciences, 112(28), 8567-8572.

Brewer, J. A., Worhunsky, P. D., Gray, J. R., Tang, Y. Y., Weber, J., & Kober, H. (2011). Meditation experience is associated with differences in default mode network activity and connectivity. Proceedings of the National Academy of Sciences, 108(50), 20254-20259.

Brewster, S. (2019). Ford is using virtual reality to design cars. Fast Company.

Bridger, D. (2015). Decoding the Irrational Consumer: How to Commission, Run and Generate Insights from Neuromarketing Research. Kogan Page Publishers.

Brown, B. (2012). Daring Greatly: How the Courage to Be Vulnerable Transforms the Way We Live, Love, Parent, and Lead. Gotham Books.

Brown, S. (2009). Play: How it shapes the brain, opens the imagination, and invigorates the soul. Penguin.

Brown, T. (2008). Design thinking. Harvard Business Review, 86(6), 84.

Brown, T. (2009). Change by design: How design thinking transforms organizations and inspires innovation. HarperBusiness.

Brown, T., & Katz, B. (2011). Change by design. Journal of Product Innovation Management, 28(3), 381-383.

Brown, T., & Wyatt, J. (2010). Design thinking for social innovation. Development Outreach, 12(1), 29-43.

Brynjolfsson, E., & McAfee, A. (2014). The Second Machine Age: Work, Progress, and Prosperity in a Time of Brilliant Technologies. W.W. Norton & Company.

Brynjolfsson, E., & McAfee, A. (2017). Machine, Platform, Crowd: Harnessing Our Digital Future. W. W. Norton & Company.

Bugden, D. (2023). The Greta Thunberg Effect: Familiarity with Greta Thunberg predicts intentions to engage in climate activism in the United States. Journal of Applied Social Psychology, 53(1), 79-89.

Bureau of Labor Statistics. (2023). Employee Tenure Summary.

Burgdorf, J., & Panksepp, J. (2006). The neurobiology of positive emotions. Neuroscience & Biobehavioral Reviews, 30(2), 173-187.

Burt, R. S. (2004). Structural holes and good ideas. American Journal of Sociology, 110(2), 349-399.

Buzan, T., & Buzan, B. (1993). The mind map book: How to use radiant thinking to maximize your brain's untapped potential. Plume.

Cameron, J. (1992). The artist's way: A spiritual path to higher creativity. Jeremy P. Tarcher/Putnam.

Cardoso-Leite, P., Green, C. S., & Bavelier, D. (2015). On the impact of new technologies on multitasking and learning. Developmental Review, 35, 98-112.

Carlozzi, A. F., Bull, K. S., Eells, G. T., & Hurlburt, J. D. (1995). Empathy as Related to Creativity, Dogmatism, and Expressiveness. The Journal of Psychology, 129(4), 365-373.

Carr, N. (2010). The Shallows: What the Internet Is Doing to Our Brains. W. W. Norton & Company.

Castaldo, J. (2018). How Tara Bosch is taking on the candy industry. Canadian Business.

Catmull, E. (2014). Creativity, Inc.: Overcoming the Unseen Forces That Stand in the Way of True Inspiration. Random House.

Celikates, H., & Boudry, M. (2020). True or false: Can AI become a reliable source of knowledge? AI & Society, 35, 1043-1053.

Chen, Y., Elenee Argentinis, J., & Weber, G. (2016). IBM Watson: How Cognitive Computing Can Be Applied to Big Data Challenges in Life Sciences Research. Clinical Therapeutics, 38(4), 688-701.

Chesbrough, H. W. (2003). Open innovation: The new imperative for creating and profiting from technology. Harvard Business Press.

Cirillo, F. (2006). The Pomodoro Technique. FC Garage.

Cisco. (2020). Cisco Annual Internet Report (2018–2023) White Paper. Cisco Systems, Inc.

Clark, A., & Chalmers, D. (1998). The extended mind. Analysis, 58(1), 7-19.

Colzato, L. S., Ozturk, A., & Hommel, B. (2012). Meditate to create: The impact of focused-attention and open-monitoring training on convergent and divergent thinking. Frontiers in Psychology, 3, 116.

Costandi, M. (2016). Neuroplasticity. MIT Press.

Cross, R., & Parker, A. (2004). The hidden power of social networks: Understanding how work really gets done in organizations. Harvard Business School Press.

Cross, R., Borgatti, S. P., & Parker, A. (2002). Making invisible work visible: Using social network analysis to support strategic collaboration. California Management Review, 44(2), 25-46.

Cross, R., Rebele, R., & Grant, A. (2016). Collaborative overload. Harvard Business Review, 94(1), 74-79.

Crossley, N., Bellotti, E., Edwards, G., Everett, M. G., Koskinen, J., & Tranmer, M. (2015). Social network analysis for ego-nets: Social network analysis for actor-centred networks. Sage.

Crunchbase. (2021). SmartSweets - Crunchbase Company Profile & Funding. Crunchbase.

CryptoNews. (2022). Vitalik Buterin: "The Merge Isn't Priced In" - ETHCC 2022 Experience [Video]. Retrieved from https://cryptonews.com/videos/vitalik-buterin-the-merge-isnt-priced-in-ethcc-2022-experience-1/

Csikszentmihalyi, M. (1988). Society, culture, and person: A systems view of creativity. In R. J. Sternberg (Ed.), The nature of creativity: Contemporary psychological perspectives (pp. 325–339). Cambridge University Press.

Csikszentmihalyi, M. (1990). Flow: The Psychology of Optimal Experience. Harper & Row.

Csikszentmihalyi, M. (1996). Creativity: Flow and the Psychology of Discovery and Invention. Harper Collins.

Csikszentmihalyi, M., & LeFevre, J. (1989). Optimal experience in work and leisure. Journal of Personality and Social Psychology, 56(5), 815-822.

Damasio, A. R. (1994). Descartes' Error: Emotion, Reason, and the Human Brain. G.P. Putnam's Sons.

de Bono, E. (1985). Six thinking hats: An essential approach to business management. Little, Brown, & Company.

De Manzano, Ö., Theorell, T., Harmat, L., & Ullén, F. (2010). The psychophysiology of flow during piano playing. Emotion, 10(3), 301-311.

Deci, E. L., & Ryan, R. M. (2000). The "what" and "why" of goal pursuits: Human needs and the self-determination of behavior. Psychological Inquiry, 11(4), 227-268.

Dell Technologies. (2023). Gen Z: The Future Has Arrived.

Deloitte. (2019). Success personified in the Fourth Industrial Revolution: Four leadership personas for an era of change and uncertainty. Deloitte Insights.

Deloitte. (2021). The Deloitte Global 2021 Millennial and Gen Z Survey. Deloitte Touche Tohmatsu Limited.

Deloitte. (2022). The Deloitte Global 2022 Gen Z and Millennial Survey.

Deloitte. (2023). The Deloitte Global 2023 Gen Z and Millennial Survey. Retrieved from https://www.deloitte.com/global/en/about/press-room/2023-gen-z-and-millenial-survey.html

DeRosa, D. M., Smith, C. L., & Hantula, D. A. (2007). The medium matters: Mining the long-promised merit of group interaction in creative idea generation tasks. Computers in Human Behavior, 23(3), 1549-1668.

Design Management Institute. (2015). Design Value Index Results and Commentary.

Di Domenico, S. I., & Ryan, R. M. (2017). The emerging neuroscience of intrinsic motivation: A new frontier in self-determination research. Frontiers in Human Neuroscience, 11, 145.

Dietrich, A. (2004). Neurocognitive mechanisms underlying the experience of flow. Consciousness and Cognition, 13(4), 746-761.

Drucker, P. F. (1985). Innovation and entrepreneurship. Harper & Row.

Drucker, P. F. (1999). Management Challenges for the 21st Century. HarperBusiness.

Duckworth, A. (2016). Grit: The power of passion and perseverance. Scribner.

Duhigg, C. (2016). What Google learned from its quest to build the perfect team. The New York Times Magazine, 26, 2016.

Dul, J., & Ceylan, C. (2011). Work environments for employee creativity. Ergonomics, 54(1), 12-20.

Dweck, C. S. (2006). Mindset: The New Psychology of Success. Random House.

Eagleman, D., & Brandt, A. (2017). The Runaway Species: How Human Creativity Remakes the World. Catapult.

Edmondson, A. (1999). Psychological Safety and Learning Behavior in Work Teams. Administrative Science Quarterly, 44(2), 350-383.

Edmondson, A. C. (2011). Strategies for learning from failure. Harvard Business Review, 89(4), 48-55.

Edmondson, A. C. (2012). Teaming: How organizations learn, innovate, and compete in the knowledge economy. John Wiley & Sons.

Edmondson, A. C. (2019). The Fearless Organization: Creating Psychological Safety in the Workplace for Learning, Innovation, and Growth. John Wiley & Sons.

Eisenmann, T. R. (2021). Why Start-ups Fail. Harvard Business Review Press.

Elliot, J. (2011). The Steve Jobs way: iLeadership for a new generation. Vanguard Press.

Ericsson, A., & Pool, R. (2016). Peak: Secrets from the new science of expertise. Houghton Mifflin Harcourt.

EY. (2023). Gen Z Segmentation Study.

Eyal, N. (2019). Indistractable: How to Control Your Attention and Choose Your Life. BenBella Books.

Federal Reserve. (2023). Survey of Consumer Finances.

Feist, G. J. (1998). A meta-analysis of personality in scientific and artistic creativity. Personality and Social Psychology Review, 2(4), 290-309.

Firth, J., Torous, J., Stubbs, B., Firth, J. A., Steiner, G. Z., Smith, L., & Sarris, J. (2019). The "online brain": how the Internet may be changing our cognition. World Psychiatry, 18(2), 119-129.

Fortune. (2021). Interview with Whitney Wolfe Herd. Fortune Magazine.

Fortunato, S., Bergstrom, C. T., Börner, K., Evans, J. A., Helbing, D., Milojević, S., ... & Barabási, A. L. (2018). Science of science. Science, 359(6379).

Fowler, M. (2019). Technical debt. Martin Fowler's Bliki.

Furr, N., & Dyer, J. (2014). The Innovator's Method: Bringing the Lean Start-up into Your Organization. Harvard Business Review Press.

Galinsky, A. D., Maddux, W. W., Gilin, D., & White, J. B. (2008). Why it pays to get inside the head of your opponent: The differential effects of perspective taking and empathy in negotiations. Psychological Science, 19(4), 378-384.

Gallup. (2023). State of the American Workplace.

Gazzaley, A., & Rosen, L. D. (2016). The distracted mind: Ancient brains in a high-tech world. MIT Press.

Gentile, M. C. (2010). Giving Voice to Values: How to Speak Your Mind When You Know What's Right. Yale University Press.

Gerpott, F. H., Lehmann-Willenbrock, N., & Voelpel, S. C. (2017). A phase model of intergenerational learning in organizations. Academy of Management Learning & Education, 16(2), 193-216.

Gino, F. (2018). The Business Case for Curiosity. Harvard Business Review, 96(5), 48-57.

Glasner, J. (2020). SmartSweets Sells To Private Equity Firm TPG Growth. Crunchbase News.

Glăveanu, V. P. (2010). Paradigms in the study of creativity: Introducing the perspective of cultural psychology. New Ideas in Psychology, 28(1), 79-93.

Global Entrepreneurship Monitor. (2023). 2022/2023 Global Report.

GlobalWebIndex. (2023). Social Media Trends Report.

Goldratt, E. M., & Cox, J. (2004). The goal: A process of ongoing improvement. Routledge.

Goldsmith, K. (2011). Uncreative writing: Managing language in the digital age. Columbia University Press.

Goleman, D. (2004). What Makes a Leader? Harvard Business Review, 82(1), 82-91.

Goleman, D. (2007). Social intelligence: The new science of human relationships. Bantam.

Goleman, D., & Boyatzis, R. (2017). Emotional Intelligence Has 12 Elements. Which Do You Need to Work On? Harvard Business Review.

Goleman, D., & Davidson, R. J. (2017). Altered traits: Science reveals how meditation changes your mind, brain, and body. Avery.

Google. (2023). Digital Wellbeing Study.

Govindarajan, V. & Srinivas, S. (2013). The Innovation Mindset: The Mentality That Enables Continuous Innovation. Harvard Business Review.

Govindarajan, V., & Trimble, C. (2010). The Other Side of Innovation: Solving the Execution Challenge. Harvard Business Review Press.

Grabher, G., & Ibert, O. (2014). Distance as asset? Knowledge collaboration in hybrid virtual communities. Journal of Economic Geography, 14(1), 97-123.

Granovetter, M. S. (1973). The strength of weak ties. American Journal of Sociology, 78(6), 1360-1380.

Grant, A. (2013). Give and take: A revolutionary approach to success. Viking.

Grant, A. M. (2016). Originals: How non-conformists move the world. Viking.

Grant, A. M., & Berry, J. W. (2011). The Necessity of Others is The Mother of Invention: Intrinsic and Prosocial Motivations, Perspective Taking, and Creativity. Academy of Management Journal, 54(1), 73-96.

Green, C. S., & Bavelier, D. (2012). Learning, attentional control, and action video games. Current Biology, 22(6), R197-R206.

Greenberg, J., Reiner, K., & Meiran, N. (2012). "Mind the trap": Mindfulness practice reduces cognitive rigidity. PloS One, 7(5), e36206.

Greenleaf, R. K. (1977). Servant leadership: A journey into the nature of legitimate power and greatness. Paulist Press.

Gruber, M. J., Gelman, B. D., & Ranganath, C. (2014). States of curiosity modulate hippocampus-dependent learning via the dopaminergic circuit. Neuron, 84(2), 486-496.

Guilford, J. P. (1950). Creativity. American Psychologist, 5(9), 444-454.

Guilford, J. P. (1967). The nature of human intelligence. McGraw-Hill.

Haidt, J. (2024). The Anxious Generation: How the Great Rewiring of Childhood Is Causing an Epidemic of Mental Illness. Penguin Press.

Hamel, G. (2007). The Future of Management. Harvard Business Press.

Hampton, K. N., Sessions, L. F., & Her, E. J. (2011). Core Networks, Social Isolation, and New Media: How Internet and Mobile Phone Use Is Related to Network Size and Diversity. Information, Communication & Society, 14(1), 130-155.

Hansen, M. T. (1999). The search-transfer problem: The role of weak ties in sharing knowledge across organization subunits. Administrative Science Quarterly, 44(1), 82-111.

Hargroves, K., & Smith, M. (2006). Innovation inspired by nature: Biomimicry. Ecos, 2006(129), 27-29.

Harvard Business Review. (2017). A face-to-face request is 34 times more successful than an email. Harvard Business Review Digital Articles.

Harvard Business Review. (2023). The Collaborative Advantage: The Impact of Digital Tools on Team Innovation.

Hatano, G., & Inagaki, K. (1986). Two courses of expertise. In H. Stevenson, H. Azuma, & K. Hakuta (Eds.), Child development and education in Japan (pp. 262-272). Freeman.

Heffernan, M. (2011). Willful blindness: Why we ignore the obvious at our peril. Simon and Schuster.

Heffernan, M. (2019). Uncharted: How to Map the Future Together. Simon & Schuster.

Heifetz, R. A., & Linsky, M. (2002). Leadership on the line: Staying alive through the dangers of leading. Harvard Business School Press.

Heifetz, R., & Linsky, M. (2017). Leadership on the Line, With a New Preface: Staying Alive Through the Dangers of Change. Harvard Business Review Press.

Hennessey, B. A., & Amabile, T. M. (2010). Creativity. Annual Review of Psychology, 61, 569-598.

Hewlett, S. A., Marshall, M., & Sherbin, L. (2013). How diversity can drive innovation. Harvard Business Review, 91(12), 30-30.

Highsmith, J. (2009). Agile project management: Creating innovative products. Addison-Wesley Professional.

Hill, L. A., Brandeau, G., Truelove, E., & Lineback, K. (2014). Collective Genius: The Art and Practice of Leading Innovation. Harvard Business Review Press.

Hoever, I. J., Van Knippenberg, D., van Ginkel, W. P., & Barkema, H. G. (2012). Fostering Team Creativity: Perspective Taking as Key to Unlocking Diversity's Potential. Journal of Applied Psychology, 97(5), 982.

Hoffman, B. G. (2012). American Icon: Alan Mulally and the Fight to Save Ford Motor Company. Crown Business.

Hoffman, R. (2011). The Start-Up of You: Adapt to the Future, Invest in Yourself, and Transform Your Career. Random House.

Holland, J. H. (1995). Hidden order: How adaptation builds complexity. Addison-Wesley.

HolonIQ. (2022). 2021 Global Learning Landscape.

Honeyman, C., Coben, J., & De Palo, G. (2009). Rethinking negotiation teaching: Innovations for context and culture. DRI Press.

Humble, J., Molesky, J., & O'Reilly, B. (2018). Lean enterprise: How high performance organizations innovate at scale. O'Reilly Media, Inc.

Hunt, V., Prince, S., Dixon-Fyle, S., & Yee, L. (2018). Delivering through Diversity. McKinsey & Company.

Huston, L., & Sakkab, N. (2006). Connect and develop: Inside Procter & Gamble's new model for innovation. Harvard Business Review, 84(3), 58-66.

Immordino-Yang, M. H. (2018). The brain basis for integrated social, emotional, and academic development: How emotions and social relationships drive learning. The Aspen Institute.

Immordino-Yang, M. H., & Damasio, A. (2007). We feel, therefore we learn: The relevance of affective and social neuroscience to education. Mind, Brain, and Education, 1(1), 3-10.

Immordino-Yang, M. H., Christodoulou, J. A., Pekrun, R., & Linnenbrink-Garcia, L. (2022). Implications of emotion regulation choice for constructive internal reflection and creative innovation. Trends in Neuroscience and Education, 26, 100168.

Ionescu, T. (2012). Exploring the nature of cognitive flexibility. New Ideas in Psychology, 30(2), 190-200.

Isaacson, W. (2011). Steve Jobs. Simon & Schuster.

Japardi, K., Bookheimer, S., Knudsen, K., Ghahremani, D. G., & Bilder, R. M. (2018). Functional magnetic resonance imaging of divergent and convergent thinking in Big-C creativity. Neuropsychologia, 118, 59-67.

Jobs, S. (2011). Steve Jobs' 2005 Stanford Commencement Address. Stanford News.

Johansson, F. (2017). The Medici Effect: What Elephants and Epidemics Can Teach Us About Innovation. Harvard Business Review Press.

Johnson, S. (2010). Where good ideas come from: The natural history of innovation. Riverhead Books.

Jung-Beeman, M., Bowden, E. M., Haberman, J., Frymiare, J. L., Arambel-Liu, S., Greenblatt, R., ... & Kounios, J. (2004). Neural activity when people solve verbal problems with insight. PLoS Biology, 2(4), e97.

Kashdan, T. (2009). Curious?: Discover the missing ingredient to a fulfilling life. William Morrow.

Kashdan, T. B., DeWall, C. N., Pond Jr, R. S., Silvia, P. J., Lambert, N. M., Fincham, F. D., ... & Keller, P. S. (2013). Curiosity protects against interpersonal aggression: Cross-sectional, daily process, and behavioral evidence. Journal of Personality, 81(1), 87-102.

Kaufman, J. C., & Beghetto, R. A. (2009). Beyond big and little: The four c model of creativity. Review of General Psychology, 13(1), 1-12.

Kaufman, J. C., & Gregoire, C. (2015). Wired to create: Unraveling the mysteries of the creative mind. TarcherPerigee.

Kellett, J. B., Humphrey, R. H., & Sleeth, R. G. (2006). Empathy and the emergence of task and relations leaders. The Leadership Quarterly, 17(2), 146-162.

Kelley, T., & Kelley, D. (2013). Creative confidence: Unleashing the creative potential within us all. Crown Business.

Kelley, T., & Littman, J. (2001). The art of innovation: Lessons in creativity from IDEO, America's leading design firm. Currency.

Killingsworth, M. A., & Gilbert, D. T. (2010). A wandering mind is an unhappy mind. Science, 330(6006), 932-932.

Knapp, J., Zeratsky, J., & Kowitz, B. (2016). Sprint: How to Solve Big Problems and Test New Ideas in Just Five Days. Simon & Schuster.

Konrath, S. H., O'Brien, E. H., & Hsing, C. (2011). Changes in dispositional empathy in American college students over time: A meta-analysis. Personality and Social Psychology Review, 15(2), 180-198.

Kotler, S. (2014). The rise of Superman: Decoding the science of ultimate human performance. New Harvest.

Kotler, S. (2021). The Art of Impossible: A Peak Performance Primer. Harper Wave.

Kotter, J. P. (1996). Leading change. Harvard Business Press.

Kowalski, R. M., Giumetti, G. W., Schroeder, A. N., & Lattanner, M. R. (2014). Bullying in the digital age: A critical review and meta-analysis of cyberbullying research among youth. Psychological Bulletin, 140(4), 1073-1137.

Krebs, R. M., Schott, B. H., Schütze, H., & Düzel, E. (2009). The novelty exploration bonus and its attentional modulation. Neuropsychologia, 47(11), 2272-2281.

Krznaric, R. (2014). Empathy: Why It Matters, and How to Get It. Penguin Books.

Kübler-Ross, E. (1969). On death and dying. Routledge.

Lakhani, K. R., & Wolf, R. G. (2003). Why hackers do what they do: Understanding motivation and effort in free/open source software projects. MIT Sloan Working Paper No. 4425-03.

Lakhani, K. R., Jeppesen, L. B., Lohse, P. A., & Panetta, J. A. (2007). The value of openness in scientific problem-solving. Harvard Business School Working Paper, No. 07-050.

Langer, E. J. (2005). On becoming an artist: Reinventing yourself through mindful creativity. Ballantine Books.

Lanzoni, S. (2018). Empathy: A History. Yale University Press.

Leonard, D., & Rayport, J. F. (1997). Spark innovation through empathic design. Harvard Business Review, 75, 102-115.

Leung, A. K. Y., Maddux, W. W., Galinsky, A. D., & Chiu, C. Y. (2008). Multicultural experience enhances creativity: The when and how. American Psychologist, 63(3), 169-181.

Levitin, D. J. (2014). The organized mind: Thinking straight in the age of information overload. Dutton.

LinkedIn. (2020). The Network Gap. LinkedIn Corporation.

LinkedIn. (2023). Workplace Learning Report.

Literat, I., & Glăveanu, V. P. (2018). Distributed Creativity on the Internet: A Theoretical Foundation for Online Creative Participation. Journal of Creative Behavior, 52(1), 16-33.

Lionesses of Africa. (2014, October 6). Video: The interview - Tara Fela-Durotoye, Founder & CEO, House of Tara International [Blog post]. Retrieved from https://www.lionessesofafrica.com/blog/2014/10/6/video-the-interview-tara-fela-durotoye-founder-ceo-house-of-tara-international

Loh, K. K., & Kanai, R. (2016). How Has the Internet Reshaped Human Cognition? The Neuroscientist, 22(5), 506-520.

Lorenzo, R., Voigt, N., Tsusaka, M., Krentz, M., & Abouzahr, K. (2018). How Diverse Leadership Teams Boost Innovation. Boston Consulting Group.

Maddux, W. W., & Galinsky, A. D. (2009). Cultural borders and mental barriers: The relationship between living abroad and creativity. Journal of Personality and Social Psychology, 96(5), 1047-1061.

Magas, J. (2022). Ocean Protocol: The Decentralized Data Exchange Protocol to Unlock Data for AI. Cointelegraph.

Mang, P., & Reed, B. (2012). Designing from place: a regenerative framework and methodology. Building Research & Information, 40(1), 23-38.

Mankins, M., & Garton, E. (2017). Time, talent, energy: Overcome Organizational Drag and Unleash Your Team's Productive Power. Harvard Business Review Press.

Manovich, L. (2020). Cultural Analytics. MIT Press.

Marion, R., & Uhl-Bien, M. (2001). Leadership in complex organizations. The Leadership Quarterly, 12(4), 389-418.

Marr, B. (2018). The Amazing Ways Chinese Tech Giant Alibaba Uses Artificial Intelligence And Machine Learning. Forbes.

Maslach, C., & Leiter, M. P. (2008). Early predictors of job burnout and engagement. Journal of Applied Psychology, 93(3), 498.

Maurya, A. (2012). Running lean: Iterate from plan A to a plan that works. O'Reilly Media, Inc.

MBO Partners. (2023). State of Independence in America.

McCoy, J. M., & Evans, G. W. (2002). The potential role of the physical environment in fostering creativity. Creativity Research Journal, 14(3-4), 409-426.

McEwen, B. S. (2012). Brain on stress: How the social environment gets under the skin. Proceedings of the National Academy of Sciences, 109(Supplement 2), 17180-17185.

McGrath, R. G. (2010). Business models: A discovery driven approach. Long Range Planning, 43(2-3), 247-261.

McKinsey & Company. (2022). True Gen: Generation Z and its implications for companies.

McKinsey & Company. (2023). The New Digital Edge: Rethinking Strategy for the Post-Pandemic Era.

McKinsey. (2017). How to create an agile organization.

Mead, M. (1984). Continuities in Cultural Evolution. Routledge.

Mehta, R., & Zhu, R. J. (2009). Blue or red? Exploring the effect of color on cognitive task performances. Science, 323(5918), 1226-1229.

Meyers-Levy, J., & Zhu, R. J. (2007). The influence of ceiling height: The effect of priming on the type of processing that people use. Journal of Consumer Research, 34(2), 174-186.

MIT Sloan Management Review. (2023). Winning With AI.

Moser, J. S., Schroder, H. S., Heeter, C., Moran, T. P., & Lee, Y. H. (2011). Mind your errors: Evidence for a neural mechanism linking growth mind-set to adaptive post-error adjustments. Psychological Science, 22(12), 1484-1489.

Mueller, J. S., Melwani, S., & Goncalo, J. A. (2012). The Bias Against Creativity: Why People Desire but Reject Creative Ideas. Psychological Science, 23(1), 13-17.

Nadella, S. (2017). Hit Refresh: The Quest to Rediscover Microsoft's Soul and Imagine a Better Future for Everyone. Harper Business.

Nakamura, J., & Csikszentmihalyi, M. (2002). The concept of flow. In C. R. Snyder & S. J. Lopez (Eds.), Handbook of positive psychology (pp. 89-105). Oxford University Press.

Neumann, N., Lotze, M., & Eickhoff, S. B. (2016). Cognitive expertise: An ALE meta-analysis. Human Brain Mapping, 37(1), 262-272.

Newell, A., & Simon, H. A. (1972). Human problem solving. Prentice-Hall.

Newport, C. (2016). Deep work: Rules for focused success in a distracted world. Grand Central Publishing.

Newport, C. (2019). Digital Minimalism: Choosing a Focused Life in a Noisy World. Portfolio.

Nordgren, L. F., & Schonthal, D. (2022). The Human Element: Overcoming the Resistance That Awaits New Ideas. Wiley.

O'Reilly, C. A., & Tushman, M. L. (2016). Lead and Disrupt: How to Solve the Innovator's Dilemma. Stanford University Press.

Obstfeld, D. (2005). Social networks, the tertius iungens orientation, and involvement in innovation. Administrative Science Quarterly, 50(1), 100-130.

Ochsner, K. N., & Gross, J. J. (2005). The cognitive control of emotion. Trends in Cognitive Sciences, 9(5), 242-249.

Odgers, C. L., & Jensen, M. R. (2020). Annual Research Review: Adolescent mental health in the digital age: facts, fears, and future directions. Journal of Child Psychology and Psychiatry, 61(3), 336-348.

Orben, A., & Przybylski, A. K. (2019). The association between adolescent well-being and digital technology use. Nature Human Behaviour, 3(2), 173-182.

Osterwalder, A., & Pigneur, Y. (2010). Business Model Generation: A Handbook for Visionaries, Game Changers, and Challengers. John Wiley & Sons.

Page, S. E. (2007). The Difference: How the Power of Diversity Creates Better Groups, Firms, Schools, and Societies. Princeton University Press.

Palfrey, J., & Gasser, U. (2008). Born Digital: Understanding the First Generation of Digital Natives. Basic Books.

Pariser, E. (2011). The Filter Bubble: What the Internet Is Hiding from You. Penguin Press.

Patnaik, D. (2009). Wired to Care: How Companies Prosper When They Create Widespread Empathy. FT Press.

Paulus, P. B., & Nijstad, B. A. (Eds.). (2003). Group creativity: Innovation through collaboration. Oxford University Press.

Paulus, P. B., & Nijstad, B. A. (Eds.). (2019). The Oxford handbook of group creativity and innovation. Oxford University Press.

Pentland, A. (2014). Social Physics: How Good Ideas Spread-The Lessons from a New Science. Penguin.

Peppler, K. A., & Kafai, Y. B. (2007). From SuperGoo to Scratch: exploring creative digital media production in informal learning. Learning, Media and Technology, 32(2), 149-166.

Peters, T. (1997). The brand called you. Fast Company, 10(10), 83-90.

Pew Research Center. (2023). Teens, Social Media and Technology 2023.

Pink, D. H. (2005). A whole new mind: Moving from the information age to the conceptual age. Riverhead Books.

Pink, D. H. (2009). Drive: The surprising truth about what motivates us. Riverhead Books.

Pink, D. H. (2011). Drive: The surprising truth about what motivates us. Penguin.

Porter, M. E., & Kramer, M. R. (2011). Creating shared value. Harvard Business Review, 89(1/2), 62-77.

Prabhu, T. (2017). Rethink: The Story Behind the App. ReThink, Inc.

Prensky, M. (2001). Digital Natives, Digital Immigrants. On the Horizon, 9(5), 1-6.

Project Management Institute. (2017). Success Rates Rise: Transforming the high cost of low performance.

Project Management Institute. (2018). Pulse of the Profession 2018: Success in Disruptive Times.

Przybylski, A. K., & Weinstein, N. (2017). A Large-Scale Test of the Goldilocks Hypothesis: Quantifying the Relations Between Digital-Screen Use and the Mental Well-Being of Adolescents. Psychological Science, 28(2), 204-215.

PwC. (2022). Workforce of the future: The competing forces shaping 2030. PwC.

Radjou, N. (2015). Frugal innovation: How to do more with less. The Economist.

ReThink. (2023). ReThink: About Us. ReThink, Inc.

Rhodes, M. (1961). An analysis of creativity. The Phi Delta Kappan, 42(7), 305-310.

Riess, H. (2017). The Science of Empathy. Journal of Patient Experience, 4(2), 74-77.

Ries, E. (2011). The lean startup: How today's entrepreneurs use continuous innovation to create radically successful businesses. Crown Books.

Robinson, K., & Aronica, L. (2016). Creative Schools: The Grassroots Revolution That's Transforming Education. Penguin Books.

Rock, D. (2009). Your brain at work: Strategies for overcoming distraction, regaining focus, and working smarter all day long. HarperBusiness.

Rock, D., & Cox, C. (2012). SCARF in 2012: Updating the social neuroscience of collaborating with others. NeuroLeadership Journal, 4(4), 1-14.

Rosen, L. D., Carrier, L. M., & Cheever, N. A. (2013). Facebook and texting made me do it: Media-induced task-switching while studying. Computers in Human Behavior, 29(3), 948-958.

Rothwell, J. (2020). The effects of COVID-19 on U.S. small businesses: Evidence from owners, managers, and employees. Brookings Institution.

Runco, M. A., & Jaeger, G. J. (2012). The standard definition of creativity. Creativity Research Journal, 24(1), 92-96.

Runway. (2021). About Runway. Runway AI, Inc.

Russ, S. W. (1993). Affect and creativity: The role of affect and play in the creative process. Psychology Press.

Saggar, M., Quintin, E. M., Kienitz, E., Bott, N. T., Sun, Z., Hong, W. C., ... & Reiss, A. L. (2015). Pictionary-based fMRI paradigm to study the neural correlates of spontaneous improvisation and figural creativity. Scientific Reports, 5(1), 1-11.

Sarasvathy, S. D. (2001). Causation and effectuation: Toward a theoretical shift from economic inevitability to entrepreneurial contingency. Academy of Management Review, 26(2), 243-263.

Sawyer, R. K. (2007). Group genius: The creative power of collaboration. Basic Books.

Sawyer, R. K. (2017). Group genius: The creative power of collaboration (Updated and expanded edition). Basic Books.

Schiller, B. (2019). After its first attempt failed, the Ocean Cleanup project is now collecting plastic. Fast Company.

Schooler, J. W., Smallwood, J., Christoff, K., Handy, T. C., Reichle, E. D., & Sayette, M. A. (2011). Meta-awareness, perceptual decoupling and the wandering mind. Trends in Cognitive Sciences, 15(7), 319-326.

Seligman, M. E. P., & Csikszentmihalyi, M. (2000). Positive psychology: An introduction. American Psychologist, 55(1), 5-14.

Senge, P. M. (1990). The Fifth Discipline: The Art and Practice of the Learning Organization. Doubleday/Currency.

Shane, S., Venkataraman, S., & MacMillan, I. (1995). Cultural differences in innovation championing strategies. Journal of Management, 21(5), 931-952.

Shors, T. J. (2014). The adult brain makes new neurons, and effortful learning keeps them alive. Current Directions in Psychological Science, 23(5), 311-318.

SignalFire. (2023). Creator Economy Market Map.

Simonton, D. K. (1997). Creative productivity: A predictive and explanatory model of career trajectories and landmarks. Psychological Review, 104(1), 66-89.

Simonton, D. K. (2000). Creativity: Cognitive, personal, developmental, and social aspects. American Psychologist, 55(1), 151-158.

Sinek, S. (2009). Start with Why: How Great Leaders Inspire Everyone to Take Action. Penguin.

Slack. (2023). The State of Work.

Small, G. W., Lee, J., Kaufman, A., Jalil, J., Siddarth, P., Gaddipati, H., Moody, T. D., & Bookheimer, S. Y. (2020). Brain health consequences of digital technology use. Dialogues in Clinical Neuroscience, 22(2), 179-187.

Smallbizgenius. (2021). The ultimate list of collaboration statistics for 2021. Smallbizgenius.

Snowden, D. J., & Boone, M. E. (2007). A leader's framework for decision making. Harvard Business Review, 85(11), 68-76.

Solk, T. (2021). Whitney Wolfe Herd: How I Built Bumble. How I Built This with Guy Raz, NPR.

Sommers, C. H., & Dineen, T. (1984). Margaret Mead: A Life. Viking.

Sparrow, B., Liu, J., & Wegner, D. M. (2011). Google Effects on Memory: Cognitive Consequences of Having Information at Our Fingertips. Science, 333(6043), 776-778.

Steinberg, L. (2008). A social neuroscience perspective on adolescent risk-taking. Developmental Review, 28(1), 78-106.

Stephens, G. J., Silbert, L. J., & Hasson, U. (2010). Speaker--listener neural coupling underlies successful communication. Proceedings of the National Academy of Sciences, 107(32), 14425-14430.

Sternberg, R. J. (Ed.). (1999). Handbook of creativity. Cambridge University Press.

Sternberg, R. J., & Lubart, T. I. (1991). An investment theory of creativity and its development. Human Development, 34(1), 1-31.

Sternberg, R. J., & Lubart, T. I. (1995). Defying the crowd: Cultivating creativity in a culture of conformity. Free Press.

Sternberg, R. J., & Lubart, T. I. (1999). The concept of creativity: Prospects and paradigms. In R. J. Sternberg (Ed.), Handbook of creativity (pp. 3-15). Cambridge University Press.

Stiglic, N., & Viner, R. M. (2019). Effects of screentime on the health and well-being of children and adolescents: A systematic review of reviews. BMJ Open, 9(1), e023191.

Straker, L., Harris, C., Joosten, J., & Howie, E. K. (2018). Mobile technology dominates school children's IT use in an advantaged school community and is associated with musculoskeletal and visual symptoms. Ergonomics, 61(5), 658-669.

Tan, L. B., Lo, B. C., & Macrae, C. N. (2014). Brief mindfulness meditation improves mental state attribution and empathizing. PloS one, 9(10), e110510.

Tapscott, D. (2008). Grown up digital: How the net generation is changing your world. McGraw-Hill.

TechCrunch. (2020). Runway raises $8.5M at a $50M valuation for its AI-powered design tool. TechCrunch.

Tedeschi, R. G., & Calhoun, L. G. (2004). Posttraumatic growth: Conceptual foundations and empirical evidence. Psychological Inquiry, 15(1), 1-18.

TEDx Talks. (2012). How the oceans can clean themselves: Boyan Slat at TEDxDelft. YouTube.

The Ocean Cleanup. (2019). Annual Report 2019. Annual_Report_2019.pdf (theoceancleanup.com)

The Ocean Cleanup. (2021). Our Story. The Ocean Cleanup.

The Ocean Cleanup. (2023). The Great Pacific Garbage Patch Cleanup. The Ocean Cleanup.

The Tilt. (2023). Content Entrepreneur Benchmark Research.

Thrash, T. M., & Elliot, A. J. (2003). Inspiration as a Psychological Construct. Journal of Personality and Social Psychology, 84(4), 871.

Throuvala, M. A., Griffiths, M. D., Rennoldson, M., & Kuss, D. J. (2019). Motivational processes and dysfunctional mechanisms of social media use among adolescents: A qualitative focus group study. Computers in Human Behavior, 93, 164-175.

Toffler, A. (1970). Future Shock. Random House.

Turkle, S. (2015). Reclaiming Conversation: The Power of Talk in a Digital Age. Penguin Press.

Turkle, S. (2017). Alone Together: Why We Expect More from Technology and Less from Each Other. Basic Books.

Twenge, J. M. (2017). iGen: Why Today's Super-Connected Kids Are Growing Up Less Rebellious, More Tolerant, Less Happy—and Completely Unprepared for Adulthood—and What That Means for the Rest of Us. Atria Books.

Twenge, J. M., Campbell, S. M., Hoffman, B. J., & Lance, C. E. (2010). Generational differences in work values: Leisure and extrinsic values increasing, social and intrinsic values decreasing. Journal of Management, 36(5), 1117-1142.

Twenge, J. M., Hisler, G. C., & Krizan, Z. (2019). Associations between screen time and sleep duration are primarily driven by portable electronic devices: Evidence from a population-based study of U.S. children ages 0–17. Sleep Medicine, 56, 211-218.

Twenge, J. M., Joiner, T. E., Rogers, M. L., & Martin, G. N. (2018). Increases in Depressive Symptoms, Suicide-Related Outcomes, and Suicide Rates Among U.S. Adolescents After 2010 and Links to Increased New Media Screen Time. Clinical Psychological Science, 6(1), 3-17.

Udemy. (2018). 2018 Workplace Distraction Report. Udemy, Inc.

Uhl-Bien, M., & Arena, M. (2017). Complexity leadership: Enabling people and organizations for adaptability. Organizational Dynamics, 46(1), 9-20.

Uhl-Bien, M., & Arena, M. (2018). Leadership for organizational adaptability: A theoretical synthesis and integrative framework. The Leadership Quarterly, 29(1), 89-104.

Uhl-Bien, M., Marion, R., & McKelvey, B. (2007). Complexity leadership theory: Shifting leadership from the industrial age to the knowledge era. The Leadership Quarterly, 18(4), 298-318.

Ullén, F., de Manzano, Ö., Almeida, R., Magnusson, P. K., Pedersen, N. L., Nakamura, J., Csíkszentmihályi, M., & Madison, G. (2012). Proneness for psychological flow in everyday life: Associations with personality and intelligence. Personality and Individual Differences, 52(2), 167-172.

Ulrich, M., Keller, J., Hoenig, K., Waller, C., & Grön, G. (2014). Neural correlates of experimentally induced flow experiences. Neuroimage, 86, 194-202.

Uncapher, M. R., & Wagner, A. D. (2018). Minds and brains of media multitaskers: Current findings and future directions. Proceedings of the National Academy of Sciences, 115(40), 9889-9896.

UNDP. (2021). The Peoples' Climate Vote.

United Nations. (2013). Malala Yousafzai UN Speech. United Nations, New York.

Upwork. (2023). Freelance Forward.

Utz, S. (2016). Is LinkedIn making you more successful? The informational benefits derived from public social media. New Media & Society, 18(11), 2685-2702.

Uzzi, B., & Spiro, J. (2005). Collaboration and creativity: The small world problem. American Journal of Sociology, 111(2), 447-504.

Vallas, S. P., & Cummins, E. R. (2015). Personal branding and identity norms in the popular business press: Enterprise culture in an age of precarity. Organization Studies, 36(3), 293-319.

Vartanian, O., Bristol, A. S., & Kaufman, J. C. (Eds.). (2013). Neuroscience of creativity. MIT Press.

Vieten C, Rubanovich CK, Khatib L, Sprengel M, Tanega C, Polizzi C, Vahidi P, Malaktaris A, Chu G, Lang AJ, Tai-Seale M, Eyler L, Bloss C. Measures of empathy and compassion: A scoping review. PLoS One. 2024 Jan 19;19(1):e0297099. doi:10.1371/journal.pone.0297099

Vogel, E. A., Rose, J. P., Roberts, L. R., & Eckles, K. (2014). Social comparison, social media, and self-esteem. Psychology of Popular Media Culture, 3(4), 206-222.

Voss, M. W., Vivar, C., Kramer, A. F., & van Praag, H. (2013). Bridging animal and human models of exercise-induced brain plasticity. Trends in Cognitive Sciences, 17(10), 525-544.

Vygotsky, L. S. (1978). Mind in society: The development of higher psychological processes. Harvard University Press.

Wallas, G. (1926). The art of thought. Harcourt, Brace and Company.

Waytz, A., & Epley, N. (2012). Social connection enables dehumanization. Journal of Experimental Social Psychology, 48(1), 70-76.

Waytz, A., & Gray, K. (2018). Does online technology make us more or less sociable? A preliminary review and call for research. Perspectives on Psychological Science, 13(4), 473-491.

Weber Shandwick. (2019). Gen Z's Influence. Weber Shandwick.

Weger Jr, H., Castle Bell, G., Minei, E. M., & Robinson, M. C. (2014). The relative effectiveness of active listening in initial interactions. International Journal of Listening, 28(1), 13-31.

Weick, K. E. (1984). Small wins: Redefining the scale of social problems. American Psychologist, 39(1), 40.

Weisberg, R. W. (1999). Creativity and knowledge: A challenge to theories. In R. J. Sternberg (Ed.), Handbook of creativity (pp. 226-250). Cambridge University Press.

Wellman, B., Quan-Haase, A., Boase, J., Chen, W., Hampton, K., Díaz, I., & Miyata, K. (2003). The Social Affordances of the Internet for Networked Individualism. Journal of Computer-Mediated Communication, 8(3).

World Economic Forum. (2020). The Future of Jobs Report 2020. World Economic Forum.

Yerkes, R. M., & Dodson, J. D. (1908). The relation of strength of stimulus to rapidity of habit-formation. Journal of Comparative Neurology and Psychology, 18(5), 459-482.

YPulse. (2020). The power of online communities. YPulse.

Zomorodi, M. (2017). Bored and Brilliant: How Spacing Out Can Unlock Your Most Productive and Creative Self. St. Martin's Press.

INDEX

Numbers

A

B

C

D

E

F

G

H

I

J

K

L

M

N

T

U

www.ingramcontent.com/pod-product-compliance
Lightning Source LLC
Chambersburg PA
CBHW031422270326
41930CB00007B/544
* 9 7 9 8 9 9 1 2 3 7 7 2 7 *